Improving Company Productivity

John W. Kendrick is professor of economics at the George Washington University and adjunct scholar at the American Enterprise Institute, as well as the president of the Southern Economic Association, 1982–83. His books include *Productivity Trends in the United States* (1961); with Daniel Creamer, *Measuring Company Productivity: Handbook with Case Studies* (1961; rev. ed., 1965); *Measuring the Nation's Wealth* (1964); *Economic Accounts and Their Uses* (1972); *Postwar Productivity Trends in the United States, 1948–1969* (1973); *The Formation and Stocks of Total Capital* (1976); *The National Wealth of the United States* (1976); and *Understanding Productivity: An Introduction to the Dynamics of Productivity Change* (1976) and, with Elliot Grossman, *Productivity in the United States: Trends and Cycles* (1980), both published by the Johns Hopkins University Press.

The American Productivity Center is a privately funded, nonprofit organization that develops practical programs to improve productivity and the quality of work life in the United States.

IMPROVING COMPANY PRODUCTIVITY
Handbook with Case Studies

JOHN W. KENDRICK,
in collaboration with the
American Productivity Center

THE JOHNS HOPKINS UNIVERSITY PRESS
Baltimore and London

The Johns Hopkins University Press, Baltimore, Maryland 21218
The Johns Hopkins Press Ltd., London

Library of Congress Cataloging in Publication Data

Kendrick, John W.
Improving company productivity.

Bibliography: p. 215
Includes index.
1. Industrial productivity. 2. Industrial produc-
tivity — Case studies. I. American Productivity Center.
II. Title.
HD56.K45   1983   658.3'14   83–48053
ISBN 0–8018–2992–5

Contents

FIGURES

TABLES

Foreword

I am truly delighted to commend to readers of this book the material that Dr. Kendrick has assembled. As anyone who knows me and/or is familiar with the goals and work of the American Productivity Center is fully aware, I agree with the author that "the plant is where the action is in productivity improvement."

Hence, I am convinced that the future of our national standard of living — resting as it does on continuing productivity growth — lies in the hands of the managers and employees of the individual establishments in the U.S. business community.

Outside factors, favorable or unfavorable (ranging from the weather and the U.S. government to Japanese exporters, Korean steel producers, and the OPEC cartel), at times strongly influence productivity at the level of the individual plant. However, in the long run it is the combined efforts of factory managers and employees which solve the problems and assure appropriate actions requisite to long-range productivity growth.

Effective managers elicit the employee cooperation essential to high productivity and make certain that resources available to the enterprise are earmarked in a manner to assure the future technological improvement requisite to increasing productivity. Similarly, the effective managers do not sacrifice long-term growth for short-term profit maximization.

Secondly, I share fully with Dr. Kendrick the conviction that plant-level *measurement* of productivity (in a manner appropriate to the needs of each situation) is an essential ingredient in the composite of actions required to continue — and maximize — productivity growth. One senior statesman of productivity noted some years ago that to know where you are going, it is essential to know not only where you *are,* but also *where you have been.* Only sound productivity measurement can provide this guideline to management.

My earlier experience as price controller in 1971–73 taught me how important productivity measurement is as a tool for management, and how few factories and offices were at the time carrying forward sound measurement programs. This resulted in my current efforts to motivate the adoption of sound measurement programs by *all* U.S. companies.

It is because of these fundamental convictions that I encouraged participation of members of the APC staff in a joint effort with Dr. Kendrick to assure the assembly of the manuscript and carefully selected case studies for this book.

I commend this book to you as the best and most complete available published guideline on practical approaches to company and plant-level measurement. As some readers who have been involved with APC productivity measurement activity already know, we regularly recommend the earlier — and now out-of-print — version of Dr. Kendrick's company-level measurement book, of which the late Daniel Creamer was coauthor.

We are delighted to have this new updated and expanded version available for future participants in APC productivity measurement and improvement workshops. Although we would like to see you in future APC workshops, even if you cannot attend one this new book can provide invaluable ideas and techniques for sound approaches to measurement.

C. Jackson Grayson, Jr.
Chairman, American Productivity Center

Preface and
Acknowledgments

This volume is a response to the great upsurge of interest on the part of managers and workers in progressive American firms and other organizations in the ways and means to increase productivity. As Dr. Grayson notes in his Foreword, productivity improvement efforts are more effective when linked to measurement. At his invitation I have been pleased to collaborate with several staff members of the American Productivity Center in producing this volume which covers both topics – the measurement and promotion of productivity at the firm and plant level.

Much of chapters 2 through 5 of part 1 on measurement represents a reissue of the core material of the handbook I wrote with the late Daniel Creamer for the Conference Board in the 1960s, *Measuring Company Productivity: Handbook with Case Studies*. The second edition of that handbook is now out of print, and we are grateful to the Conference Board for permission to use much of the text and two of the case studies from the handbook in the present volume. I have, however, taken the liberty of editing the handbook material to a minor extent in order to update it and fit it into the present context. I have also added a fair amount of new material in chapters 2 and 3, as well as providing a new introductory chapter 1.

Part 2, "Uses of Productivity Measures," is truly collaborative. In chapter 6 I go well beyond the summary treatment in the handbook to provide an overview of uses. Chapter 7, "Productivity and Profitability Analysis: The APC Performance Measurement System," was written by Carl Thor, APC vice-president for measurement. Thor has drawn on his experience in applying the APC system to client companies, and in designing the APC's courses on productivity measurement. Chapter 8, "Interfirm Comparisons," was written by George Sadler, retired APC senior economist. Sadler draws not only on his APC experience but also on his years with the Bureau of Labor Statistics in plant-level productivity measurement and comparisons. In chapter 9, "Industry and Economy Comparisons," I draw on my past work at both the micro- and macroeconomic levels to show how firms can compare their own productivity performance with that of the industries in which they are classified.

The two chapters of part 3, "Promoting Company Productivity," were written by John McClure, former APC vice-president for productivity management. McClure came to the APC from Honeywell, Inc., where he was manager of productivity programs, and has designed and taught APC courses in that area.

The positive effects of company employee involvement programs have been documented in a recent New York Stock Exchange survey, results of which were summarized in the report *Productivity and People,* released in November 1982. Indeed, the beneficial effects of productivity promotion programs and their rapid spread in the past few years hold out hope that U.S. productivity advance may be significantly higher in the 1980s than in the previous decade.

C. Jackson Grayson has been a leading figure in the productivity enhancement movement in American industry. It has been my privilege to be associated with him and his colleagues on the board of the APC since its inception in 1977. I am grateful for his encouragement in preparation of this volume which we feel will fill a need in the movement which has now gathered sufficient momentum to make a difference in the years ahead.

We are also indebted to Anders Richter, Miriam Kraft Tillman, and their associates at the Johns Hopkins University Press, who have handled this product of several authors with their customary skill. Mr. Richter and an anonymous referee made a number of suggestions that helped to improve the volume significantly. We are confident that it will be of value to company officials and others who are seeking to measure and improve the productivity of their organizations.

John W. Kendrick

1

Introduction and Preview

During the last decade, interest in productivity has greatly increased. Such an upsurge reflects more than a passing fad, however, since changes in productivity are of perennial importance at all levels — national, industrial, company, and personal. For present purposes we define productivity as the ratio of output to inputs of labor and other resources, in real terms. Productivity increases as output grows faster than the inputs used in the production process.

At the national level, productivity is a major element of economic growth and progress. In the first two decades after World War II increase in total factor productivity in the United States accounted for more than half the growth of real gross national product (GNP). Productivity growth was responsible as well for all of the increase in real income per capita, since input grew only about as fast as population. At the national level, productivity growth also provides a proportionate offset to increases in wage rates and other input prices, thereby reducing the rate of inflation of output prices. Moreover, since the growth of total productivity means reduction in requirements for labor, capital, and natural resource inputs per unit of output, it contributes to greater leisure time, to increased consumption, and to conservation.

At the industry level, above-average productivity growth leads to relative declines in costs and prices. In both domestic and international markets, this increases the competitiveness of the firms of the progressive industries, which consequently tend to grow faster than average. To the contrary, industries with below-average productivity performance generally suffer relative declines in output since their above-average price increases discourage sales.

At the level of the firm, productivity is fundamental to profitability and survival. Companies with higher productivity than the industry average tend to have higher profit margins. Moreover, if productivity is growing faster than that of competitors, the margins will rise. Conversely, below-average levels and rates of growth of productivity will ultimately lead to bankruptcy.

At the personal level, increasing productivity in all of one's activities is an important aspect of self-fulfillment. To the individual, as a member of a firm or other organization, it serves as a key to advancement since it helps increase the productivity of the organization. In the last analysis, the productivity advance of the nation, with all its attendant benefits, depends on the increasing productivity of all of us as individuals and of the organizations in which we work.

The Purpose of the Volume

The widening recognition in recent years of the importance of productivity has been due in large part to the problems created by the marked slowdown after 1973 — the accelerating inflation through 1980, a leveling of real income per worker, an upward trend of unemployment, and the growing difficulty in the international market. Since 1981, federal government policies have been adopted and administered to promote a renewed upsurge in productivity growth.

More relevant to the theme of the present volume, the number of U.S. firms that have instituted some type of productivity measurement system for their internal operations has taken a quantum jump. Increasingly, productivity measurement also is being linked directly to special programs to promote company productivity. Various other uses of productivity measures have been developed to enhance the value of both measurement and promotion as major management tools to increase efficiency, improve the quality of products and working life, and maintain or enhance profitability.

The purpose of this volume is to summarize the current state of the art with respect to the measurement of company productivity, the various practical uses to which productivity measures may be put, and the development of productivity improvement programs. Much of the material has been drawn from the seminars and courses offered by the American Productivity Center (APC) over the past four years, and the volume will be used in conjunction with such courses in the future. We hope that other organizations will also find it to be a useful textbook. But it is also truly a "handbook," which company officials can read on their own as background for instituting productivity measurement and / or promotion programs or for improving and enriching existing programs. In this connection, the case studies of individual measurement systems (which include examples of uses of productivity measures) and of productivity promotion programs will suggest various features of successful programs that the reader may wish to try in his or her own firm. Although it is addressed primarily to the business community, which is where most work is being done on increasing productive efficiency, this volume will also interest government officials and academicians who are concerned with the measurement, analysis, and promotion of productivity in the firm or other type of organization.

We recognize, of course, that the socioeconomic environment within which business operates importantly affects decisions that impact productivity — particularly government regulations and tax policies. In recent years the attempts to reduce and rationalize regulatory policies, the Economic Recovery Tax Act of 1981, and the effectuation of a significant reduction in the inflation rate have all contributed to a more favorable climate for private saving, investment, and innovational activity.

Of greatest importance is that company managements take maximum advantage of the improved business climate in order to improve productivity through enhanced efficiency and cost-reducing innovations. We sincerely believe that further diffusion and refinement of productivity measurement systems and promotion programs can materially assist in realizing that objective. Improved productivity at the company level, if widespread, adds up to accelerated productivity growth nationally, contributing to further disinflation and increased international competitiveness of domestic industries.

A Preview of the Volume

In preparing this handbook we had three major objectives, indicated by its three major parts. The first is to provide an authoritative guide for measurement of productivity in the company and its organizational components for which separate accounts are maintained. Obviously, programs to improve productivity can be more effective if they are linked to measures that help to identify problem areas and that can be used to track the progress resulting from new investments, innovations, and other aspects of productivity improvement programs.

Part 1, on productivity measurement, covers the fundamental points of the handbook written by John Kendrick and the late Daniel Creamer for the Conference Board in the 1960s, *Measuring Company Productivity: Handbook with Case Studies.*

Chapter 2 introduces the productivity concept and discusses the meaning and significance of changes or differences in the various productivity ratios. Following a discussion in chapter 3 of general measurement problems, chapter 4 covers the measurement of output aggregates, including both major approaches — weighting physical units and deflating production values by appropriate price index numbers. Chapter 5 deals with the measurement of inputs and their combination to produce multi-input productivity measures. To supplement these discussions, two of the six case studies included in the Conference Board handbook have been reproduced, and a recent case has been added, to form appendix A.

Uses of productivity measures were discussed in general terms in the original handbook. But with the subsequent spread of company productivity measurement programs, particularly during the past decade, the application of the measures to their various potential uses has broadened and intensified with gratifying results. Accordingly, after an overview of uses in the initial chapter (6) of part 2, three subsequent chapters explore in some depth the special types of uses developed by the APC and included in its course offerings: productivity and profitability analysis (chapter 7); interfirm and interplant comparisons (chapter 8); and comparisons of company measures with the corresponding measures for industries and for the business economy as a whole (chapter 9). The latter chapter also summarizes the relative industry productivity trends in the U.S. business economy from 1948 to the present as a background for appraisal of company performance. This summary is based on the APC multi-input productivity measures for various sectors and industry groups reproduced in appendix C, as well as on the official estimates of output per labor-hour for individual industries not covered in the APC's service, as published by the U.S. Department of Labor Bureau of Labor Statistics (BLS).

Part 3 deals with the essential features of company productivity programs. It is desirable to link improvement programs (chapter 10) with productivity measurement as a means of enhancing productivity-mindedness and tracking the results of the programs. But even though strongly recommended where feasible, it is not necessary to measure productivity in order to improve it. Thus, productivity improvement programs (chapter 11) are much more than a "use" of productivity measures even when they are linked. They represent a valuable organizational technique intended to become a part of the corporate culture to involve employees at all levels in promoting the objectives of the company, as well as society, with respect to cost-reduction and productivity growth and improvements in the quality of products and in the quality of working life. If successful, they obviously contribute to companies' profits, which also have the social function in our type of private-enterprise, market economy of directing resources to the more efficient firms. The role of competition in promoting the growth of high-productivity firms is, of course, a significant aspect of national productivity advance.

The wide variety of productivity improvement programs ranges from joint labor-management productivity teams and group financial incentive schemes to Japanese-style quality circles. Within each category are variations of procedures among firms. For this reason we supplement the discussion of basic principles in part 3 with a number of case studies of company productivity improvement programs in appendix B, and other published case studies are included in the bibliography. Company productivity coordinators will find the cases useful in helping to develop or enrich their own programs, drawing on relevant features of the tested programs of others.

For companies whose officers desire help in instituting or improving productivity measurement systems or improvement programs, either through courses or personal consultation, appendix D comprises a list of productivity and quality of working life centers. A glossary is provided in appendix E to assist those readers who may not be familiar with all the terminology used in the productivity literature.

I

MEASURING COMPANY PRODUCTIVITY

2

Concept and Meaning
of Productivity

Productivity cannot be measured directly. Instead, it must be measured indirectly as a relationship between physical outputs and inputs that can be assembled. The relationship can better be understood with reference to the notion of the production function.

The Production Function Framework

Simply speaking, the quantity of goods and services produced by an establishment or firm depends on (and is a function of) the quantity of labor and other resource inputs used in production and on the efficiency with which they are used, i.e., their productivity. This is also true of aggregations of firms up to the levels of the industry and the national economy. This theory implies, of course, that the production of individual firms can be increased and the whole economy can grow by increasing the quantity of labor and other inputs used, and/or by increasing productivity. These are all supply-side concepts. The potential expansion of market demand must be in place if increased production is not to result in unwanted inventory accumulation.

Although productivity cannot be measured directly, it can be indirectly estimated most simply as a ratio of aggregate output to the sum of inputs. Quantities of outputs of the various types are usually combined (weighted) by their costs per unit or prices as of a base period, which indicate their relative importance. The inputs are combined on the basis of their proportions of total costs in the base period to indicate their relative contributions to output. Output must be related to all associated inputs or cost elements in order to measure the net saving in real cost per unit of output, and thus the increase in productive efficiency. Real unit cost reductions are the

9

mirror image of total productivity gains, as output increases in relation to input (real cost). In the next section we will discuss the various *partial* productivity ratios obtained by relating output to labor or other individual input classes, increases in which are reflected declines in labor or other input requirements per unit of output.

The ratio of output to input at a point in time has no meaning. Rather, productivity ratios are meaningful only in measuring changes over time, or differences among plants or firms producing the same range of goods and services or among the same industries in different countries. In this volume we are concerned mainly with intertemporal comparisons.

Ratioing output to input is not the only way to measure productivity changes. Output may be statistically regressed on inputs and a time-trend, the coefficient of the latter variable reflecting the trend rate of growth of productivity. This does not have the flexibility of the ratio approach since it misses short-term productivity changes. An alternative approach is to subtract a weighted average of the rates of change of the inputs from the rate of change of output. The difference has been called "the residual," which focuses attention on trying to explain the reasons why output generally grows faster than input. The residual can be calculated between successive periods, or from rates of change over long periods. But since the results are the same as those obtained by calculating percentage changes in the ratios, usually expressed as index numbers, the latter approach is the one most generally used.

The chief cause of productivity growth over the long run is cost-reducing innovation in the technology and organization of production. This provides a sharp distinction between the aforementioned average production ratios and the "marginal productivity" and cost curves of what economists call "static equilibrium theory." Such static theories assume that technology and quantities of resources are given and constant in the short run and then inquire as to the conditions of equilibrium. In comparative statics, technological change is depicted in terms of *shifts* in production functions, productivity, and cost curves. The real economy, under the dynamic conditions of technological progress as well as changes in resources, tastes, preferences, values, and institutions, is in a continually moving disequilibrium. The average productivity ratios explained in this handbook reflect the net impact of all the dynamic forces at work on productive efficiency. In a final section of this chapter we shall explore in greater depth the various factors that produce changes in productivity in the firm and at more aggregative levels in the short run as well as the long run. But the meaning of changes (or differences) in productivity ratios depends on the definitions and scope of the output and input measures. In the following sections we will discuss these matters from the operational standpoint of framing concepts that are amenable to measurement. Methodological specifics are treated in subsequent chapters of part 1.

The Relation of Output to Input

Since we are interested in a technical relationship, it is necessary to deal with the "physical volumes" of outputs and inputs. In a market economy, however, accounting records of firms and estimates for industries and sectors are stated in terms of values in the first instance — dollar volumes of sales, labor compensation, and so on. In value terms, output (sales plus inventory change) is equal to costs plus profit.

This current dollar accounting identity is not of particular interest for present purposes, except possibly as the composition of costs may change. But underlying the values are physical units of various sorts and the prices of these units. Changes in values are thus owing to changes in prices as well as in numbers of units of outputs and inputs. It is fundamental in productivity measurement to disentangle the price and quantity components of values, in order to see what has happened to physical requirements for each and all the input items relative to each other and to the physical volume of output. The heterogeneous character of outputs and inputs creates the problem of what set of constant prices to use in combining outputs and inputs. This is best discussed in the next section.

Ratios between output and individual types or classes of inputs are useful in showing economies that have been achieved over time in the consumption of these inputs per unit of output. In many cases, however, a reduction in unit requirements for certain inputs are accompanied by increases in unit requirements for other inputs. Only by relating output to both labor and capital can it be determined whether there has been a net saving of factor inputs per unit of output, and, if so, how much of a saving. The ratio of output to all associated inputs has been called "total productivity"; in contrast to the "partial productivity" measures, it reveals advances in overall productive efficiency — the same output with lowered total input.

It is true that labor cost is the major factor cost of the national product and of "value added" in most industries. Partly for this reason, "output per labor-hour" measures have been widely used as indicators of changes in productive efficiency. But these measures are biased to the extent that capital per labor-hour has not remained constant. As a matter of fact, real capital stocks and inputs — in the economy and in most industries — have increased faster than labor input. Thus, some part of the increase in output per labor-hour has reflected the substitution of capital for labor, in addition to advances in productive efficiency as such. In many cases, measures of output per labor-hour may not be seriously misleading, but when the goal is to measure changes in productive efficiency, it is better to attempt to deal with all inputs. The total productivity index, as a measure of the efficiency of the business as a whole, must occupy a central position in the spectrum of possible productivity measures.

Scope of Output and Input

Firms generally produce several, and often many, types and models of products. Against this gross output are the major input classes of labor, purchased materials and services, and capital goods, the latter consisting of plant, land, machinery and equipment, and inventory stocks, plus financial working capital.

In the economy as a whole, the national product is defined as consisting of final production; that is, services and goods that are not resold in markets during the period acquired: consumer goods, capital goods (including the change in inventories and net investment abroad), and government purchases. The inputs are the basic "factors of production" — labor and capital, including land. The intermediate materials and services are already included in the value of final products; and total labor and capital inputs include those that contributed to intermediate as well as final products. Thus, intermediate products should not be added either to final product or to factor input, if double counting is to be avoided.

For the entire economy, production in the component companies and industries consists of the value added to materials and services purchased from other companies and industries. This net output, or "real product," of a company or industry is then related to the labor and capital inputs only.

Asymmetry of Labor and Capital Inputs

Note that the basic factors of production — labor and capital (including natural resources) — are actually resource stocks, in contrast to intermediate products, which are themselves consumed during the production period. The services, or "inputs," of the basic factors are measured in terms of the time rate of actual or potential utilization of the stocks, for which compensation is made. However, in a private economy there is some asymmetry of the labor and capital inputs in this regard: labor is a direct cost only when employed, whereas reproducible capital and land represent a continuing charge to private owners, regardless of the degree of utilization.

Therefore, we adjust the labor-force "stock" for rate of utilization (average hours worked per year) in order to obtain estimates of total labor-hours worked, of various types, as the basic input. In the case of capital, we assume that the input moves proportionately to the real stock, which is made up of the various types of land, plant, equipment, and inventory weighted by their base-period prices (with the fixed stock adjusted for accumulated depreciation). The labor-hours are weighted by base-period average hourly labor compensation, while the real capital stock is weighted by the base-period rate of capital compensation. Thus, both inputs are reduced to constant dollars.

Note that the inputs are in units of standard, unchanging efficiency within each category. This is necessary, since changes in productive efficiency are to be measured by changes in the output-input ratios. If increases in productive efficiency were imputed to the factor inputs, as is done by the market in determining current incomes, the resulting output-input ratio of unity would be of little interest.

Causes and Meaning of Productivity Change

We have demonstrated that changes in partial productivity ratios reflect changes in the composition of inputs, or "factor substitutions," in addition to the changes in productive efficiency that are measured by the total productivity ratios. But what causes the changes in productive efficiency? In discussing the production function we noted that over the long run it is primarily cost-reducing innovations in the technology and organization of production which cause shifts that are reflected in productivity changes. In the short run, cyclical, seasonal, or erratic changes in demand and supply conditions affect productivity.

In this section we dig a bit deeper and look at more fundamental factors behind productivity growth. Also, some additional forces that conduce to rising productivity are brought into the picture explicitly.

Fundamental Factors

Behind the changes in technology and other proximate determinants of productivity advance stand the basic values and institutions of a society. Relevant values have to do with attitudes toward work, propensities to save and invest, and willingness to innovate, take risks, and adapt to the changes wrought by scientific and technological progress. It was only gradually that traditional societies accepted the goal of material progress and were loosened up enough to initiate and accept the changes associated with the technological advances that are responsible for most of the increases in real income per capita. Even today, many of the less-developed countries are still in the process of creating the social conditions necessary for take-off into economic growth. Some of the industrialized countries, on the other hand, have experienced an increase in questioning the goal of material progress and a greater willingness to trade off at least part of their growing affluence in order to pursue other social goals. Some observers even think that the "work ethic" in the United States has declined. The important point is that the values of a people and its leaders condition the rate of technological progress and other forces directly affecting productivity.

This is also true of a nation's institutional forms and practices, particularly those in the economic sphere. In our type of predominantly competitive private-enterprise, market-directed system, powerful forces spur productivity. Each firm can increase its profit margins, at least temporarily, by cost-reducing innovations. This is one reason why research and development (R&D) activities have become institutionalized. But as other firms imitate the successful innovators, real prices fall and the above-average profits of pioneering firms drop unless they continue to exploit new inventions and other means of staying ahead of their competitors.

Costs and profits are, of course, affected by tax laws, public expenditures, regulatory policies, and other governmental actions. That is why it is so important in our type of economy that government attempt to maintain an environment that is conducive to saving and the associated investments that are a major carrier of innovations. It is also important that the central government try to maintain a relatively high level of aggregate demand and thus reasonably steady growth, and promote the mobility of resources in response to the shifts in patterns of demand that characterize a dynamic economy. There are obviously many other aspects of economic, social, and political institutions that affect productivity which we cannot treat here. An article of faith in the West is that democratic processes promote the institutional changes that are necessary to maintain vigorous economic advance. Yet safeguards are necessary to prevent democratic freedoms from being subverted by hostile tendencies that have had a measurable negative impact on productivity.

Proximate Determinants

Within the firm, productivity can be increased not only by cost-reducing innovations in technology and organization, including those required to take advantage of economies of scale, but also by increasing actual efficiency relative to potential efficiency as reflected in work measurement data at successive levels of technology. To make these broad statements more concrete, some of the specific measures associated with productivity advance can be listed.

Beyond a certain size, firms in most industries find that it pays to support in-house R&D, to invent and develop not only new and improved products but also cost-reducing processes. Smaller firms, as well as the larger ones, can stay abreast of advancing technology (even if they do not create it) through technical and trade literature, consultants, representatives of supplying firms, conferences, and educational programs.

Because of problems in measuring quality changes in consumer goods, productivity is affected directly mainly as a result of the use of new and improved producer goods and cost-reducing process innovations. But the development of new and improved products, consumer as well as producer, indirectly affects the productivity measures because of the learning curve effect. That is, productivity generally rises faster in the early stages of producing new goods than it does in later, more mature, stages of production. Thus, the continual introduction of new and better products results in higher productivity growth than would otherwise prevail.

Productivity increases may also reflect internal and external economies of scale as plants, firms, industries, and the economy grow. These result from greater specialization of personnel, equipment, and plants and because some functions do not expand proportionately to production, resulting in a decrease in the associated inputs and real costs per unit of output. In order to realize potential economies of scale, managements must usually invest in new plants and equipment, in training or retraining of personnel, and in reorganization of production. So, scale economies are generally associated with technological and organizational innovation. Technological advances, in turn, may open up new potentialities for further scale economies. In practice, it is difficult to disentangle scale economies from technological progress in analyzing the causes of productivity growth.

Tangible investments in new plants and equipment, both to replace obsolete units and to expand capacity as needed, will increase net income and productivity if the expected rate of return exceeds the borrowing rate of interest. Increasing amounts of capital goods per worker increase labor productivity. More important, investment increases total productivity if the efficiency or quality of the new capital goods is greater than that of the old, which is generally the case because of continuing R&D in the equipment and materials industries.

Total productivity is also enhanced by purchase or manufacture of new or improved materials and other intermediate products. Consumption of materials and energy per unit of output can further be reduced, not only by innovation but by conservation measures to reduce waste and defects. Inventory requirements can be reduced by better scheduling and synchronization of purchases, production, and shipments.

The quality of the work force can be increased by improved personnel procedures that result in hiring workers with the appropriate aptitudes, interests, and educational attainments and training and retraining workers to perform to the best of their ability. But beyond this, the motivation of workers at all levels to perform at optimum sustainable efficiency is crucial. It involves more than competitive pay and benefit systems; it requires nothing less than creating an atmosphere in which employees can identify with the objectives of the firm. Many firms have found that productivity improvement programs of the types described in part 3 can significantly increase the ratio of actual to potential efficiency and stimulate innovative suggestions for raising productivity, which may be even more important for long-term progress.

Improvements in plant and office layouts, in work flows, and in the organization of the firm and its constituent units can all increase productivity. Periodic reviews of the organizational structure are particularly necessary as a firm expands. So also are reviews of activities, in order to reduce or eliminate unprofitable lines and expand those in which the current or prospective returns are on or above target rates.

In other words, improving productivity is an aspect of good management generally, and managers can never forget that theirs is the ultimate responsibility for efficient operations under given technology and for innovations in technology and organization. As we have already noted, however, and will discuss further in chapter 7, profit rates depend not only on productivity but also on "price recovery" — the changes in prices charged in relation to prices paid. So, effective strategies in purchasing, marketing, and financing all contribute to profitability but exceed the scope of this volume. It should be stressed, however, that no matter how skillful management is in these areas, unless its productivity increases are in line with those of its competition over the long run, the firm will eventually be a casualty of the impersonal forces of the market.

This leads to the point that within an industry the rate of productivity growth reflects not only that of the constituent firms but also the relative growth of those firms in which productivity shows above-average increases and the decline of those that are not keeping up technologically. Relative industry productivity trends reflect a whole host of factors covered in chapter 9.

In the business economy as a whole, the rate of productivity growth reflects the industry rates of growth and the relative shift of resources among industries — not only from industries with lower levels of productivity to those with higher levels but also among industries with different rates of productivity change.

3

General
Measurement Problems

Having clarified the concept of productivity and its meaning, we shall demonstrate the techniques of measuring outputs, inputs, and productivity. Before a discussion of some of the general measurement problems in this chapter, however, it will be of some interest and value to the reader to refer to the historical development of productivity measurement in the United States, covered in the annex to this chapter. There we begin with productivity measurement for industries and the business economy as a whole, which generally antedates company measurement programs. In any case, the macroeconomic measures are useful in providing yardsticks with which company measures can be compared.

The lag in the development of company productivity measurement behind that of industry was due in part to reliance on the bottom line of the profit and loss statement as an indicator of relative company efficiency. The idea of separating the influence of relative changes in prices of outputs and of inputs on profit margins, as distinguished from changes in productivity, was slow to spread until after World War II. By the 1950s U.S. corporations were hiring an increasing number of economists, and a new breed of management scientist, such as Peter Drucker, emphasized the basic importance of cost-reducing technological and organizational innovation as measured by productivity in the profit equation. By that time, there was greater receptiveness to the application of productivity measurement techniques, which had been developed in industry studies, to the firm and its constituent elements. (After all, the notion of the production function obviously is as applicable to firms as it is to industry aggregations of producing units. Indeed, the underlying data for outputs and inputs, which are the raw materials for productivity measurement and analysis, are usually more reliable at the company level than at the industrial and general economy levels, where they are based on secondary sources.) Once the stage was set, company productivity measurement programs expanded rapidly.

Various types of "work measurement," which relate actual output to

17

statistical or engineering norms (as distinguished from productivity measurement), spread quickly in the second and third decades of this century, following the pioneering studies of Frederick W. Taylor on scientific management. Indeed, the development of management science together with the rapid expansion of industrial laboratories, fostered by the increasing numbers of schools of business administration and of engineering, were major elements in the acceleration of American productivity, which began about the time of World War I. But company productivity measurement, in the sense used in this volume, began to take hold only after World War II.

Introduction to Measurement Problems

The operational concept of productivity involves many detailed definitional and statistical problems, including (1) measuring outputs whose characteristics may change over time; (2) defining and measuring real capital stocks and inputs as well as labor inputs when the characteristics of both factors are diverse and changing; and (3) aggregating heterogeneous units of output and of input. These problems would exist even if data were perfect, and there are data problems and occasions when ingenuity must bolster inadequate information. However, the informational gaps (which, it is hoped, will eventually be filled when the need for additional data becomes known) must be limited in size if the productivity estimates are to have the requisite degree of accuracy.

Reasons for Imprecision

It is necessary to understand in using and producing productivity indexes that the measures will not be wholly precise or even unique. This is true whether the measures relate to industries and the economy or to individual firms, plants, or products — although it would seem that company measures might be somewhat more accurate because of the greater control that can be maintained over basic data. But the chief cause of ambiguity is that alternative definitions and statistical methodology (each of which can logically be defended) will produce somewhat different results. For example, changes in models of a given product may be treated in different ways; capital stock may or may not be adjusted for changes in rate of utilization, depending on one's concept of capital input; and, in aggregating any heterogeneous collections of items, the weighting system chosen will usually influence the result.

In these cases of alternative procedures, the one must be chosen that seems most reasonable. The procedures selected and the result as contrasted with that obtainable from the use of alternative conventions should be made explicit by the producer of the estimates and understood by the user.

The use of conventions is not peculiar to productivity measures; business accounting practices involve many conventions. If, for example, management were not aware of the effect of inflation on conventionally reported depreciation and profits estimates, decisions could be adversely affected. At the national level, widely used measures, such as the consumer and the producer price indexes, real GNP, and the Federal Reserve index of industrial production, all embody conventions (such as the frequency of weight-base revision) that affect their movements.

Despite certain ambiguities, company and national accounts are useful. Productivity measures need be no more ambiguous or have larger margins of error than most other aggregate measures, and certainly they are as useful. As with all measures, however, the major conventions and their effects should be understood if the user is to derive maximum benefit. Alternative procedures frequently make little difference in the movement of economic measures; it is the absolute levels that are more seriously affected.

Fitting the Method to the Circumstance

The reader should be forewarned that the following discussion of productivity measurement is not and could not be an exhaustive "manual of instructions." We attempt to explain basic concepts and present methods for dealing with most of the major types of measurement problems that will be met by the estimator. But, in view of the many diverse industries and the even greater diversity among companies, specific instructions for all conceivable situations that might arise obviously cannot be supplied. In some instances, alternative methods of approach are discussed when it is not clear whether one method would be best under all circumstances. The company statistician will often have to use ingenuity in adapting the general principles and methods set forth here to particular company situations. But this is, after all, more challenging and interesting than attempting to process data according to cut-and-dried rules. Further, certain instances where the output defies measurement in constant prices (e.g., shipbuilding) or where data deficiencies are acute, it may be that no estimates at all should be prepared.

Isolating Physical Volume

In the preceding section, we noted that productivity estimates are based on the possibility of estimating changes in the physical volume of output and input. That is, if monetary values can always be considered as being the product of the physical units bought and sold and the prices at which they exchange, then value changes can be broken down into these basic constituent elements.

In dealing with individual types of output or input, one can work with the quantity data alone for the periods being compared. But as soon as two or more different types of output or input are aggregated, each physical volume series must be "weighted" by its relative unit values in a "base" period, since the prices generally represent their relative economic importance. This transforms the physical unit measures into "constant price" measures. These real value measures are still referred to as physical volumes; the purely physical measures have now been combined with economic valuations but in such a way that fluctuations are due to changes in the component physical units rather than in the prices, which are held constant.

If complete data are at hand with respect to value, price, and quantity, it is immaterial whether the quantities of various types are combined according to base-period prices or the aggregate values are "deflated" by index numbers of prices (combined by changing quantity weights).* In either case, a constant-dollar aggregate representing units combined by base-period price weights results.

In practice, the choice between weighting units by price or deflating values by price index depends on the relative availability and reliability of the alternative sets of data. Often in the case of large aggregates, much time is saved by deflating values by an index of representative prices, if it is known that prices of a whole product "family" tend to fluctuate with the prices of certain major items in the family.

The Weighting System

The other part of the basic problem of measuring aggregates in real terms has to do with the selection of the base period from which relative prices are chosen for weighting quantities (that is, the period in which the price deflators are set at 100.0). There is a tendency for relative movements in quantity and in price (both of outputs and of inputs) to be negatively correlated. That is, purchases tend to be shifted toward items that are becoming relatively cheaper. Thus, the more recent the base period, the smaller the apparent increase in the real aggregates. Since both outputs and inputs tend to be similarly affected by alternative weight bases, the differential effect on the movement of productivity ratios is generally not great. But to a lesser or greater extent the movement of aggregates is affected by weighting conventions.

A usual convention is to weight series for recent years by the relative prices of a recent, relatively normal, high-level production year. This is especially important for the computation of rate of return for capital. A year in which a company sustains a loss must be avoided. The base year or

$$*^i \Sigma Q_1 P_0 = \Sigma Q_1 P_1 \div \frac{\Sigma P_1 Q_1}{\Sigma P_0 Q_1}$$

period should be one in which the profit rate is close to the average over one or more business cycles. As the structure of production and prices change, the weight base can be changed every five or ten years, or, in more dynamic companies, in successive pairs of years, and the new series linked to the old. In this way, the weights reflect the contemporaneous structure of production and price in successive segments of the time span over which comparisons are being made.

Bases of Company Productivity Measurement

Company productivity measures must be built up from the basic statements that summarize data for net sales, costs and expenses, income before taxes, and assets. Data from subsidiary records on production, prices, payrolls and labor-hours, various cost accounts, and the balance sheet are needed both for detail on current dollar transactions and for conversion to constant prices. Essentially, however, company productivity measures may be viewed as a relationship between revenue and cost in real terms, as estimated from items in the operating statement and underlying records.

How many partial productivity estimates should be prepared depends on the number of important classes of inputs in which significant resource savings may be achieved. Further, total and partial productivity ratios may be prepared for divisions, departments, plants, and other "profit centers" for which separate sets of accounts are maintained. Finally, cost accounts frequently permit the calculation of variable inputs per unit of output for individual products—and estimates of total productivity, too, if one is willing to apportion indirect costs by product on the basis of data for direct costs, mainly labor and materials.

Units of Output

The starting point in estimating the gross physical volume of company production is the data on dollar volume of sales and other operating revenue. For purposes of deflation by appropriate price indexes, this should be broken down by type or class of product or service. Alternatively, the numbers of physical units of each type of commodity or service produced may be weighted by base-period prices. To each of these measures the real cost of the increment (or decrement) to goods in process should be added; to the deflated sales measure there should also be added the real value of the change in finished goods inventories.

For nonfinancial firms, income from investments should be excluded from the output computation. On the other hand, imputations should be added to cover the output of subsidiary and investment-type activities, such as interplant transfers, subsidiary sales, transport and other distributive activities, service functions such as cafeterias, "force-account" construction, and long-range research and development activity.

An alternative for R&D, and possibly for some of the other subsidiary types of production that present major problems of estimation, is to exclude the output from the production measure and the associated input from the total input measure. The drawback to this treatment is that the final output, input, and productivity measures are not wholly comprehensive. It can be justified only if exclusion of the subsidiary activities leads to significantly more accurate results.

The Four Major Cost Categories

To convert costs and expenses plus profits into real terms, the first step in a companywide analysis is to break these down into four major categories: labor compensation, cost of materials and contractual services, capital costs (interest, rent, and royalties, as well as profit before taxes), and indirect business taxes. For multiunit companies, these cost categories would further be grouped according to division or plant and would involve an allocation of central office expenses, possibly in proportion to the value of production of each division or plant. If further elaboration of the productivity measures is desired and cost accounting records permit, direct costs can be allocated by product class. The indirect plant and overhead costs that are not allocated to "cost centers" can be assigned to product classes, as suggested above.

Labor Input

Like output, real labor cost can be estimated in two ways. Most firms keep track of production-worker hours, and hours of nonproduction workers can be estimated. Hours worked can be weighted in each significant classification by base-period average hourly labor compensation to arrive at real labor input. Or payrolls, net of supplements to wages and salaries, can be deflated by a composite index of average hourly earnings and raised by the ratio in the base period of total labor cost to payrolls to achieve substantially the same result.

In many companies, time cards are kept for direct labor by product, so that direct hours can be allocated by product or product class. In other cases, "standard" hours or labor costs are calculated by product, and the actual can be computed by applying the ratios of actual to standard for the relevant department or the plant as a whole in successive time periods. If indirect and overhead labor costs (or hours) have not already been allocated by product in the cost accounts, this can be done on the basis of the plant ratios of indirect (and overhead) labor cost to direct labor cost. This was essentially the procedure followed by the BLS in its direct productivity comparisons of plant performance by product.[1]

Inputs of Materials and Services

The cost of materials, energy, and purchased or contractual services must be assembled by main types from basic cost accounts. In some cases, records are kept of the physical quantities of materials consumed; in these cases, the base-period cost may be extrapolated by the quantity series. In other cases, the dollar costs can be deflated by appropriate price indexes. Deflator indexes can be compiled if the company keeps records of prices paid, or appropriate components of the producer price index of the BLS can be used. In some cases, approximate deflators may have to be employed, as discussed in more detail later.

Direct materials costs are generally available in terms of products. If the company wishes to estimate productivity by product class, the indirect materials, supplies, and business service costs may be apportioned by product in proportion to relative direct costs.

Capital Input

The remaining costs (other than indirect business taxes) represent capital costs, including depreciation allowances and income or profit on equity capital before corporate income tax. Here, a somewhat different procedure is employed. Essentially, the approach uses the balance sheet, from which is estimated in constant dollars the value of the plant, land, equipment, and inventories used by the firm (division and plant). This is done by applying appropriate capital-goods price indexes. The base-period "rate of return," obtained as the ratio of property income before tax to the value of the capital stock, is then applied to the real capital stock throughout to obtain estimates of real capital input. Special problems, such as whether to use real stocks gross or net of depreciation and whether to adjust fixed capital for utilization rates, are discussed in chapter 5.

Allocation of capital input by product will be less precise than in the case of labor and materials input. Here, it may be necessary to employ a proportionate allocation of the total capital input of each division or plant in accordance with the value of output of each product class, or some other criterion. In some firms, records may make it possible to identify particular machines, inventories, and portions of plant floor space as "direct" requirements for production of particular outputs. In these cases, "indirect" capital can be allocated in proportion to the value of direct capital used by each product class.

Indirect Business Taxes

Finally, since indirect business taxes are not direct payments for specific governmental services, there is no equivalent input behind the tax expense — and in any case the services of government are mostly too intangible and general to be measured. Therefore, a workable convention is to measure the real value of output *exclusive* of indirect business taxes by deducting in each time period the base-period ratio of indirect business taxes to value of output. This procedure preserves the base-period equality between the value of output and input. It is true that governmental inputs are not taken into account. But given a certain minimum level of public services, the output of the firm is generally not significantly affected by changes in governmental outlays. This same reasoning suggests that the exclusion of indirect business taxes from inputs in the base and measured periods is an acceptable alternative and has the advantage of reducing the number of adjustments.

To obtain the productivity ratios for the company, the real value of output is divided by the total real cost of inputs. If the ratio is unity in the base period, the ratios may be multiplied by 100.0 to yield productivity index numbers. Alternatively, output and input in constant prices may first be converted to index numbers prior to calculation of total and partial productivity ratios.

Complementary productivity measures can be computed by first deducting real purchases of materials and other "intermediate" products from the real value of gross output in order to obtain estimates of "net output" or "real product originating." Net output may then be divided by total *factor* input and by labor and capital inputs separately in order to obtain factor productivity measures. As we shall show, the factor productivity measures of the firm are comparable with productivity measures for the economy as a whole and its industrial divisions based on the real product concept.

ANNEX

Historical Development of Productivity Statistics

Economy and Industry Measures

The basic concepts of the production function and of productivity had been well established for more than a century before economic statisticians attempted to measure productivity changes in American industry. The lag was due, in part, to the paucity of data on production, employment, and other costs of production. Beginning in 1840, however, the U.S. decennial censuses were expanded to include increasing amounts of economic data, and in 1919 a biennial census of manufactures was inaugurated.

The first studies were done by the then–Bureau of Labor in the late-nineteenth century, comparing output per worker in handicraft and mechanized operations, and measuring changes through time. In the 1920s the BLS published a series of spot articles on productivity in various manufacturing industries. In all cases, the motivation for these studies was the fear of technological displacement of workers, rather than relative efficiency evaluations or trend analyses.

Efforts accelerated and expanded in the 1930s, in part because of the suspicion by some that economic stagnation and high unemployment rates were due, at least to a degree, to rapid technological advance. The National Bureau of Economic Research began a series of studies of productivity in various industrial sectors and published a number of volumes on the subject beginning in the 1930s. The National Research Project of the Works Progress Administration (WPA) also published many monographs on output, employment, and productivity in various U.S. industries and generated, for the first time, productivity trend data for over one hundred industries plus "all manufacturing." As the WPA was being phased out with the advent of World War II these studies were transferred to the BLS of the Department of Labor. The BLS has continued ever since to publish productivity estimates for various industries of the economy — now approximately 100 series, with more unpublished series available on request.

The development and publication of estimates of GNP in constant prices by the Department of Commerce, beginning in 1951, opened the way to estimates of productivity in the private domestic economy as a whole and for major sectors. Since 1959 the BLS has published such estimates for farming, manufacturing, nonmanufacturing, and nonfinancial corporations on an annual and quarterly basis. The BLS computes, but does not publish, comparable series for each of the nonmanufacturing sectors.

The estimates discussed so far were all of partial productivity ratios — output per worker or per hour. Studies at the National Bureau of Economic Research of capital in the American economy by Simon Kuznets, Raymond Goldsmith, and others opened the way to development of estimates of "total factor" or "multiple-input" (multi-input) productivity. Beginning in the 1950s, academicians published a number of studies on this basis. In 1961 John Kendrick's summary study for the National Bureau of Economic Research, *Productivity Trends in the United States,* appeared, containing estimates of total factor productivity for the U.S. private domestic economy by thirty-two industry groups from the late-nineteenth century through 1957 as well as estimates of labor productivity for many additional industries. This study was subsequently updated, and now the multi-input productivity estimates are being extended on a regular, quarterly, and annual basis under sponsorship of the APC (see appendix C). In 1983, the APC inaugurated the publication of total productivity series for manufacturing, with energy and materials introduced on both the output and input sides. The BLS has completed development of multi-input productivity estimates for the private business economy and certain major segments and publication began in April 1983.

Company- and Plant-level Measures

It was in the latter 1940s that the BLS began a program of plant-level productivity measurement and analysis that covered a number of plants in a succession of industries, ultimately totaling about twenty. In addition to measurement of both levels and trends, the BLS analyzed the reasons for differences in levels and rates of change in output per labor hour among the plants of each industry. Because of its relatively high cost compared with studies based on census and survey data, the plant-level program was abandoned in 1953, but some of the larger firms involved continued the measurement program for their own uses.

In the late 1950s and early 1960s the Conference Board offered courses on company productivity measurement, eventuating in the Kendrick/ Creamer handbook, which first appeared in 1961 and was revised in 1965. A sample of the measurement programs of participating firms were included in the case studies that accompanied the handbook, two of which are reproduced in appendix A.

It is indeed ironic that little else occurred in plant-level productivity measurement in the United States in the first twenty postwar years, in sharp contrast to European and Japanese experience. Under the Marshall Plan program of technical assistance, the BLS, drawing upon its experience in both plant-level and industrywide productivity measurement, trained a substantial number of Japanese and European economists and statisticians in the data sources and techniques for structuring measures. Concurrently, the BLS generated, also with Marshall Plan funding, a substantial number of spot measures for U.S. plants producing designated products, with a wealth of both statistical and engineering detail, as "prototypes" or reference points for use by European industry in its economic rebuilding process. The BLS then dispatched a team of U.S. productivity measurement experts to work with European officials in the use of this material, and in structuring an expanding array of plant-level productivity measures. The Japanese and European plant-level measurement programs grew during the late 1950s and the early 1960s into one of the key tools for improving plant efficiency and national recovery. By the mid 1960s, when U.S. funding for the technical cooperation program phased out, many of the European nations had developed procedures and analytical approaches far more sophisticated than any known in the United States. Japan also was rapidly shaping an impressive assembly of plant-level productivity data, which is now certainly the most massive in the world, with several hundred establishments regularly tracked.

The next major impetus to company measurement in the United States came with Phase II of the price control program, 1971–73. In the forms filed by firms to cost-justify applications for price increases, estimates of increases in productivity were requested in order to translate wage increases into changes in labor costs per unit of output. As noted by C. Jackson Grayson, then the chairman of the Price Commission, and later the founder of the APC, neither did most firms have internal measures of productivity nor did managements know how to measure it. Assisted by management consulting firms, many companies instituted productivity measurement systems at that time, although subsequently industry rates of productivity change based on BLS studies were substituted by the Price Commission for the company rates.

The wage and price control program was phased out in 1974, but, with the slowdown in productivity growth then affecting most industries, additional firms began instituting productivity measurement and promotion programs. The APC, founded privately in 1977, and other productivity centers, which were structured under the aegis of the National Center for Productivity, began offering courses on the subject. (The APC now also performs interplant comparisons and consultancy, as described in chapter 8.) The productivity measurement movement continued to spread, increasingly linked to productivity promotion and improvement programs.

4

The Measurement of Output and Intermediate Inputs

If each firm produced goods and services of standard specifications, the characteristics of which remained constant over the years, there would be no special problem of measuring the physical volume produced. Further, if the output of each type of product changed proportionately, or if there were no systematic correlation between relative changes in prices and output, there would be no problem involved in aggregating all types to obtain measures of total output of the firm, or of the industry, or of the economy.

The choice of a weighting system was discussed earlier. At this point we are concerned with delineation of output and the practical solutions to the problems that changes in model or quality create, that new goods or services introduce, or that result from unstandardized custom-built output. These problems confront the statistician whether measuring physical units directly or compiling price indexes in order to deflate values.

What Is Being Measured

We are interested in measuring total current production, not just the physical volume of shipments. This means, first of all, that estimates of net sales billed or the value of shipments must be adjusted for inventory change — an addition if inventories have increased over the period, a deduction if sales have reduced inventory stocks. Goods in process are generally valued at cost; thus, to obtain the real change, weighted index numbers of average hourly earnings of labor and of the prices of raw materials used in the production process may serve to deflate the value of inventories at the beginning and end of the period. Finished-goods inventories, if valued at market, would be deflated by an index of the corresponding prices weighted in accordance with the relative values of the various goods in stock. The procedure is even more direct if records of finished inventories in terms of numbers of units are kept: changes in numbers of units of each type of commodity are simply multiplied by base-period average price.

Some firms, as illustrated in case 1 of appendix A, have used real net sales as the output measure and excluded from input the real costs attributable to production for inventory. Over the long run, the two productivity measures would show much the same trend. The production numerator for productivity calculations instead of sales is probably simpler than the input adjustment.

Interest and dividend income should be excluded from revenue of non-financial firms. The financial assets from which the property income is derived should likewise be excluded from the real capital stock and input measures.

Variable Purchased Goods and Interplant Transfers

Next, the company's operations should be surveyed to determine which of its intermediate goods and services outputs are variable with respect to the final output of the company. That is, if certain kinds of intermediate goods, components, or services are not wholly integral to the operation but may be purchased from outside in varying ratio to internal production, it is desirable to count these intermediate outputs separately and weight according to the unit cost or value assigned in interplant transfers. When this is done, the weights given to the company's final output should be reduced correspondingly. This procedure prevents a switch (from internal production to outside purchase of an intermediate product) from showing up as a productivity change, since output and input will be reduced in like amounts. For example, if an oil company were to divest itself of custodial and cafeteria services during the period reviewed, this would reduce labor input but would not affect final output; the productivity ratios would have been undisturbed if these ancillary services had been separately measured and included with the company's final outputs.

Similarly, imputations should be made for activities that supplement the chief productive function; in manufacturing, examples of supplementary activities are selling, transportation, and other distributive functions. In distribution, the output may be measured in terms of the physical volume of goods sold or transported through the company's facilities, with the weights based on the value added by such activities.

Finally, account should be taken of the production of capital goods by the firm for its own use. Metalworking establishments may produce some of their own machinery and equipment. Many companies carry out a certain amount of new construction or major alterations and repairs with their force-account construction crews. These expenditures, which are typically charged to capital account, should be deflated and added to other current production for purposes of productivity measurement since the real costs are counted as part of total input.

Intangible Capital Outlays

A more difficult problem is posed in the case of intangible capital outlays, such as long-range R&D expenditures and possibly those made in connection with some basic types of educational and training programs and for advertising and public relations. These outlays, though generally charged to current expense, represent a kind of investment in that they are not related to results in the current accounting period but are expected to enhance the productivity of the firm in future years.

The "output" of these activities, however, is extraordinarily difficult to define operationally. One way to treat the matter is to include the real costs of intangible investments in output as well as in input. The drawback to this procedure is that no productivity advance is attributed to such outlays. But since intangible investments are usually a minor fraction of total outlays, the understatement of output is not significant. Even so, the amount of understatement decreases if some allowance is made in output, assuming that R&D and related expenditures constitute an increasing fraction of real costs.

An alternative technique is to exclude the real costs of intangible investment from both input and output, but this method diminishes the comprehensiveness of the measures. Another avenue is to compute productivity changes on the narrower basis and then impute the estimated productivity changes in current production to the real costs of intangible investment. This procedure removes the downward bias noted earlier from the comprehensive output measure.

The area of intangible outlays illustrates the need for ingenuity on the part of the statistician and for understanding on the part of the users of the underlying conventions employed and their effect on the productivity measurements.

Quality Change

If changes in average quality of output take place as a result of relative shifts of production among coexisting "qualities" (i.e., price lines of a given product or product family), this is easily handled by separately measuring output in terms of each type or "quality" of the product. Thus, even if the same number of units of a product category were produced in two periods but with a larger proportion of higher-quality types in the second period, the change would show up in the weighted aggregate as an increase in physical volume. An increase would also be registered if the values of production in the two periods were deflated by a price index; for example, if there were no price changes between the two periods the values in both current and constant prices would rise, owing to a larger proportion of higher-quality items in the second period. In this procedure, relative market prices are accepted as indicative of relative qualities of products or product types.

Difficulties arise when a change in quality is introduced in the same product type. The change may be ignored, however, if it is minor, involving little or no difference in unit cost of production. The product type is then considered for all practical purposes to remain the same between the two periods, and if there should be an accompanying price change it would count fully as a change in price and not at all as a quantitative change. When the qualitative change is significant (as in the introduction of a new model of a durable good) and is accompanied by a change in price reflecting a change in unit cost of production or a difference in the utility afforded the purchaser, or both, some adjustment is appropriate.

Quality versus Quantity

A minimal adjustment is that employed by the BLS in estimating the "pure" price change accompanying the introduction of a new model. The manufacturer estimates the difference in cost (at constant prices) of the bill of materials and labor required to produce a unit of the new model compared with the old one. If there were a 3% increase, for example, while prices were raised 5%, the pure price increase would be set at 2%, with the 3% increase representing additional quantity embodied in the new model relative to the old. The model change would not affect the productivity measure, since initially the increased quantity per unit, by definition, would be offset by a corresponding increase in input per unit. If no adjustment had been made, there would have been a spurious decline in the productivity index.

Alternatively, the entire price increase in the case just cited might be counted as an increase in quantity. It can be argued that if purchasers are willing to buy the new model at the higher price it must represent an improved quality and thus a larger quantity of utilities to them. The relevant prices are, of course, the net realized price to the producer and not necessarily the quoted or list price, since the latter may be adjusted by various changes in the surrounding terms of sale, including variables such as service, transportation, installation, guarantee, and credit provisions.

Quality and Increase in Utility

The foregoing procedures, though better than no adjustment, still do not solve the whole problem. The new-model or quality of the product very likely yields the consumer some surplus of utility or use value over and above the change in price compared with that of the old-model product. This is strikingly evident in the early history of certain products, such as automobiles, radios, and televisions, when notable improvements in quality were associated with reduction in unit costs and prices.[1] To cope with this problem it is necessary to try to assign values to the improvements in the various product characteristics. This is possible when there is an array of qualities of a product available at the same time, but over time the lower-price qualities gradually improve to incorporate characteristics of the previously higher-quality types. It is then feasible to study the effects of differences of various characteristics on relative prices and to assign values to these differences.

In the case of automobiles, for example, the author of a classic study has calculated the relation of prices to characteristics of new automobiles.[2] His regression equation explaining 1959 prices relative to 1950 prices is:

$$\log P = .026H + .200W - .014L_0 - .025D_1 + .091D_2 + T + \text{constant}$$

where

P is list price
H is brake horsepower (in 100 HP)
W is shipping weight (in 1,000 lb.)
L_0 is overall length (in 100 in.)
D_1 is dummy variable for 6 or 8 cylinders
D_2 is dummy variable for hard-top or not
T is dummy variable for earlier and later years

If one takes account of the implicit values of the characteristics included in the estimating equation, the corrected average price of an automobile rose by 18% from 1950 to 1959, compared with an increase of 31% reported in the consumer's price index (which takes account of dealers' concessions from list prices). Therefore, the increase in the real product per car, on average, is estimated at 12%.

Even this elaborate procedure, which is of potentially wide applicability, must fail to take account of certain highly intangible factors, such as comfort, safety, and style. With respect to style, however, it is doubtful whether it is desirable to attempt to quantify the effect of change. This is because style is relative to taste, and different styles in different years may well be equally good in relation to the tastes of the era (which, of course, are heavily influenced by the producers of the goods themselves).

Some price-determining characteristics may be evaluated directly. If certain equipment is an optional "extra" one year but becomes "standard" the next, the real volume of the item must be increased in proportion to the price of the new equipment as a percentage of the price of the basic commodity, and the price change of the new as compared with the old model would be reduced in like proportion.

In other cases, one technological characteristic of a product may be dominant and provide the basis for determining the relative volume of new, as compared with old, models. For example, an increase in the average mileage obtained from a tire (holding driving conditions constant) represents "more" tire in proportion to the greater durability.

Comparing Old and New Producer Goods

Producers' durable equipment furnishes a particularly fertile field for comparing the real worth of old-model and new-model items objectively. The present value of the reduction in real cost per unit of output when using a new-model machine as compared with an old model over the lifetime of the new model indicates how much more, proportionately, it is worth. Its price will generally reflect only a portion of its increased real value, however, since sales are promoted by sharing part of the technological advantage with the purchaser. Naturally, this standard cannot wholly be objective, since the imputed interest and depreciation charges on the new model will depend on the estimate of its length of life, which can definitely be determined only retrospectively.

A final method may be suggested for both consumer and producer durable goods when new models are constructed from essentially the same parts and components as the old. The total cost of producing the new model can be deflated by a composite index of unit cost of the components. Or, conversely, the physical volumes of output of the components going into new models may be weighted by base-period unit costs. (The deflation variant of this method is used by one of the largest producers of electronic machinery and equipment in this country.) The advantage of deflating by composite unit cost indexes is that the index may be constructed using only those parts and components that are produced in successive periods, linking in new parts after they have been produced for at least two periods.

Frequently No Problem

Finally, the problem of quality change is pronounced only in those products that undergo relatively frequent and often significant changes in model. For the majority of products, characteristics remain relatively stable over substantial time periods. In the former case, if simple adjustments based on differences in unit real cost are to be supplemented by more elaborate adjustments, it may be wise to maintain two output and productivity indexes. The more elaborately adjusted index is somewhat speculative, at best, and it may not be practical to maintain it currently even if it can be computed retroactively. Thus, the historical company record would be shown in two variants: one, the simple calculation used for current estimates; the other, a complex adjusted index designed to portray more fully the historical effects of quality improvement.

New Products

Some new products, such as home computers, represent major innovations in that they are distinctly different from previously existing commodities or services. Many new products, however, are merely varieties of existing products. In either case, new products present a different set of problems from those rising from quality change since new products coexist with different varieties of the same product, or with functionally related products. This makes the problem easier, in that transaction prices are simultaneously available for the new and the older products or product varieties.

The main problem is created by the fact that the new product, by definition, is introduced *after* the weight-base period. One convention is to extrapolate the initial period price back to the base period by the price movement of a closely related product or product group. Thus, television sets were introduced into the consumer price index in 1947 at the level of the radio-phonograph group index. An alternative procedure is to cost the new item in terms of standard costs of the base period.

Following developmental and market-testing periods, a new product should be included in a production or price index as soon as it is produced in commercial volume. Typically, if the product is successful, its relative price falls as its volume increases. Thus, the average price in the initial period (as a ratio of prices to related products) will be high. One advantage of a system of occasionally changing weights is that the weights will be reduced relatively in the new base consonant with their expanded volume.

Custom-built Products

When most units of a product class are built to order and differ considerably from one another, a precise meaning cannot be attached to comparisons of numbers of units produced over successive time periods. Neither can the product be priced in a comparable way over time, since its characteristics are not constant. However, if the custom-built products are constructed from more or less standardized components, one solution is the procedure already mentioned of deflating cost of producing the components by an index of unit costs.

If the proportion of total output built to customer specification is relatively small, the value of this production can be deflated by a price index of the firm's (or industry's) standardized products. In effect, this is based on an assumption that productivity changes in the standard and nonstandard areas are comparable. Even if this is not so, the total output index is not seriously distorted owing to the small size of the custom-built portion of output.

When the bulk of output is nonstandardized, the measurement problem must be attacked directly, as in the case of construction, shipbuilding, aircraft manufacture, and certain metalworking industries, not to mention some of the noncommodity areas. One method that may apply to certain types of manufacturing or construction is averaging the prices of parts and components. The Bureau of Public Roads, for example, measures the composite cost for furnishing and installing fixed quantities of (1) excavation, (2) concrete paving, (3) structural concrete, and (4) reinforced steel and structural steel as represented in a specified composite mile of highway.

Use of a Common Denominator

Another possible approach is to find a physical common denominator of output, which may at least be applied within categories, to minimize the variation in real cost per unit owing to differences in other characteristics. For example, square footage of floor space is a common denominator in building construction; but in residential building the price per square foot differs considerably, depending on other criteria such as size, development, custom work, material, floor level, and amount of equipment. So, output may be measured in terms of square footage for significant categories within which shifts in product mix over time would not be expected to cause significant changes in real price per square foot. Price brackets themselves could be used as categories. Changes in mix among categories would, of course, affect unit value.

These approaches may miss the effect of qualitative changes in the product. In some cases, output is so heterogeneous that it may be the better part of wisdom for company management not to try to measure physical production or productivity. In almost 10% of real GNP, for example, real input is used as a proxy for real product — as in governmental services and certain types of private, professional, or personal services. Insofar as productivity may have increased in these areas, the Commerce Department's expedient obviously imparts a downward bias to real product.

Imputations

If physical volume measures are readily available and satisfactory for the major part of the value of production, the corresponding real output estimates can be raised to full coverage by dividing the real value of covered output by ratios of the current value of covered production to the total value of production. This "coverage adjustment" is based on the assumption that the average price of uncovered output moves with that of covered items. It has been used in deriving total industry production indexes, and tests show that it gives better results than does assuming that uncovered output moves with that for which data are available.

Similarly, if prices are available for items that account for the bulk of sales or for a representative sample of the output, an index of these prices may be used to deflate the total value of production. Occasionally, however, one should check, if possible, to see whether the prices of uncovered items, on average, have moved with the average price of products represented in the index. The BLS indexes themselves involve fairly extensive imputations of price movements of particular specifications to broader product families as a whole, but the reasonableness of the imputations is checked occasionally. It will also be noted in case 1 that the deflator used by the Mideast Manufacturing Company was composed only of prices of principal products. With more than a thousand products to consider, it saved a significant amount of time for the statistician's office to omit the prices of product items and groups that were unimportant in the total sales picture.

Intermediate Product Inputs

Since the materials, supplies, energy, and contractual services purchased by firms represent the output of other firms, the methods of estimating these inputs in constant dollars are exactly the same as the methods of estimating physical output.

Just as it is important to estimate production by basic types of output, so it is necessary to break down the direct materials and the indirect supplies and contractual service costs of goods sold by type. This analysis can be based on records of the purchasing departments or other accounts. In some cases, there may be records of physical units consumed; in other cases, the dollar cost estimates will have to be deflated by the appropriate price indexes. Most appropriate are deflators based on average prices actually paid by the company and computed from the records of the central purchasing section, as in case 1. For many materials, it would be permissible to use price indexes taken from relevant trade journals or from the BLS producer price index detail. In some services, such as lawyers' fees, the statistician will not find any appropriate price index and may have to resort to expedients such as using the average hourly rate of compensation as the deflator. So long as the areas in which "proxy" price indexes are used are not large, distortion will not be significant.

When obtained, real intermediate purchases may either be added to real factor cost (described in chapter 5 below) to obtain total input or be deducted from real gross output to obtain real value added — or net output — as discussed earlier. It is suggested that "real" indirect business tax payments should be obtained by applying to measured-period production the base-period ratio of such taxes to the value of production. This preserves the equality of output and input in the base period and neutralizes the effect of this variable on the productivity ratios. In case 1 the statistician attempted to deflate indirect business taxes directly. Such an attempt is doomed to failure. Since a firm's taxes are not a payment for specific public services, there is no relevant price measure.

5

The Measurement of Factor Inputs and the Productivity Ratios

Labor Input

The input of services of human resources is measured as the hours worked by all persons engaged in production, by occupational categories, weighted by base-period average hourly compensation.

Scope

Some so-called productivity indexes have related output to labor-hours of production workers only. Not only does this measure miss the substitution of capital for labor, but it also neglects the substitution of one type of labor for another. In manufacturing as a whole, the proportion of non-production workers to total workers rose from 16.3% in 1947 to 33% in 1980. Obviously, the ratio of output to production-worker hours over-states the increase in productive efficiency since the hours in the denominator have risen less rapidly than total hours, not to mention that capital input has increased even in relation to total labor hours.

So, total hours worked by all persons productively engaged must be included in the labor portion of an input measure designed as the denominator of a total factor productivity measure. This means not only employees — whether production or general management, engineering, marketing, personnel, and other nonproduction workers, whether direct or indirect — but also proprietors and unpaid family workers in unincorporated firms and in industries where proprietorships are a significant form of organization. This is not to say that ratios of output to particular classes of labor are not useful in showing changes in requirements for each type. This meaning is more clearly implied by inverting the productivity ratio to read "labor-hours per unit of output."

In order to facilitate analysis of changes in unit labor requirements and to provide a basis for weighting as discussed later, it is desirable to provide the labor-hour estimates by all the significant occupational categories into which the work force can be classified.

Unit of Measurement

Some people have argued that labor input should be measured in terms of the number of persons engaged in production, converted to "full-time equivalents" to take care of part-time workers. The argument is that changes in weekly hours do not have a proportionate effect on output per person. This may be so, particularly when hours per week are very long, but in general, work output is closely correlated with hours worked, even if the relation is not proportionate.

More important, from the viewpoint of workers, the real cost of their labor in the sense of disutility to them and opportunities forgone for alternative activities is best measured in terms of hours. When such terms are used to measure labor input of various types, changes in average hours worked per week or per year may be viewed as one of the forces affecting productivity.

Hours Actually Worked

Labor-hours should be measured as those worked rather than those paid for. This is a significant distinction because, beginning with World War II, time paid for but not worked has markedly increased. It has been argued that time paid for is the significant variable in terms of real cost to the employer. But actually, an employer is hiring time on the job, and increasing time paid for off the job is merely an indirect way of increasing the compensation per hour actually worked. In other words, the hour paid for but not worked is fictitious from the technological viewpoint of the production process (although not for the payroll), and productivity measures are concerned with real input-output relations.

One reason why measures based on hours paid for have been used in industry productivity ratios is that this is the concept underlying BLS collection of data for its estimates of average hours worked per week. Such a concept was adopted by the BLS when it initiated its series some decades ago, since this was a prevalent basis of company payroll accounts. Since the war, however, most companies have kept separate figures for hours worked and have reported on this basis to the Census Bureau and, more recently, to the BLS for its special studies of payment practices. Data on average hours worked per week are, of course, merely a means of obtaining average and total hours worked per year. Surveys of hours based on data for only one week a month, however, have obvious limitations for estimating monthly and annual totals.

At the present time, companies do not customarily keep account of hours worked by nonproduction workers. The personnel department can usually make a good estimate, however, by multiplying standard hours per week times fifty-two and adjusting for holidays and the average amount of leave. With the increasing relative importance of white-collar workers, hours worked is an area in which many companies might well consider keeping more precise records.

Weighting of Labor-Hours

Although the hour is a basic unit for measuring like types of work, labor-hours as a whole are about as diverse a collection as is the capital stock. That is, there are many occupational groupings within each large firm and industry, and the occupational mix differs among firms and industries and changes over time within the same producing unit. Occupational specialties differ not only in what they do but in the level of their pay. Economic theory teaches that average hourly pay tends to reflect the relative contributions of different types of factors to the value of output. If this is so, then a worker of one specialty who is paid $7.00 an hour is presumably furnishing twice as much labor as one paid $3.50 an hour, from the viewpoint of contribution to production values.

Even if total hours worked were not to change, but there was a shift in the distribution of hours toward higher-paying occupations, weighted labor-hour input would rise. A shift toward higher-paying jobs and industries has actually occurred in the American economy, reflecting the gradual upgrading of the labor force as a result of increasing education and training, coincident with the increasing skill requirements of technology.

A practical advantage to the firm of weighting hours by occupation in calculating productivity ratios is that productivity indexes based on the weighted measures do not reflect the effect of changing occupational mix. Since one use of productivity indexes is to indicate the average increases in rates of factor compensation that would be consistent with stable prices, the weighted measures are appropriate. Unweighted labor-hour inputs are inappropriate since some of the apparent "productivity" gain has already accrued to workers in the form of upgrading. Even if it is not feasible to collect hours data by all occupational categories, it is still desirable to use the broad breakdowns that are available.

Total Average Hourly Compensation

The weights by which labor-hours of various types are combined should be average hourly labor compensation of all types, including fringe benefits, such as employer contributions to welfare funds. If total labor compensation for a period is divided by hours actually worked, the effect of time paid for but not worked shows up in compensation per hour actually worked. This weight is consistent with the labor-hour data used in the productivity ratio.

Finally, instead of weighting labor-hour data by average hourly earnings, the same result may be obtained by deflating total labor compensation by an index of average hourly compensation, including fringe benefits, representing a (variable) weighted average of wage rates of the most important occupational groups. The deflated compensation automatically reflects the effect of employee shifts. It has the same weight base as the reference base chosen as 100.0 (which should, of course, be the same base as that used for output and the other inputs).

Capital Input

Some companies now estimating labor-hour input and productivity shy away from estimating capital input (sometimes called "investor input") and the related measures of capital and total productivity. The estimator's reluctance has usually stemmed from a lack of information on possible procedures for estimating capital input, an admittedly more complex task, conceptually and statistically, than estimating labor input. However, certain estimating procedures do provide reasonable results in most instances. We will discuss first the measure of capital in constant prices, and secondly the measure of capital's contribution, or unit rate of return, in the base period. The latter applied to capital resources in real terms (i.e., in constant prices) is the capital or investor input.

Scope

The first measurement problems concern definitions. The capital of a company is composed of tangible assets (structures, machinery and equipment, land, and inventories) and intangible or financial assets (cash, notes, and accounts receivable, as well as portfolio investments in government securities and in other enterprises). Except for portfolio investments, both tangible and financial assets are required for the production of a company's output. Therefore, a comprehensive measure of a company's capital resources devoted to its production would include tangible capital and financial capital except portfolio investments. The latter are used to create output in government or other enterprises.

Need to Include All Capital Resources

It is this comprehensive coverage that is used in actual company measures described in the cases in appendix A. However, if one is obliged to be less than comprehensive (owing, e.g., to a lack of adequate staff or time), probably little distortion would be introduced by restricting capital input to tangible fixed capital (land, structures, and machinery and equipment) and, more particularly, to the depreciable component. The rationale for this is that technological innovations, the source of much of a company's productivity gains, affect fixed capital much more than working capital. Indeed, capital input is restricted to machinery and equipment. This is not recommended unless there were no changes in the company's structures during the interval being measured.

Ideally, all capital resources used by the company, whether rented or owned, should be included. Furthermore, there is no justification for distinguishing between assets financed by equity funds and those financed by debt. In practice, however, one may not be in a position to make a reasonable estimate of the value of rented capital based on the accounts of the lessee company. Frequently, the lessor company will provide the needed information; or it can be worked out from information available from trade sources; or the value may be approximated by applying an appropriate capitalization rate to the rental payments. If rented fixed capital is quantitatively important in a company's operations, every effort should be made to include it.

An alternative procedure to including the capital value of rented capital in capital input is to include the deflated rental payments in intermediate product inputs. However, in this case it might be informative to retain it as a separate entry related to output if such payments are relatively large or subject to trend.

Some analysts favor adjusting the real fixed capital estimates for rates of utilization of capacity. Weighing against this is the consideration that capital represents a cost regardless of intensity of use, besides which utilization data are not always available. If the capital estimates are not adjusted, then the productivity estimates will reflect the effects of cyclical and erratic changes in capacity utilization rates.

Another consideration is that the capital measure should have the same scope as the output measure. If the output measure excludes R&D activities, for example, the plant and equipment supporting these activities should also be excluded from capital input.

Gross or Net Depreciable Assets

A crucial question is whether the real stocks of fixed, depreciable assets (plant and equipment) should be measured gross or net of accumulated depreciation reserves. The answer to this question determines whether or not depreciation allowances will be counted as part of the return to capital. Use of gross capital return rather than net results in a significantly larger weight accorded to capital input in most firms.

We believe that the real capital measure should approximate movements in the capacity of the fixed reproducible assets to produce output. With proper maintenance and repair outlays, plant and equipment should retain its output-producing capacity up to the time it is retired (usually due to obsolescence). As an item ages, it may require some additional down-time, which would be reflected in a bit less gross output per year and some increase in purchased intermediate products for repairs, both of which would result in some decline in measured productivity.

The possible mild decline in productive capacity of plant and equipment as it ages, however, is nowhere as sharp as the decline in real net depreciated value. Depreciation is an economic concept, representing the decline in value of a reproducible fixed asset as it ages. It reflects the decline in net income-producing capacity of the asset due to eventual obsolescence, as well as the shortening of its economic life with time. Depreciation has little to do with physical productivity.

Another argument in favor of real gross, rather than net stock, measures is that they are consistent with the gross output and gross product numerators of productivity ratios. Market values of production, in current and constant prices, both before and after deduction of intermediate purchases, cover gross factor costs, including depreciation. Moreover, since labor compensation is not adjusted for depreciation of human capital, it would not be symmetrical to adjust property compensation downward for depreciation of nonhuman capital.

As noted earlier, input is the real capital stock times the base-period rate of return. If the real stock is gross, capital compensation including depreciation would be divided by the base-year gross stock for the percentage return to apply to the real gross stock estimates in other years. But the appropriate rate of return to apply to nondepreciable assets (land and working capital) is the *net* rate of return, since depreciation is not relevant. To estimate the net rate, net property income must be divided by the net stock of all capital in the base period, and the resulting percentage multiplied by the real stock of nondepreciable assets in other years. An alternative procedure is to multiply the net rate of return by the real *net* capital stock, including depreciables, in all years, then add real depreciation charges to come up to gross capital input. In the following section, then, we discuss the measurement of both gross and net capital and depreciation in constant prices, so that either approach may be followed.

Capital in Constant Prices

As in all such measures, the accounting records provide the starting point for deriving a measure of capital resources. Such records include balance-sheet statements and, depending on estimating method, expenditures on structures, machinery and equipment, and the depreciation account.

Two characteristics of typical balance sheets should be recognized. One relates to the time period covered by balance sheets — they disclose a company's resources on a given date — a moment in time; it is a stock concept. Output, on the other hand, is measured over a period of time, say, a calendar quarter or one year; it is, therefore, a flow concept. This difference does not create any estimating difficulties but does suggest the desirability of taking an average of the capital used at the beginning and end of each period.

The other characteristic is the practice of carrying assets on balance sheets at purchase price, even though the purchase may have been made years ago (typically the case with structures) and prices may have changed in the intervening years, which clearly has been the case in the post–World War II period. This characteristic, together with the durable character of fixed capital, makes the deflation of the latter a more complicated process than the deflation of working capital. Our discussion respects this distinction.

Working Capital. The first step transcribes from accounting records the working capital items (cash, notes and accounts receivable, and inventories — ideally, distinguishing raw materials, good in process, and finished goods) for the base and measured periods. For these items, the balance-sheet values at purchase price are virtually identical with values at current prices. This must be true for items that have an annual turnover rate of one or more, which is typically true of this category of asset. The estimating assignment, then, is to find a price index or series of indexes that accurately show the relationship of prices in the measured period to prices in the base period.

An aid in selecting the most appropriate price series is to ask what use is made by the company of each particular asset. Cash, for example, is used for the payment of wages and salaries, goods and services purchased, and construction. The appropriate deflator, therefore, is a composite index of average hourly earnings, prices of operating materials and other supplies, and a construction cost index for industrial structures.

Company records usually provide average hourly earnings. A price index of purchases may not already exist; it may, however, be relatively easy to compile (depending on the complexity of a company's operations) by restricting the coverage of the index to those purchases that are quantitatively important. Alternatively, some combination of the official producer price indexes compiled and issued by the BLS may serve the purpose. Still another possibility is the use of market prices reported in trade journals. For construction, existing indexes of costs can be used. The more widely used indexes are those compiled by the *Engineering News Record* (ENR) and the Turner Construction Company.

To combine the three series into a composite index, each should be weighted by its relative importance in the production process. This information should be available from the accounts dealing with the costs of goods sold.

Since accounts receivable originate in the financing of the company's sales, the appropriate deflator is the price index of its own sales. This same index could also be used to deflate finished inventories. For the adjustment of prices of raw materials inventories, the most suitable is a price index of purchased materials, as mentioned in the discussion of the deflation of cash. For semifinished inventories, the relevant index would be a composite of the purchased materials prices and average hourly earnings weighted by the relative contribution of each to the cost of semifinished inventories.

Fixed Capital. The starting point can be either the entries on the balance sheet or the accumulation of annual expenditures on structures and machinery, both gross and net of depreciation charges over their lifetimes. As we have noted, the value placed on fixed capital assets in the balance sheet is typically the value at the time of acquisition. Equally important, the assets in use at any given time usually were not acquired in a single year but over many years during which the price level may have fluctuated widely. Therefore, on any given date varying amounts of the original acquisitions will be included in net and gross fixed capital, the exact amounts depending on the length of the interval between acquisition and the base and measured periods and the length of life assigned to each depreciable asset. Since the two main categories usually have substantially different lengths of life, a separate deflator should be used for structures and another for machinery and equipment.

The arithmetic of the derivation is illustrated in table 1. The immediate problem is to express the book value of machinery in company X's balance sheet at the end of 1982 in 1982 prices.

In column 1 are the purchases of machinery at cost in each year of the ten-year period ending in 1982. The next step is to determine what these machinery purchases would have cost had they been acquired at 1982 prices. In column 2 is shown the price index of machinery, where 1982 = 100. Ideally, this price index should be based on company X's records; if this is not possible, the appropriate producer price indexes for machinery as compiled by the BLS or trade sources could be used. Purchases at cost divided by the machinery price index equal purchases in constant (1982) prices.

The sum of column 3 equals the gross value of machinery in constant prices at the end of 1982. Since we are also interested in net value after depreciation we must continue with the computations in columns 4 and 5. Assuming a ten-year life, only 10% of the purchases in 1973 would be in use in 1982, 20% of the 1974 acquisitions, and so on.

The sum for the ten years of purchases in constant prices multiplied by the percentage in use is equal to the net value of machinery in 1982 prices in use at the end of 1982 (column 5). To derive a price deflator for book values of machinery, which, as we shall soon see, is required in the calculations of the input represented by depreciation, the outlays in column 1 are weighted by the percentages in column 4 — from which are obtained the figures in column 6. The sum of column 6 divided by the sum of column 5 is the price deflator for the net book value of machinery at the end of 1982 in 1982 prices. Now, if the measured period to be compared with the base period is 1983, this series of computations in essence is repeated, starting with purchases in 1974 and extending them to 1983.

The same set of calculations should be used for structures, which typically have a length of life of forty to fifty years. Indeed, even in the machinery and equipment category, any types of importance that have a significantly different length of life from other types should have their own

TABLE 1
Derivation of Price Index of Book Value of Machinery and Equipment, Company X, 1982
(in millions of $) (average life: ten years; depreciation rate: 10%)

Year of Purchase	Value of Machinery Purchased	Price Index of Machinery	Gross Value of Machinery, 1982	% in Use, 1982	Net Value	
					1982 price, (3) x (4)	Original price, (2) x (5) = (1) x (4)
	(1)	(2)	(3)	(4)	(5)	(6)
1973	18.9	71.8	26.3	10	2.63	1.89
1974	17.2	75.1	22.9	20	4.58	3.44
1975	18.9	76.9	24.6	30	7.38	5.67
1976	21.3	83.6	25.5	40	10.20	8.52
1977	21.3	84.2	25.3	50	12.65	10.65
1978	22.3	85.5	26.1	60	15.66	13.38
1979	20.8	86.4	24.1	70	16.87	14.56
1980	23.1	88.6	26.1	80	20.88	18.48
1981	27.0	94.1	28.7	90	25.83	24.30
1982	27.9	100.0	27.9	100	27.90	27.90
Total	218.7	84.9[a]	257.5		144.58	128.79

[a] Deflator index for gross book value $= \dfrac{\Sigma \text{Col. (1)}}{\Sigma \text{Col. (3)}} = 84.9$; deflator index for net book value $= \dfrac{\Sigma \text{Col. (6)}}{\Sigma \text{Col. (5)}} = 89.1$.

deflator. However, it is important that realistic lengths of life be used. Special amortization arrangements for defense facilities, for example, which in effect are tax inducements for the expansion of certain types of facilities, should be avoided.

The next step is to divide the fixed capital gross and net of depreciation in the company's balance sheets for the base period and the measured period by these deflators of book values for structures, machinery, and equipment. This expresses all fixed assets in base-period prices.

The approach to the revaluation of fixed assets by way of the cumulation of annual expenditures (generally referred to as the perpetual inventory method) is a variant of the methodology just described for computing a deflator of book values. The underlying computations are those set out in table 1 (stopping short of the derivation of book-value deflators). This method is illustrated in case 1.

The two approaches can result in somewhat different estimates of fixed capital in constant prices. This occurs whenever depreciable capital is retired before it is fully depreciated. In the perpetual inventory method the undepreciated amount of the obsolete capital would continue to be part of fixed capital, since this method assumes that a depreciable asset is retired only when it is fully depreciated. The balance sheet, on the other hand, would reflect this unexpected obsolescence and show fixed assets as less by the amount of the undepreciated but retired capital. This discrepancy must be considerable in periods of rapid technological innovation, such as characterized the years 1948–67. For this reason, balance sheets, despite their limitations, provide the more realistic measure of resources retained for production. The approaches share the failure to reflect instances of the continued use of fixed capital after it has been fully depreciated. Which approach is used may well depend on how detailed the available accounting records are.

Investors' Input

The enquiry had led to a consideration of real net capital (i.e., capital after depreciation in constant prices), which is an intermediate stage in the derivation of investors' input. The latter is defined as real net capital weighted by the rate of return in the base period. The computation of the rate of return starts with the reported net income before tax and interest payments, but after depreciation, in the base period. Two adjustments of this reported figure are required. One is to eliminate the effect on net income of the inclusion in reported profits of inventory gains or losses. Such gains or losses result entirely from price changes (i.e., the difference between the book value of inventories and the current value) and not from changes in physical volumes. Net profits are decreased by the amount of such inventory gains and increased by the amount of inventory losses.

The other adjustment is required because reported net income is based on depreciation in book values. For this purpose, net income should be calculated after depreciation is valued in base-period prices. Since the depreciation charge based on book values reflects the same time curve of purchases as the book values of fixed capital, the deflator for the latter can be used to express book-value depreciation in base-period prices. If this adjustment raises the amount of depreciation, then reported net income should be reduced by the increased amount. Conversely, if depreciation is lowered by the adjustment, the difference should be added to reported net income.

Once reported net income of the base period is adjusted, it becomes the measure of investors' net input in the base period and is related to (divided by) the total of working and fixed capital revalued in the prices of the base period. This base-period rate of return is applied to total capital of the measured period expressed in base-period prices to obtain the investors' net input of the measured period. To this is added deflated depreciation allowances to obtain the gross capital input of investors; or, the alternative method suggested in the previous section can be used.

Total Productivity Summary

How all inputs (labor, capital, and intermediate goods and services) for the base period and measured period are expressed in base-period prices has now been explained. In the base period, the sum of the inputs in base-period prices, by design, equals the output in base-period prices. In the measured period, the difference, if any, between the sum of inputs in base-period prices and output in base-period prices is the productivity gain (or loss). The total productivity index is calculated by dividing measured-period output in base-period prices by measured-period inputs in base-period prices.

If it is desired to exclude the effect of intermediate goods and services, a total factor productivity index is computed. Total factor input equals the sum of the labor-hour input of the measured period weighted by base-period average hourly earnings (preferably including fringe benefits) and the total capital of the measured period expressed in base-period prices and weighted by the base-period rate of return plus depreciation. Since intermediate goods and services are excluded from inputs, they must also be excluded from output. So, net output is derived by subtracting intermediate goods and services from output. Net output and factor input are identical in the base period and in the measured period in current prices. However, if there has been a productivity change, net output in the measured period in base-period prices will differ from factor input in the measured period valued in base-period prices. The absolute productivity gain or loss is the same as that obtained from use of the gross output comparison. However, the factor productivity index shows larger proportionate increases (or decreases) than the total productivity index, since the base of the former is smaller by the amount of intermediate product purchases.

If partial productivity measures are desired, each factor input in base-period prices (labor and capital) is related in turn to the output in base-period prices. The respective quotients for the base period and the measured period can be converted to index numbers by expressing the measured-period quotient as a relative of the base-period quotient. As we argued in chapter 2, a fuller understanding of a company's productivity changes is obtained by measuring and analyzing total productivity indexes together with the partial productivity indexes.

In addition to analyzing the relative changes in the partial productivity indexes, the absolute constant dollar savings in each type of input can be compared with the total real productivity gain (or loss) described above. This indicates the relative amount of economizing for each type of resource input.

The absolute productivity gains, in conjunction with the net gains (or losses) of revenue owing to relative changes in prices received for outputs and in prices paid for inputs, can also be used to analyze changes in profit from one period to the next (see chapter 7). After all, the ultimate justification of productivity analysis in a free enterprise setting is its contribution to the understanding and promotion of productive efficiency in the profitable operation of the firm.

II
USES OF PRODUCTIVITY MEASURES

6

Overview of Potential Uses

The initial costs of installing a productivity measurement system are modest, and the annual costs of maintaining the system are even more so. But the costs will not be recovered unless productivity measures are used along with other information to enhance the efficiency of the enterprise and thus widen profit margins above the rates that would otherwise obtain. It is our conviction that in most companies the intelligent use of productivity data can repay many times over the costs of producing them.

A major motivation for managements to develop productivity measurement is the realization of the importance of levels and changes in productivity to profit rates and the need to track productivity explicitly as an aspect of cost control. Accordingly, the first section of this chapter is devoted to some further comments on the relationship of productivity to profit. Next, we consider the uses of productivity measures as a management tool for promoting efficiency and discuss the utility of comparisons. Finally, we discuss the use of productivity measures as a background for projections of input requirements and costs in connection with budgeting and longer-term projections required for planning purposes.

Productivity and Profits

One reason why productivity measurement was slow to spread among companies was their primary reliance on profit and loss statements to reveal levels and changes in efficiency relative to competitors. It is true that if a firm sells its outputs at the same prices as do its competitors and pays the same wage rates and other input prices, its profit margins on sales will be higher only if it uses fewer inputs per unit of output — that is, if its productivity is higher. Likewise, its profit margins will rise relative to those of competitors if its relative productivity rises, all else being equal. Competition is seldom perfect, however, and rates of return on investment reflect the net results of activities on many fronts — product planning and development, purchasing, financing, selling, and other activities besides the primary production function. This makes it all the more important to try to separate the p's and q's in production values and in costs so as to measure real outputs, inputs, and productivity changes explicitly. For, over the long run, probably the most important factor influencing profit margins is the relative rate of productivity advance, reflecting primarily the rate of cost-reducing innovations in the technology and organization of production. In the short run, the effects of productivity trends may be obscured by the relative efficiency of managements in other functions and by variations in rates of utilization of capacity. But direct measurement of productivity makes it possible to track continuously this basic ingredient of the profit equation.

Chapter 7 explains just how productivity measures can be used in profitability analysis. The rest of this chapter deals with the other, direct uses of the productivity measures. It should be stressed, however, that awareness, and measurement if possible, of the role of productivity in levels and rates of change in profits strengthens the motivation of managers to improve productivity.

The objective of increasing productivity, important as it is, is not the primary goal of rational management, since it is subject to the profit maximization constraint. To the extent that productivity gains are the results of investments, tangible and intangible, the investments should be pushed only up to the point at which the rates of return on the investments from the expected cost savings are equal to the rate of interest or alternative cost of funds to the firm. Current costs of productivity improvement, such as for productivity measurement and promotion programs, should be incurred only up to the point of equality with the present value of the cost reductions achieved as a result of the programs.

Measurement as a Management Tool for Increasing Efficiency

It is sometimes claimed that productivity measurement by itself raises productivity-consciousness when the figures are disseminated and thus may act to increase the efforts and efficiency of managers and other employees. There is some truth in this claim, although the psychological effects of measurement are greater and longer lasting if they are linked to productivity promotion programs that seek to involve workers at all levels in addressing problems and taking actions that increase productivity. Conversely, productivity promotion programs can be made more effective by the preparation and dissemination of productivity indexes that show employees the results of their efforts and reveal problem areas requiring further attention. Part 3 discusses employee involvement programs at some length. Here we merely emphasize that such programs can be more effective if linked to measurement systems, if at all possible, and we discuss other uses of productivity measures as a management tool.

By themselves, the productivity indexes are of little value. They must be analyzed and interpreted to be of use in sparking action. This involves comparisons — comparisons over time within firms, distinguishing the movements of the various partial productivity ratios; comparisons among components of a firm; and comparisons with competing firms or plants, or with averages for the industry or industries within which the firm and/or its establishments are classified.

For intertemporal comparisons, it is desirable to push the productivity measures back at least five to ten years, in order to establish the underlying trend across two or more business cycles as well as to reveal cyclical patterns of change. Measures should be at least annual, and preferably quarterly (with seasonal adjustment), to provide greater timeliness. Usefulness is also enhanced by preparation of the estimates in as much detail as possible with respect to product lines, types of inputs, and organizational components: divisions, plants, and cost centers. We are not concerned in this handbook with functional measures relating outputs of particular types of workers or groups to standards or norms, as in industrial engineering work-measurement studies. Although such measures are very useful, they do not reveal productivity trends due to technological change since the standards are set with respect to given technologies.

If the productivity performance of a firm and/or particular organizational components falls below past trends (after allowance for normal seasonal and cyclical variations), there is cause for concern, investigation, and possibly corrective action. If the firm has several plants, it can be determined which are showing relatively poorer performance. The partial productivity ratios further reveal which inputs are falling behind the average productivity changes. For example, a decline of energy productivity (increasing real energy costs per unit of output) suggests that investigation of that factor is necessary. In some cases, the movements can be rationalized, as in the case of conscious factor substitutions, to take advantage of changing relative prices. In other cases, corrective action may be indicated.

The intertemporal comparisons within the firm are more meaningful if they can be coupled with comparisons against competing firms, or the relevant industry productivity measures. Trade associations or productivity centers in the United States have occasionally made interfirm or interplant productivity comparisons when firms in the same industry have requested them and have been willing to furnish the necessary data on a confidential basis. Such comparisons are more common in Canada and in Europe than in the United States. (Chapter 8 describes this approach in some detail.) It should be noted that levels of productivity and unit costs, by type of input, as well as changes over time can be compared. The results can help management not only in appraising the firm's overall relative performance but also in identifying specific areas in which further economies in use of resources could be achieved. Similar comparisons can be made based on industry data obtainable from the Census Bureau on a grouped basis, such as quartiles or deciles of establishments with respect to the value of production, or value added, per worker.

It is simpler to compare productivity of the company with that of its industry, or in the case of a multiplant company to compare the productivity indexes of its establishments with those of the several industries in which they are classified. Although multi-input productivity indexes are available only for broad industry groupings, the Bureau of Labor Statistics (BLS) has indexes for many four-digit industries as defined by the Standard Industrial Classification Codes.[1] These comparisons are also revealing. As an example, the executive vice-president of the Mill Products division of the Aluminum Company of America (Alcoa) wrote with reference to the measurement system installed in his division in 1968:

> It was a terrible shock to discover that although output per man-hour in Alcoa had increased 20% from 1958 to 1965, the increase in the industry for the same time period was about 60%. Believe me, that stimulated real action on our part. The record since 1968 would indicate that the mechanism used in Mill Products to insure productivity growth has been relatively effective . . . measured against our 1968 base, output per man-hour in Alcoa's Mill Products has increased more than the output per man-hour of the aluminum rolling and drawing industry as a whole. If that were not the case, I might not be here to tell you about it.[2]

In addition to their utility in triggering action in competitive industries, productivity measures and comparisons are frequently used by utility companies before regulatory commissions to demonstrate efficiency gains. Detroit-Edison, for example, instituted its productivity measurement and promotion programs in response to pressure from the Michigan Public Services Commission to demonstrate productivity increases before being allowed to pass rising unit costs on to customers through rate adjustments. The Bell Telephone system used productivity measures in the 1981 Justice Department antitrust case to demonstrate the superior productivity performance of the system in order to bolster its argument against being broken up (see chapter 9).

Productivity measures may also be used as a vehicle for setting goals for performance in the period ahead. The goals can be set based on past trends, modified by other factors within the purview of management, such as expected changes in volume, or changes in technology that are being implemented. At the end of the period, actual performance can be compared with the goals. If there is a shortfall, it is a useful exercise to try to determine the reasons why.

It should be apparent from this discussion that productivity measurement does not automatically raise productivity. As is true of information systems generally, productivity measures are useful as a management tool only insofar as they provide warning signals for further investigation and institution of measures to correct the conditions that have caused productivity to lag in relation to past performance, other organizational units, company goals, competing firms, or the industry generally. It should also be emphasized that productivity measures are not all-purpose tools but must be used in conjunction with other elements of management information systems.

Budgeting and Projections

A firm's historical productivity measures provide a useful background for more accurate projections of input requirements both for the period ahead, as part of the budgeting process, and for the long run, as a basis for planning. The basic technique for both short- and long-term projections is to project productivity (O/I) and thus, the requirements for inputs per unit of output, in as much detail as possible; then, by projecting sales and output (O), total input requirements can be estimated, since $O \div O/I = I$.

As noted earlier in connection with goal setting, productivity for the period ahead should not be obtained merely by projecting the past trend. Account must also be taken of the output projection and its implication for changes in rates of utilization of capacity. If there is a cyclical movement toward more efficient rates of utilization, productivity increases would be above average, as established by past cyclical patterns. In addition, the engineers can attempt to estimate the effects on the average productivity trend of any new capacity that would be coming on stream or in the "shake down" stage, possibly replacing less efficient plant and/or equipment.

In the short-term budgeting exercise, the input requirements for the coming period would be multiplied by the projected average price per unit to arrive at total costs. In some cases, such as labor under contract or interest on embedded debt, future costs are already known. In other cases, such as prices of purchased materials and services or interest on new debt, prices must be projected by the usual economic forecasting techniques. The cost projections may be of aid in pricing policies if the firm is a price-maker. However, if the projected unit costs are not consistent with the initial price projection used in the sales forecast, a second approximation of future sales and output and related variables would be in order. If the firm is a price-taker, projections of sales and of costs would provide the basis for forecasting profits.

The historical and projected labor productivity numbers are also relevant to wage negotiations. Basically, wage changes are heavily influenced by competitive forces, and in the long run, trends in real average hourly earnings in all sectors tend to approximate the trend of labor productivity in the business economy as a whole. In the short run, however, when the productivity changes of an industry and a firm are below average, unit costs and prices tend to rise more than the economy average with adverse effects on sales and profits; so management has a good case to argue for below-average increases. Conversely, a favorable productivity, cost, price, and sales outlook means that wage increases can be more generous. What is important is that management be knowledgeable concerning past and prospective productivity movements before entering wage negotiations.

Long-range projections of output, productivity ratios, and input requirements are generally based on trend extrapolations without adjustment for cyclical variations since it is not possible to forecast the cyclical position of an economy, industry, or firm ten or fifteen years out. The real sales projection is usually based on projection of real GNP by type of expenditure, linked to industry outputs by means of input-output matrices. The firm then projects its expected share of industry markets. The productivity projections are based on extrapolations of past trends, modified by expert engineering views of probable major cost-reducing innovations that are likely during the ten or fifteen years ahead and the probable rate of diffusion of current and prospective innovations.

Account should also be taken of probable interfactor substitutions designed to economize on factors whose prices are rising relatively, such as energy and selected types of labor and materials. The projections of output and of factor productivities together yield the projections of input requirements for the future year.

Both the short- and long-range input projections are obviously useful as a background for planning capital outlays, financial requirements, personnel recruitment and training policies, and materials procurement strategy. Since company planning is done against the backdrop of macroeconomic trends and structural changes, we summarize them in chapter 9, with particular regard to the productivity factor.

7

Productivity and Profitability Analysis: The APC Performance Measurement System

Introduction

We have seen that a total productivity measure has substantial advantages over individual partial measures for the business analyst. Not only does it ensure that all the factors of production will be reflected in business decisions, but it makes available information on trade-offs between factors that individual partial ratios alone do not provide. Since many of the types of productivity improvement common in American industry are reducible to a factor trade-off, it is essential, at least at higher levels of the organization, to have a measurement tool that produces trade-off information.

However, total productivity measurement is *not* required at all levels of an organization. Day-to-day operational control can effectively be exercised through work measurement techniques, partial measures, and old-fashioned subjective judgment. But as organizations become more complex, and as the managers of those organizations become more responsible for factor trade-offs, the need for total productivity measures increases.

Even total productivity measurement, supplemented by simpler operational measures, will not satisfy all management data needs. Top management (and its Wall Street observers) is accustomed to thinking in terms of profitability — the impact on earnings per share of the decision in question.

Corporate management, therefore, analyzes its various divisions on a profitability basis. Any form of measure other than profitability risks being sidetracked if it is not reconcilable directly with profitability planning data. It would be futile (and unnecessary) to suggest that there is anything wrong with profitability as a basic measure of business performance. However, financial accounting has not evolved in a way that assures complete faith in current dollar financial statistics; one of the adverse effects of inflation has been to erode confidence in the financial accounting system. An important feature of total productivity measurement is the inflation-free analysis of overall business performance. Thus, if a total productivity measurement system directly connects to the profitability planning system, it will complement profitability analysis and continue to be useful.

The connecting link between profitability analysis and productivity analysis is the relative change of input prices and output prices. This relationship reflects the combined efforts of both purchasing and product-pricing decisions. Most approaches to total productivity measurement make price and cost information of subordinate interest or reject it entirely. General purpose deflators are used to adjust dollar data into constant dollars or physical-equivalent data. These deflation indices, however, generally do not directly reflect the experience of an individual corporate entity but rather some surrogate macroeconomic compendium. If a company does have its own cost and price information and can put it into usable index form for profitability-productivity analysis, the link between profitability and productivity can then be completed.

We will discuss a method of total productivity measurement that was developed under the auspices of the National Productivity Institute of the Republic of South Africa. The key developer, Basil Von Loggerenberg, outlined the basic system to associates of the APC in early 1978. The APC has reviewed and revised the basic approach and has developed procedures that are being applied increasingly by U.S. industrial firms. APC measurement seminars provide details throughout the United States. Computer software is available to aid in calculations. Independently, Von Loggerenberg and Data Resources Incorporated (DRI) have developed a productivity model called REALST, which is similar to the APC Performance Measurement System.

The key elements of the APC Performance Measurement System are profitability, productivity, and price recovery. The relationship is illustrated in figure 1. Reading across the output and input rows, one can see that everything starts from that keystone of cost accounting, value = quantity × price. For any output and for any input, the dollar value expressed on the income statement can be said to be made up of a physical quantity (or its equivalent) multiplied by a unit price or unit cost. Reading vertically, and thinking in terms of relationship over time, one can define the relative change of output value compared to the relative change of the input values as change in profitability. This profitability can be expressed as a rate of contribution to "economic" earnings from the operation being analyzed. This is directly related to earnings-per-share improvement, which is the apparent target of all financial analysis.

The relationship between quantity of output and quantity of input in the second column at a point in time and over time is called *productivity*, as defined previously. These quantities are expressed in physical terms or,

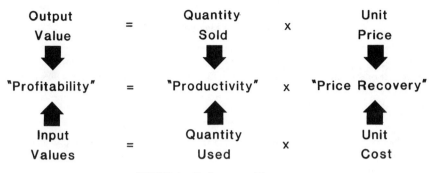

FIGURE 1. Performance Measures

alternatively, in constant dollar terms, which is the best available surrogate. The third columnar relationship, price recovery, is defined as the relationship between change in unit price and change in unit cost over time. It is an index of relative inflation or, in other words, an index of the ability (or desire) of an organization to pass on its unit cost changes through price changes.

The APC Performance Measurement System essentially provides a matrix that connects change in profitability, productivity, and price recovery with each of the input factors as demonstrated in table 1. The change is expressed as an improvement ratio and as a dollar effect. Both are necessary, because an organization is typically interested in knowing which factors show the largest percentage changes, but it is also interested in identifying those factors that provide the largest net impact in dollars.

Most businesses keep very good track of profitability, but they are usually unable conveniently and routinely to analyze whether their profitability changes are the result of productivity or of price-cost movements. In a period of high and greatly fluctuating inflation, where unstable price and cost relationships mask quantity changes, this sort of tool is vital for an understanding of likely future direction of the firm.

Methodology

The data required for the APC Performance Measurement System are value, quantity, and price for each time period for each output and input of the entity being analyzed. For each data element, the third variable can automatically be obtained if two are available. This system can treat (1) two time periods, (2) actual versus budget, or (3) any other two-element comparison. The two-period ratios can be linked to other pairs of periods to trace changes over a time span. Value, quantity, and price of the various outputs and most of the inputs (labor, capital, materials, and energy) can be derived from most basic accounting systems. Care must be taken to

TABLE 2
APC Performance Measurement System

Product or Resource	Period 1			Period 2		
	Value	Quantity	Price ($)	Value	Quantity	Price ($)
	A	B	C	D	E	F
OUTPUT						
Chairs	50,000	1,000	50.00	66,000	1,200	55.00
Tables	40,000	200	200.00	33,600	160	210.00
Total output	90,000			99,600		
INPUT						
Materials						
Maple stock	20,000	20,000	1.00	25,200	21,000	1.20
Varnish	1,000	100	10.00	1,200	100	12.00
Screws	200	200	1.00	160	148	1.08
Total materials	21,200			26,560		
Labor						
Woodworker	24,000	4,000	6.00	30,400	3,800	8.00
Finisher	8,000	1,000	8.00	8,320	800	10.40
Total labor	32,000			38,720		
Energy						
Electricity	3,000	30,000	0.10	3,780	27,000	0.14
Capital						
Cash	600	8,000	0.075	560	7,000	0.080
Leases	1,800	24,000	0.075	1,920	24,000	0.080
Inventory	900	12,000	0.075	810	10,125	0.080
Depreciation	15,000	300,000	0.050	15,300	300,000	0.051
Pretax return	14,100	300,000	0.047	15,120	315,000[b]	0.048
Total capital	32,400			33,710		
Miscellaneous						
Taxes & insurance	1,400	1,000	1.40	1,500	1,000	1.50
Total input	90,000			104,270		
DIFFERENCE	0			(4,670)		

Source: American Productivity Center.

Note: Parentheses signify negative value.

include the inputs *consumed* and the outputs *produced* by the defined process, rather than purchases and sales, unless the "process" being analyzed purposely includes inventory responsibility. Each input category generally should further be broken into appropriate subinputs (e.g., labor type 1, labor type 2, indirect factory labor, head office personnel allocations).

Special care is needed in development of value, quantity, and price data for capital, because the method suggested represents a departure from most accounting systems. The APC Performance Measurement System includes as an input not only lease expense and the depreciation of fixed assets but also a return component (opportunity cost) that arises from

Change Ratios			Performance Ratios			Effect on Profits		
V_2/V_1	Q_2/Q_1	P_2/P_1	Chg. in Profit-ability	Chg. in Produc-tivity	Chg. in Price Recovery	Chg. in Profit-ability	Chg. in Produc-tivity	Chg. in Price Recovery
G	H	J	N	R	S	T	U	W
1.3200	1.2000	1.1000						
0.8400	0.8000	1.0500						
1.1067	1.0222[a]	1.0826[a]						
1.2600	1.0500	1.2000	0.8783	0.9735	0.9022	(3,067)	(556)	(2,511)
1.2000	1.0000	1.2000	0.9222	1.0222	0.9022	(93)	22	(115)
0.8000	0.7400	1.0800	1.3834	1.3814	1.0014	61	56	5
1.2528	1.0447[a]	1.1992[a]	0.8834	0.9785	0.9028	(3,099)	(478)	(2,621)
1.2667	0.9500	1.3333	0.8737	1.0760	0.8120	(3,840)	1,733	(5,573)
1.0400	0.8000	1.3000	1.0641	1.2778	0.8328	533	1,778	(1,245)
1.2100	0.9125[a]	1.3260[a]	0.9146	1.1202	0.8165	(3,307)	3,511	(6,818)
1.2600	0.9000	1.4000	0.8783	1.1358	0.7733	(460)	367	(827)
0.9333	0.8750	1.0667	1.1857	1.1682	1.0150	104	88	16
1.0667	1.0000	1.0667	1.1429	1.0222	1.1180	72	40	32
0.9000	0.8438	1.0667	1.2296	1.2115	1.0150	186	161	25
1.0200	1.0000	1.0200	1.0850	1.0222	1.0614	1,300	333	967
1.0723	1.0500	1.0213	1.0320	0.9735	1.0601	485	(392)	877
1.0404	1.0151[a]	1.0249[a]	1.0637	0.9878	1.0768	2,147	(230)	1,917
1.0714	1.0000	1.0714	1.0329	1.0222	1.0105	49	31	18
1.1586	0.9815[a]	1.1804[a]	0.9552	1.0415	0.9171	(4,670)	3,661	(8,331)

[a] Weighted.
[b] Added land was purchased for $15,000 at the beginning of Period 2.

forgoing that capital's alternative use. This covers both fixed assets employed and whatever working capital is appropriately charged to this entity. Thus, included in capital input is a factor that represents either a profit "standard" for that entity or simply the actual base-period profit level for that entity. If the latter approach is used, the total base-period output value will equal the total input value (by definition) and there will be no residual. If a fixed "standard" approach is taken to capital, then little expectation remains that the profit level specified will exactly equal the actual profit level in the base year. Thus, there will be a residual between output and input viewed as "profit above (or below) standard," or "economic" profit. In year two, there will be a residual regardless of approach. The difference between these residuals represents the year-to-year change in profitability, and that becomes the number the rest of the exercise aims at explaining.

Once an array is constructed with value, quantity, and price data for each subinput and suboutput in both time periods, ratios of change for each item from period to period are calculated. These results are called "change ratios." The change ratios of the individual outputs are straightforward. For later calculations, however, change ratios are also required for *total* output. This is done using base-period price-weighting for the total output quantity change ratio and current-period quantity-weighting for the total output price change ratio. To the extent that either weighting system is judged to be inappropriate for the particular circumstance, other weighting systems might be used. The APC's experience to date is that for most general purposes, particularly long-range planning, the price-weighting of quantities, for example, is not distorting.

Next, each change ratio for each subinput is divided into the corresponding change ratio for *total* output, resulting in a "performance ratio." The performance ratios on value relationship, quantity relationship, and price relationship are as previously defined: profitability, productivity, and price recovery. Thus, productivity performance ratios are the change in quantity of output between the two periods compared to the change in quantity of each of the individual subinputs. Similarly, the change in price of total output is compared to the change in price (i.e., unit cost) of each subinput. Productivity and price recovery together fully explain changes in profitability.

The performance ratios can be organized vertically in such a way that relative improvements or declines in productivity of each subinput factor can be read from the quantity performance ratio column, and changes in price recovery can be read from the price performance ratio column.

The total performance ratios for the sum of all inputs (i.e., total input) are the "total productivity" and "total price recovery" ratios, which in one sense, can be considered the purpose of the analysis. Although having a total productivity ratio is clearly valuable, the importance of the total price recovery ratio is often overlooked. However, overall ratios alone are not sufficient for interpretation. The APC system goes beyond these ratios and also translates them into their dollar effects on profitability.

The APC Performance Measurement System indicates the number of dollars involved when a performance ratio is above or below unity. Thus, for example, if a productivity ratio for one subinput is 1.05 instead of 1.00, the system calculates the dollar effect of the 5% change in productivity. The total dollar effects of both productivity and price recovery are combined for all inputs and collectively become the total explanation of the change in profit (i.e., the difference in the residuals) from one period to another.

The APC Performance Measurement System is completely reconcilable with normal accounting systems. The major differences are:

- Since capital return has been included as an input, it must be removed to comply with standard accounting practice.
- Outputs are normally based on sales value of production or its equivalent rather than on sales; materials inputs are based on consumption rather than purchases. The appropriate inventory adjustments are required to get to a correct basis.
- An economic depreciation basis is used where possible, using replacement values and "true" lives rather than official accounting lives and patterns, which are increasingly unrealistic.
- Materials enter the process on a replacement value basis rather than on the normal historical cost basis.

With these adjustments, and assuming that all expense categories have been included in the subinputs for productivity analysis, reconciliation should be straightforward.

Conclusion

The APC Performance Measurement System coexists with and complements an overall system using partial measures at individual plants and staff departments and/or work measures at still lower levels in the organization. The prime factor in selecting the proper tools is managerial need; measures are required by all organizations but for different purposes.

Top profit-center levels of an organization need measures that are appropriate for their strategic planning considerations. For example, analyzing sensitivity to assumptions made on the relationship among productivity, profitability, market share, and the like requires an all-inclusive, general productivity model in which all factors of production need to be considered. But they do not need to be considered with microscopic precision. On the other hand, price and cost relationships, often assumed away in long-range planning applications, should not be ignored.

At lower levels of the organization, managers do not need the kind of detail presented in this system. Typically, cost centers below the plant-manager level seldom require price recovery information and quite frequently cannot effect trade-offs among factors. It is not necessary to over-burden them with total productivity detail (except, perhaps, for training purposes).

The success of a measurement system often depends on the clarity with which its results can be displayed and understood. Examples of data

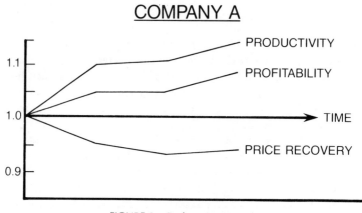

FIGURE 2.   Performance Trends

display are included (figure 2) to demonstrate graphical relationships of trends in productivity, profitability, and price recovery. If these rather simple curves are presented on a total basis and for each of four major individual factors at each review period, several organizations have found that this provides a readily understood and dramatic demonstration of important economic interrelationships.

8

Interfirm Comparisons

Comparisons of the performance levels and trends of plants producing a common range of products may be quite useful to company managers as background for developing strategies for improving productivity. As an eminent businessman once said, "The secret of success is to copy success." Interplant comparisons reveal the operational patterns of successful firms which may serve as exemplars for those that are less successful. Further, the revelation of the ranking of the establishments of various firms within an industry helps provide the incentive to raise productivity and otherwise improve rates of return on investment.

The comparative measures may be based on financial data, physical output and input data, or on a combination of financial and productivity statistics. Typical of financial measures customarily developed and used in industry are the so-called operating ratios or financial ratios, which are regularly collected by trade associations and accounting firms, based on individual company data for specified industries. Such figures are customarily published both in the form of industry averages and as interfirm comparisons (IFCs).

Physical productivity measures are developed for the economy as a whole (with deflated value data as a surrogate for nonexistent physical productivity facts) and for specific industries. In addition, some trade associations regularly produce and assemble physical productivity measures based on individual-plant records, showing either industry averages or direct, computer print-out interplant comparisons.

The "direct reports" productivity series published some years ago by the BLS, and the BLS "factory performance" case studies for selected factories in a number of industries (under the Marshall Plan program of technical assistance) also typify physical productivity measures based on factory data. The direct reports series provided information for individual products, for groups of plants categorized by significant operational characteristics, and for the "total industry." At present, however, the federal government is not assembling or publishing plant-level productivity data. The productivity series published by the BLS provides only summary labor productivity trend data based on statistics collected for other purposes.

During the 1950s and 1960s, a number of European and Asian national productivity centers carried out detailed plant-level productivity studies and structured some interplant comparisons. After a several-year hiatus following the mid-1960s during which little plant-level measurement work was carried out, those centers and some other public and private institutions renewed efforts for interplant (and/or interfirm) productivity comparisons, which provide firms in the covered industries with a meaningful basis for analyzing their own experience as compared with other firms in their industry.

Since its establishment, the APC has been developing a physical-productivity-oriented multiplant comparison program, elements of which are outlined later in this chapter. Concurrently, in recognition of the extreme disparity in productivity levels and trends among producers (even those fabricating identical products), the APC has been assembling and distributing comparative within-industry dispersion figures.

Just as the data composites for major segments of the economy are averages of individual industries, so data for a particular industry are an average of constituent individual plants. The early BLS direct reports studies revealed differences in productivity levels as great as eight to one between plants in the same industry. Further, level and trend variations were noted among groups of plants when classified by size, geographic area, extent of technological change, production method, extent of product diversification, and other relevant characteristics.

More recently, a series of BLS special studies on technological change and its impact on labor requirements provided further useful information on the productivity variance between plants in fourteen industries, with average ratios of productivity in the "most efficient" quartile to the "least efficient" quartile of the plant sample ranging from more than 4 to 1 (see table 3). (A leading European economist and statistician, Angus Maddison, emphasized the pervasiveness of such differentials in all countries. He cited figures for Swedish pulp and paper for 1964 with spreads from best to worst deciles of 3.8 to 1.0 and 4.4 to 1.0, respectively.)

APC Census Comparisons

More recently, the APC undertook a project with the Census Bureau to capture illustrative productivity data from the computer tapes that store data supplied by some seventy thousand plants each year for the Annual Survey of Manufactures. Data on shipments, output, value added by manufacture, and inputs of labor, materials, energy, and capital are assembled. Recognizing that this annual survey data constituted a valuable

TABLE 3
Productivity Variance among Plants, 1967

Industry	Mean Ratio of Productivity, Most Efficient Quartile to Avg.	Mean Ratio of Productivity, Most Efficient to Least Efficient Quartile
Hydraulic cement	1.71	2.97
Blast furnaces and steel mills	1.41	2.96
Steel pipes and tubes	1.58	2.89
Aircraft	1.28	4.54
Aircraft engines and engine parts	1.58	4.05
Other aircraft equipment	1.65	3.57
Cotton weaving	1.50	2.40
Women's hosiery (except socks)	1.60	2.80
Knit fabric	2.20	4.90
Tufted carpets	1.90	5.20
Sawmills	1.70	4.10
Tires	1.40	3.20
Aluminum rolling and drawing	1.50	4.00
Footwear (except rubber)	1.50	2.50

Source: American Productivity Center, based on data from the U.S. Department of Labor, Bureau of Labor Statistics.

Note: Value added per production-worker hour.

but as yet untapped source of productivity measurement data, the APC funded a pilot project for generating data for plants classified in eight industries deemed to reflect a cross section of U.S. manufacturing: blast furnaces, steel works, and rolling mills; metal-cutting machine tools; metal-forming machine tools; electronic computing equipment; petroleum refining; wood household furniture; men's shirts (except workshirts) and nightwear; and men's and women's footwear (except athletic footwear). Using the most recent available industry data (1976), the Census Bureau then generated statistics on the extent of variations in productivity levels among the selected industries and among plants within each industry.

The productivity dispersion series provides statistics for quartile groups of plants, with averages and high / low readings in the inner quartiles. These comparisons include:

- value added per employee
- value added per production-worker hour
- value added per production worker
- production-worker wage per production-worker hour
- production-worker wage per production worker
- value of shipments per employee
- value of shipments per production worker
- value of shipments per production-worker hour

The data reveal substantial variations in value added per production worker between industries (figure 3). The series also pinpoints the extreme

TABLE 4
Productivity Levels, 1976

Industry	Avg. All Plants	Low Quartile Avg.
Blast furnaces, steel works, and rolling mills	21.71	9.63
Machine tools, metal cutting	21.66	8.56
Machine tools, metal forming	19.01	11.45
Electronic computing equipment	42.95	4.74
Petroleum refining	78.73	16.87
Wood household furniture	8.55	5.99
Men's, youths', and boys' shirts (except workshirts)	9.11	4.56
Men's and women's shoes (except athletic)	8.06	4.54

Source: American Productivity Center, based on data from the U.S. Census Bureau.

Note: Value added per production-worker hour.

differences in productivity level for high versus low productivity segments within each industry. Industry comparisons based on value added per production-worker hour provide an obvious example of such interplant differences. The ratios of the averages for the highest to the lowest quartiles within given industries range from 2.4 to 1.0 (wood furniture) to 18.2 to 1.0 (computing equipment). Similarly, the same measures illustrate variations in the ratio of the lowest productivity quartile to the average for the industry. These ranged from 1 to 10 (computing equipment) to 7 to 10 (wood household furniture). The ratios of highest productivity quartile to the industry average ranged from 1.4 to 1.0 to 2.3 to 1.0 (table 4 and figure 4). The information about value added per employee illustrates the obvious — but not fully recognized — truth that each industry exhibits its own unique pattern. For productivity data to be useful, these individual patterns must be analyzed separately rather than as part of an economic aggregate.

In using interplant group comparisons, it is important to keep in mind that many influences may combine to determine a particular plant's level. These may include, for example, variations in

- size
- diversification of output
- age and condition of machinery
- processes applied
- average product or product line
- percentage of designed plant capacity utilized

The APC's productivity dispersion data tables, though for 1976, provide the most up-to-date material of this kind available.[1]

Past experience has shown that in a significant percentage of cases, measures of productivity trends for individual industries, based on individual factory records, proved to be more reliable than were indices

2d Quartile			3d Quartile			4th Quartile, Avg.
Avg.	High	Low	Avg.	High	Low	
17.32	19.74	14.44	22.73	25.99	19.79	34.69
15.57	17.38	11.82	19.52	21.77	17.38	29.56
16.44	17.93	14.95	21.79	26.92	17.98	35.05
14.52	21.26	6.09	30.27	40.40	21.26	86.21
39.83	58.94	26.27	80.77	106.50	58.94	184.02
8.29	9.12	7.42	10.01	11.22	9.12	14.44
7.10	8.40	5.91	9.59	10.36	8.40	17.67
6.48	7.19	5.79	8.09	9.09	7.20	11.75

calculated from statistical series computed and published for other purposes. Of much greater significance, however, is the fact that the data for individual plants can be matched with analytical information on operating characteristics to provide valuable insights as to the factors that have determined relative levels and trends of productivity in specific industries.

In interplant comparisons, especially with respect to levels (as opposed to trends), studies show that differences in all the factors listed here greatly affect productivity. Interestingly enough, however, even groups of similar sized plants making the same product line and sharing dominant technological characteristics, still showed significant dispersions in productivity levels. The BLS analyses concluded that such dispersion was most likely the result of differences in management style, capability, and the condition of labor / management cooperation.

Differences in Approach

There are a number of basic differences in concept and approach to analyzing the plant-level physical or financial productivity data generated under existing IFC programs in various industrialized nations.

Some programs (including the Canadian, New Zealand, and British) assemble primarily, but not exclusively, *financial* ratios. Other programs (including the initial efforts of the APC and the South African IFC service) focus mainly on *physical* productivity comparisons, combined in some instances with financial "cost performance" data. The content of the studies is determined by the particular needs or wishes of the participating industries and is also affected in some countries by government policy. Table 5 shows the types of ratios computed under the IFC program conducted by the Canadian Department of Industry, Trade, and Commerce. Some programs, such as the Canadian and South African, collect data from the several plants by means of plant visits by full-time staff experts,

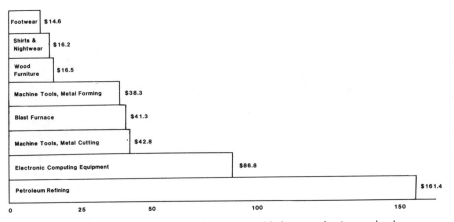

FIGURE 3.   1976 Industry Productivity Levels (value added per production-worker hour; in thousands of $)

working with accountants, engineers, and others at each plant. These programs, by their nature, yield generally excellent data but are relatively costly.

Other programs, such as that being undertaken by the APC (see table 6), rely on a mail questionnaire approach, with schedules based on appropriate developmental work in a few plants in the industry. Upon occasion, the mail questionnaire approach also requires some regional or subregional meetings with factory personnel to go over the schedules and instructions to assure that those who will prepare the data fully understand the preparation instructions and methodology.

Programs such as the British and the BLS direct reports project involve one or more regularly scheduled plant visits by productivity experts to each plant in the sample to assure that requisite records are available; to answer questions relating to the methods for assembling and reporting the data; and to review reported data with factory personnel, in order to carefully identify factors in the operational environment at the plant which, in combination, determine both the level and trend in productivity. The results make the statistical data more useful and assure identification of the most important causal factors. In some instances, the productivity analyst might counsel factory personnel on how to use the computed productivity figures in shaping logical actions to eliminate weak points and improve plant productivity. If this action is pursued systematically and in any depth, it may be categorized as a "productivity audit."

In general terms, decisions as to which course to follow in operating an interfirm comparison program will be based on several factors:

- size of the industry — number of firms (determines total operational time, and hence, cost)
- desires of the individual firms of an industry working through its

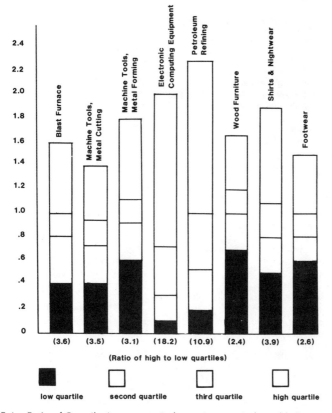

FIGURE 4.   Ratio of Quartile Averages to Industry Average (value added per production-
worker hour)

trade association, an industry publication or other organization,
and willingness to pay (if industry financed)
- whether the government or an independent foundation funds the
operation, and whether the appropriations are sufficiently large to
permit a substantial amount of plant contact

Some programs will collect data only for the total plant, whereas others
will collect such data plus information for individual products, processes,
departments, or operations. This may well be, in most instances, an
industry-by-industry decision, which will depend both on the nature of the
industry (e.g., product pattern, product mix, availability of detailed internal output and input records) and on management desires as to uses of the
completed study.

In this connection, it is relevant to note that total plant data (which
often must be derived through deflated dollar values rather than by the
aggregation of physical productivity data for the individual products or
departments) is generally of more interest to comptrollers, accountants,

TABLE 5
Interfirm Comparison, Sample Consumer Products Sector, 1977

		Highest	Median	Lowest
Return on assets				
Operating profit/operating assets	%	17.8	6.3	1.2
Profit margin, turnover of assets, & gross profit				
Operating profit/sales	%	12.4	5.8	0.9
Sales/operating assets	times	1.6	1.3	0.7
Gross profit/sales	%	22.5	19.1	12.9
Prod. costs (/sales value of prod.)				
Prod. costs	%	87.1	80.9	77.5
Materials & components	%	51.1	45.8	35.8
Total prod. labor cost	%	37.3	27.9	23.0
Mfg. overhead	%	13.1	8.4	5.2
Operating expenses (/sales)				
Total operating expenses	%	17.3	12.0	8.9
Selling & promotion	%	9.9	5.5	3.6
Administration	%	8.9	6.2	3.7
Asset utilization ratios (/$1,000 of sales)				
Total operating assets	$	1,343	775	631
Current assets	$	874	404	348
Fixed assets	$	504	321	200
Current asset utilization (/$1,000 of sales)				
Raw material inventory	$	458	95	43
Work-in-process inventory	$	59	23	9
Finished goods inventory	$	238	83	41
Total inventory	$	653	182	144
Accounts receivable	$	424	195	150
Other current assets	$	52	5	1
Fixed asset utilization (/$1,000 of sales)				
Land & buildings	$	292	118	57
Machinery & equipment	$	360	187	121
Road vehicles	$	16	5	2
Furniture & fixtures	$	29	9	3
Productivity ratios				
Sales/prod. employee	$	40,250	31,572	18,790
Value added/prod. employee hours	$	17.45	8.39	5.27
Value added/prod. floor area	$	134.63	73.16	51.39
Sales increase (decrease) over prec. year	%	26.6	(2.5)	(34.5)
Prod. labor costs/prod. employee hours	$	5.74	4.41	3.65
Machinery & equip./prod. employee	$	10,349	5,680	4,005

Source: Reprinted, with permission, from Imre Bernolak, "Interfirm Comparison in Canada," in *Productivity Measurement,* ed. David Bailey and Tony Hubert (Westmead, Eng.: Gower, 1980).

Note: Each row of ratios shows the median and extremes of that particular ratio. As such, ratios in this table are not additive vertically. Also, parentheses signify negative value.

and factory managers than to production supervisors or industrial engineers. The latter, in most instances, find of more direct interest and use physical productivity data relating to individual products, processes, cost centers, or machining stations, whereby unit labor-hour inputs may be matched against both the output and machine-hour inputs or energy consumption. Both of these types of measure are conceptually valid and

TABLE 6
APC Schema for Interplant Comparison

	Data for Your Plant			Data for Your Competition			
			Avg.	High	Low	Quartiles 1–4
Productivity			%				
Ratio	80	81	Change	80 81	80 81	80 81	80 81

| Total plant |
| Output per |
| Employee |
| Labor-hour |
| BTU of energy |
| Value added per |
| Employee |
| Labor-hour |
| $ capital input |

	Production Method	Plant Size	Technical Improvement	Product Quality Line
	Job Lot Line	High Med. Low	Signif. Some None	High Med. Mass Mkt.

| Total plant |
| Output per |
| Employee |
| Labor-hour |
| BTU of energy |

	Data for Your Plant			Data for Your Competition			
			Avg.	High	Low	Quartiles 1–4
			%				
	80	81	Change	80 81	80 81	80 81	80 81
Ratio of
Labor cost/
labor-hour
Energy BTUs/
labor-hour
Machine hours/
labor-hours
Capital input/
employee

	Data for Your Plant			Data for Your Competition			
			Avg.	High	Low	Quartiles 1–4
			%				
	80	81	Change	80 81	80 81	80 81	80 81
Specific products,
processes, or
departments
Output per
Machine-hour
(by type)
Labor-hour
$ material input

(continued on next page)

TABLE 6, continued

	Data for Your Plant			Data for Your Competition			
				Avg.	High	Low	Quartiles 1–4
Productivity Ratio	80	81	% Change	80 81	80 81	80 81	80 81
Ratio of Waste/good product Labor cost/ $ machine use							

Source: American Productivity Center.

useful — and to a reasonable degree, the APC program attempts to cover both levels, where the nature of the industry permits.

Plant data can be used for comparative analyses of factors determining productivity levels and trends. In some instances (such as in the BLS direct reports series, the South African studies, and the APC Multifirm Comparison Program), it is essential to collect a substantial amount of information on factory operational characteristics. These data are then used as an integral part of the development of productivity ratios for groups of plants with similar characteristics, compared or contrasted to data for other firms with different characteristics. The results, when properly processed, are a useful appraisal and an analytical tool.

Unlike some of the other IFC programs, that of the APC attempts to provide respondents with a feedback of comparisons of a variety of physical productivity ratios, relating inputs of energy, labor, capital, and materials to factory output by product, process, or department, in addition to the factory total. Industry officials indicate an increasing interest in such multi-input comparisons.

Profile of the Projected
APC Multifirm Comparison Program

The APC is planning to conduct Multifirm Comparison Programs to provide data for individual (unidentified) plants and for specific products or processes of importance in the industry. Such studies will provide series on both levels and trends in productivity, utilizing disguised individual factory statistics, with an update and feed-out. The initial comparison printouts will provide respondents with averages and dispersions of their competitors' productivity levels and trends, both aggregated and broken down into groups of plants with like characteristics (such as size, location, diversification of output, production method, percentage of capacity utilization, and other factors of specific relevance to each industry). The printouts will identify the respondent's own data by a code number, which will serve as the only mode of identity. The reports will provide information deemed of analytical value to the users in understanding their comparative performance as background for appropriate activities.

In most cases, a later report will provide data for the entire industry. The approach of the APC in conducting this program will involve prior arrangement with one or more appropriate trade associations or other entities (for example, a specialized trade journal, such as *Plastics Technology*) with which the APC is working for each industry covered. The industry entity will facilitate work by the APC technical staff in determining the relevant scope and approach to the study. In general, the "association(s)" will approve the final data collection package and will either fund or arrange for coverage of the APC operational costs for the project.

Data will be collected by mail questionnaire, with either the association or an appropriate third party (such as an accounting firm) handling the mailing of schedules in a manner to preserve anonymity of the reporting firm. A computer will process data, with the report to respondents in the form of a computer print-out.

Types of data to be collected and the measures computed and provided for each industry will be those deemed of most usefulness to the respondents. In general, the requisite data for IFCs can be assembled from factory accounting records on outputs and inputs of labor, capital, materials, and energy along the lines outlined in an article in a recent issue of *Plastics Technology,* which lays the groundwork for a planned interfirm productivity comparison program for the plastics products industry.[2]

Most of the interplant comparisons in which the APC will be involved will include measures of levels and trends of outputs (physical production, shipments, or value added by manufacture) related to some or all of the inputs (labor, capital, materials, and energy).

In addition to the averages for all plants, the reports will customarily involve various average productivity ratios for plants grouped according to the basic characteristics noted earlier. Although the nature of the computer print-out will vary with each industry, table 6 indicates in a general way the form and content for the presentation.

Status of IFC Programs and Follow-up Consultancy

The Austrian, Canadian, and South African programs are conducted by the federal governments, as are those of Turkey, New Zealand, and Ireland. The German IFC program is one element of the activities of the federally sponsored RKW (German productivity center), with funding derived both from revenues for services rendered and from government grants. The British and Australian IFC programs are privately organized and funded. Fees for services in each instance represent a substantial element in coverage of operational costs (see table 7).

TABLE 7
Interfirm Comparisons in Ten Countries, October 1979

	Australia	Austria	Canada	Germany (West)	Hong Kong
Name	Aust. Inst. of Mgt. (other IFCs: Dept. of Prod., Univ. of New England)	WIFI (Institute for Economic Development)	Dept. of Industry, Trade & Commerce (Business Services Branch)	RKW (Mgt. & Prod. Centre)	Hong Kong Prod. Centre
Status of organization	Private; attached to AIM: nat. mgt. organ., funded by participants	Public-private; public corp. in Fed. Econ. Chamber (*all* employers are members)	Public; fed. govt.	Public-private; private non-profit, publicly sponsored: fed., regional, & SMEs	Public; nonprofit
Main objective	Mgt. analysis & info. for firms & assns.	Info. for firms & recommendations for sector for future	Solid info. & advice for firms & govts.	Solid group analyses, recommendations for future	Assess prog. of tech. assis. for local
Staff on IFC	1 exec. sec., 2 consultants (part-time)	4 execs., 20 freelance consultants under contract	3 execs., 20 consultants (part-time)	2 execs. & freelance expert consultants	2 execs. (part-time)
Coverage	Mainly mfg., some trade & health care (13 projects underway)	Mfg. (300 firms/yr.)	Mainly mfg., some services (240 firms/yr., 12 sectors/yr.)	Mainly mfg. 3 projects (10-50 firms each/yr.)	Mfg.
Scope & content	Each IFC designed to meet specific sector needs (assets, costs, specific problem areas) 20–70 ratios, other stat. info.	Analysis of financial statements, sector econ. situation, & operational analysis; profit & loss analysis & 40 ratios	25–30 ratios, mainly production performance; background info.	Combines macro & micro; sales, technology, mgt. qualifications; trends affecting structure; proposals to eliminate sources of loss	Prod. measurement based on official production stats.
Frequency	Varies — most annual, some mo. or quar.	Every few yrs. — ad hoc	2 annual, then every few yrs.	"Once for all," i.e., every 10 years	Ad hoc
Data collection	Coded questionnaire; late returns followed up	Personal visits (using questionnaire); opportunity to ask for consultation	Personal visits & personal follow-up interviews; consultation	Questionnaire & visit; analyzing co. & branch stats.; work with assn.	Interviews with questionnaires
Who gets the results	Participants only; if agreed, sector report & averages to assns.	Participants only (confidential); sector report to WIFI & govt.; summaries to the press	Participants only; sector reports to govt.; summaries to assns.	Participants only; neutral report to assns. & govt.; summaries to the press	Firms & sponsor

Source: Reprinted, with permission, from David Bailey and Tony Hubert, eds., *Productivity Measurement* (Westmead, Eng.: Gower, 1980).

Ireland	Japan	New Zealand	Turkey	U.K.
Irish Prod. Centre	Japan Prod. Center	Dept. of Trade & Industry (Productivity & Tech. Div.)	Nat. Prod. Centre (MPM)	Centre for Interfirm Comparisons
Public; state agency, controlled by employers & unions, funded by govt.	Private; nonprofit	Public; govt. agency	Public; semi-autonomous, set up by law; funded by govt. & industry	Private; nonprofit; funded mostly by firms; some govt. funds for research
Comparative performance standards for firms	Assess prod. growth & its fruits, foster mgt. policy, help econ. growth pol.	Organized comp. of key business data for mgt.	Info. for mgt.; promotes interfirm co-op. & flow of info.	Helps firms improve prod.; research into factors
At max., 4	4 execs.	1 exec., 4 external consultants	12 execs.	10 execs.
Services (retail, wholesale, advertising), mfg.	25 p.a., mainly mfg., primary & services sectors (5–160 firms/IFC)	Mfg. services	Mfg. (150 plants)	Mfg. & various services (30–35 sectors/yr.)
29 – ratios plus other production stats.	28 index nos. based on public financial statement: VA produced, VA dist., labor share, cost, capital profit, dist. net profit groups	±30 ratios of profit cost/sales, turnover of assets, staff performance, bldg. utilization, growth	43 ratios: basic, technical, cost structure	60–100 mgt. ratios, and background data
Mfg. & wholesale every 3 yrs.; retail annual	Annual	Annual	Annual	Most annual, some quar. or mo.
Questionnaire & visit; in many cases, only personal visits provide good data	Financial statements issued by Minis. of Finance	Questionnaire & personal visits to non-respondents	Questionnaire & visit; need to convince firms of advantages	Questionnaire & some visits; assure comparable definitions & measures; discount for quick returns
Participants only; summary sometimes to the press	Part to govt. agency; part sold to firms & trade unions	Participants only; summary with upper & lower quartiles to assn. & prod. c.	Participants only; in future, anonymously also to assn.	Participants only; if agreed, also assn.

Note: All dollar amounts are in U.S. currency. (continued on next page)

TABLE 7, continued

	Australia	Austria	Canada	Germany (West)	Hong Kong
Format of presentation	Ratio print-outs to participants with guide to interpretation showing own data & averages, deviations, sometimes rank-ing. Written reports at extra charge. Follow-up group seminars.	Results to par-ticipants with individual & econ. com-ments, with rec's. Explana-tions for inter-pretation. Follow-up visits. Neutral sector report with only averages, com-ments & ranges.	Tabular results of all firms anonymously to participants, with detailed practical com-ments. Follow-up visits. Neutral reports to govt. with averages and ranges.	Averages & ranges & written explanations & rec's to firms, with no com-ments on other firms. Follow-up visits to discuss action.	Tabular
Finance	No grants. Paid by participants, through assn., in advance. Fee $70 – depends on depth & & type of report.	Subsidies from Min. Trade & Industry case by case. For econ. studies gen. costs funded by WIFI. Each firm pays $160 of total.	Funded by Gov't. Cost $1,400 per company for consultants plus $350 in-house cost. Sector reports included. Some form of cost recovery is being con-sidered.	Usually 50% of costs covered from govts. through RKW, 50% by industry Estimated cost per firm: $2,300.	Sponsor & general overhead budget
Promotion	Very much a personal presen-tation exercise. Through trade assn. set up pilot study, address assn. meet-ings. Some arti-cles also written	Trade assns. seminars, leaflets, info. in trade journals	Word of mouth, letters to presidents, personal visits and phone calls of dept. assn. meetings	Trade assns. primarily	Letters
Problems of measure-ment & definitions, etc.	Currently focus-ing on perform-ance measure-ment: little done before in Australia	Definitions and interpretation given. Recently computerized	Issues: choice of measures, breadth, confi-dentiality, financing evaluation of effectiveness, desirable fre-quency inter-national comparisons	RKW works with committee of sector & govt. to avoid problems, set out tasks & procedures, develop action programs. Imple-mentation of recommendations emphasized	How to convince leading trade assns. to support IFC?
Address	18/65 Queens Road Melbourne 3004	Hoher Markt 3 1011 Wien	235 Queen St. Ottawa Ontario K1A 0H5	Dusseldorf Str. 6236 Eschborn	173 Des Voeux Rd. P.O. Box 16132 Central Hong Kong

Ireland	Japan	New Zealand	Turkey	U.K.
Individual anonymous results with ranges & explanations to participants. Comments included on performance.	Individual firm's results shown separately – grouped results by industry.	Firm gets own results for each ratio plus written comments. Prod. c. offers assist. of its field officers.	Anonymously all ratios given to firms & quartiles & medians. Plans to expand reporting.	Firms get anonymously all ratios with averages & written report on how to use. Comments on request. Visits if required.
60% govt. subsidy for IPC. No specific for IPC. Participants pay partial fees, varied greatly. Fees: $65–$210 per firm, not depending on service.	JPC receives regular MITI subsidy of 1.7% of total income.	Partial degressive state subsidy for total gp. cost. Firm contributes $40 to first IPC, rising later.	From Treasury 13% State enterprise 32% Chambers 40% Misc. 15%. Costs per firm in 1978 $420.	No govt. subsidies but grants for R&D work. Usually paid by firms. Sometimes support of assn. Fees vary by complexity & service provided. Fees per firm: UK: $450–1,100 International $1,850.
Direct canvassing of potential participants, assns. meetings, printed media.	Promo. lit. for selling results	Ind. assns., field officer contracts, seminars & literature.	Trade assn. & promotional material.	Promotional literature. Trade assns. meetings & seminars, contacts with previous participants.
Most work in retail distrib., where technical problems not great. Main problems: lack of comparability, overcoming reservations re confidentiality & practical benefits; meaningful international comparisons	Problems of intl. comparison	Measurement problems discussed with ind. reps. & consultants. How to help unsophisticated small firms implement conclusions?	Variations of accounting practices of private enterprises. Interested in developing common basis for international comparisons.	Interest: choice of measures, treatment of assets & overheads, transfer prices, international comparisons, balance between need for detail vs. paperburden. How to obtain maximum participation & quick returns.
35 Shelbourne Road Dublin 4	No. 1–1 Shibuya 3-Chome Shibuya-Ku Tokyo 150	Private Bag Wellington	Mithatpasa Caddesi 46 Ankara	25 Bloomsbury Square London WC1A 2PJ

A number of the country IFC programs collect some information on factory characteristics, such as size, geographic location, and production methods. The BLS program and the approach used by the APC include a number of other factors, such as age and condition of machinery, extent of technological change, diversification of output pattern, production methods, quality line of product, payment systems, and others that have been found significant for some industries. The South African program also involves an in-depth "productivity audit" of factory operational characteristics, productivity experience, and approaches for improvement.

Some countries follow-up with company officials as a built-in part of the IFC program, with personal visits to review results with company executives and, in some instances, consultancy on indicated productivity improvement actions. Generally, the nature and the extent of follow-up is governed by the desire of the customer and his willingness or ability to fund the professional costs involved. In the case of South Africa, the government pays a substantial portion of the basic cost but requires the recipient to fund some of the consultancy charges. In the German program, where average costs per firm are quite high, consultancy is considered a built-in part of the IFC and the government and the company split the costs equally. Follow-up consultancy is a standard part of the British IFC program, with the respondent funding all or part of the charges.

An Example of Follow-up Consultancy: The APC "Productivity Focus"

Focus is a diagnostic structure for assessing how an organization is functioning with regard to productivity and quality of work life. Its primary objectives are to:

- identify those significant opportunities that improve the quality of work life and the productivity of the human, material, capital, and technological assets available to the organization
- develop strategies for capitalizing on the key opportunities
- obtain commitment from the client organization to take action in accordance with planned strategies

The diagnostic structure is built around data gathering, analysis, and action planning in seven key areas vital to productivity and through which improvements in productivity can be attained:

- assets — human, capital, material, and technological
- goals
- awareness and promotion
- reward and recognition
- measurement and analysis
- employee participation
- organization and leadership

Although it can vary with the organizational unit being studied, a

typical focus project requires about eight weeks and involves a multidisci-
plinary team of three with skills in operations management, behavioral
science, productivity measurement, and project management. The process
can be applied to any level of an organization, but the APC's initial projects have been conducted at the plant, mill, or regional operations level of
divisions within large, diversified corporations.

Heavy emphasis is placed throughout the project on the close involvement of key personnel in the organization in the assessment process and
development of action plans. This type of involvement is critical to
reaching consensus on what the key opportunities are; to creating a sense
of ownership within the organization of the strategies developed; and to
obtaining commitment to the actions and changes required to take full
advantage of the identified opportunities for improvement.

Subject to this emphasis, the project phases are fairly traditional. Considerable stage setting is done during *project initiation* to develop a working relationship with the management team, to assure that everyone
understands the process and project objectives, and to introduce the project effectively to the organization at large. *Data gathering* is accomplished
by observation, analysis of statistical data and other documents, and
extensive interviewing at all levels and in all functional areas of the organization.

Analysis is generally done in Houston by the project team members and
is followed by an intensive *feedback* phase in which their findings and conclusions are reviewed in depth with the management team. This phase is
critical to reaching agreement between the APC team and management
about what the current situation is, where the real opportunities lie, and
which projects have the highest priority.

Strategic planning flows logically from the feedback phase and again
requires close interaction with management to codevelop the responsibilities, timing, resources, work steps, and other areas necessary for
improvement. It is APC's objective to have managers view the action plans
as their own rather than as the recommendations of the APC. A *final
report* is prepared to document the project and resulting strategies.
Follow-up is provided periodically after the on-site work to review progress against plans and facilitate attainment of benefits from the project.

ANNEX

Elements Involved in Establishing a
System of Plant Productivity Measures

For readers who are actively involved with company information
systems and those charged with organizing and carrying out programs of
productivity measurement and/or interplant comparisons, the following

notes will supplement usefully the earlier material on productivity measurement concepts and systems.

A primary element at the initial phase of developing simple or complex plant-level productivity measures for any industry is to identify the types and forms of records extant and to verify actual and potential interfaces of the accounting, engineering, and production records that are required — whether they exist or must be developed.

The early identification of the specific *level* and *nature* of the outputs and inputs to be tracked and related through the productivity measurement system should follow. For example, in the context of company policy and the particular features of the industry and plant setup, at what level can the outputs and inputs be identified, recorded, and reported out? Plant total? Department? Cost center? By process? For specific machine operations?

Next to be considered is the nature of the measures to be framed. Will they be for the total plant only, at least in the beginning? Will they tie into individual processes or products? If so, is there a product mix or noncontinuous operation structure that will require the identification of individual models (or a product) or production cycles or runs (for process operations), selected to represent fairly the broader category? How will the input records be shaped to match up, to assure comparability — both on a one-time basis and over a span of years? Should the inputs for the selected departments, subproducts, processes, or cost centers be matched up in such a way that energy, materials, labor, and other requirements are tied into specific partial outputs, or to the finished output at the plant level? (For example, can or should the inputs for the cutting department in a garment plant be related to the dozens of parts cut, or to the number of finished garments?)

The next productivity measurement question to arise is, What interfaces — if any — are to be made in the unit output patterns and the ratios? Is material to be related to waste and to the amount of good product? Are machine hours — for a department or for individual major items — to be tracked and related to labor-hour inputs, or to standard staffing quotas? Can energy be related in an appropriate manner to other inputs at the level of individual cost centers, departments, processes, and for products, or only at the plant level? For the labor inputs, how effectively can factory records identify direct labor inputs for the measured production being tracked, and how best may one measure the related indirect or overhead labor — by cost center, by department, or for the plant as a whole? Is the measurement system to be shaped to track *only* physical productivity relationships (including any or all of the above), or are financial figures to be included and related — wages, energy cost, material cost, capital input, dollar value of output?

The analysis of unit costs for the inputs and the output, including their relationship to changing input *prices* per unit and to the changes in physical productivity, can provide useful insight into the true sources of bottom-line profitability of the operation. Whether or not to include this adjunct element in the measurement system must be decided on the basis of company policy. The physical productivity measures are of more value when they are geared to show clearly the productivity cost performance contribution to ultimate profitability of the operation. Some managers, however, may feel more comfortable with their existing financial ratio analyses.

Once the foregoing questions have satisfactorily been answered, the firm should ask, What is the best way to shape appropriate aggregations of the data identified for components, products, processes, departments, models of representative products, or other items? If the target is a single-plant company, and if the measures are only at the plant-total level, the question answers itself. However, if submeasures are shaped, and if the company is a multi-plant operation, then the aggregation approaches are very similar in concept to the array of possible approaches to aggregating productivity data for an industry. Since appropriate weighting systems will be involved, one should ask, Must they be in deflated-value terms, or can they be in equivalents appropriate to the input of reference — labor-hour equivalents? Materials? Machine-hours? [3]

Once the firm's productivity measurement system is in place and functioning, how will management compare its experience to that of others? For this purpose, even in the absence of an interplant comparison program such as those discussed here, management may use industrywide measures such as those published under the APC's multi-input index service, or the labor productivity series published annually by the BLS or available on request, as noted in chapter 9. Also, management may compute, if it wishes to do so, industry summary measures from statistics published by the Census Bureau in the *Annual Survey of Manufactures.*

Finally, the last, but far from the least important, consideration: How and to what extent will management want to track cause and effect in its productivity experience, the analysis of the factors which determined the space and direction of productivity change? For such tracking to be truly effective, a parallel data collection and analysis system is required. Some of the requisite information is certainly already in the company records — but some must be generated *de novo.* A few examples of such "factors" should suffice:

- changes in plant machinery and equipment
- revisions in plant layout and work flow
- introduction of new product lines or changes in product design
- switches in the type of power used and how it reaches the individual machine center
- changes in the structure and average skills of the work force

- introduction of new hours worked and shift schedules
- adoption of additional and/or newer types of computer controls, automation, and robotization of plant equipment
- variations in the utilization of the plant's designed capacity
- new on-stream operation of major plant installations

The assembly and use of analytical information of this type in conjunction with the statistics on productivity dynamics provide management with another effective tool for decision-making.

9

Industry and
Economy Comparisons

More readily feasible for most companies than interfirm comparisons (IFCs) are comparisons of productivity changes of the firm with those of the industry or industries in which it is classified. The BLS publishes time-series of output per labor-hour or per employee for more than one hundred industries and can provide unpublished estimates for most of the rest on request. The multi-input productivity estimates sponsored by the APC are available for thirty-one major industry groups (see appendix C). Additional industry coverage is being added pursuant to industry request and support funding.

If productivity growth of a firm is significantly below that of its industry or industries for an extended period of time, that is indeed a warning signal. The case of Alcoa recounted in chapter 6 dramatically illustrates the action that can be triggered by recognition of poor productivity performance. Unless unfavorable relative productivity trends are turned around, it is almost certain that profit margins will fall until bankruptcy ensues. Conversely, favorable relative productivity performance is likely to be associated with above-average or rising profit rates, which confirms that management is on the right track, although that should not become grounds for complacency. In the case of regulated companies, demonstrably superior productivity performance can be a useful lever in dealing with regulatory authorities, as illustrated by the case study presented later in this chapter.

Before getting down to cases, we will review postwar productivity trends in the U.S. business economy, by industry groupings. This provides some feel for the orders of magnitude involved and the range of interindustry differentials in productivity growth. The summary of causes of the industry differences serves as an example of the type of analysis that is possible at the company level, which will also be illustrated by the case study.

For the business economy and the thirty-one industry groups, rates of change are shown for real gross product and the partial- and total-factor productivity ratios.[1] Business-cycle peak years were chosen as boundaries for the long period 1948–79 and for the subperiods into which it is divided. This minimizes the effects of the business cycle on the trend rates of growth as calculated by the compound interest formula. Industry estimates for the 1979–81 subperiod are also shown but are not included in the trend calculations because of the atypical nature of those years.

Productivity Trends in the
U.S. Business Economy

First, it is useful to review the trends of productivity in the U.S. business economy as a whole, with which we will later compare the trends in the various industry groups. The business sector comprises about 85% of the GNP as estimated by the Commerce Department, and it is for this sector that independent estimates of real product and of factor inputs are available. They are not yet available for the other domestic sectors of general governments, households, and nonprofit institutions, and for the "rest-of-the-world" sector (net income from abroad). Productivity in the business (enterprise) sector is, in effect, a weighted average of productivity in the component industries.

Economic historians estimate that during most of the nineteenth-century total factor productivity in the U.S. domestic economy increased at the modest pace of only about 0.3% a year, on average. During the subsequent ninety-year period, 1889–1979, however, productivity growth accelerated markedly — to annual rates of 1.7% 1889–1919, 2.2% 1919–48, and 2.8% 1948–66 (see table 8).[2] Actually, the thirty years 1889–1919 were a transition to a new and higher long-term trend, which began around 1917, and, excepting the Great Depression of the 1930s, continued for about half a century. Then, as the table shows, since 1966 there has been a deceleration in the rate of productivity growth.

As shown in table 9, during the "golden era" of the U.S. economy, 1948–66, total factor productivity grew at an average annual rate of 2.8%, then slowed to 1.7% 1966–73, and only 0.4% 1973–79. The decline of 0.4% a year between 1979 and 1981 reflects the economic contraction in the first half of 1980, the subsequent incomplete recovery, and renewed contraction in the latter half of 1981. Further, in terms of the broad industry groups shown in the table, the slowdown was quite general, with four of the groups actually experiencing absolute productivity declines between 1973 and 1979, and eight showing declines 1978–81. As we will see later, the retardation was also quite general within the manufacturing sector, with only two of the twenty two-digit industries showing higher productivity advance after 1973 than before. Although the focus of this chapter is on U.S. productivity developments, it is worth noting that productivity

TABLE 8
Real Gross Product, Factor Inputs, and Productivity Ratios, U.S. Domestic Business
Economy, 1800–1978 (average annual percentage rates of change)

Variable	1800– 55	1855– 90	1889– 1919	1919– 48	1948– 66	1966– 78
Real gross product	4.2	4.0	3.9	3.0	3.9	3.2
Population	3.1	2.4	1.8	1.2	1.6	0.9
Real product per capita	1.1	1.6	2.1	1.8	2.3	2.3
Total tangible factor input	3.9	3.6	2.2	0.8	1.1	1.8
Labor	3.7	2.8	1.8	0.6	0.4	1.4
Capital	4.3	4.6	3.1	1.2	2.8	2.6
Total factor productivity						
ratio	0.3	0.3	1.7	2.2	2.8	1.4
Labor	0.5	1.1	2.0	2.4	3.5	1.8
Capital	−0.1	−0.6	0.7	1.6	1.1	0.6

Source: 1800–90 from Moses Abramovitz and Paul David, "Economic Growth in America: Historical Parables and Realities," reprint no. 105, Center for Research in Economic Growth, Stanford University, 1973, tables 1–2; 1889–1948 based on John W. Kendrick, *Productivity Trends in the United States* (Princeton, N.J.: Princeton University Press, for the National Bureau of Economic Research, 1961); 1948–78 from John W. Kendrick and Elliot S. Grossman, *Productivity in the United States: Trends and Cycles* (Baltimore: Johns Hopkins University Press, 1980), app. table, p. 114 (1978 estimates revised).

TABLE 9
Rates of Change in Total Factor Productivity, U.S. Business Economy,
by Major Industry Group, 1948–81

Industry Group	1948–79	1948–66	1966–73	1973–79	1979–81
Private business economy	2.0	2.8	1.7	0.4	−0.4
Farming	3.5	3.9	3.4	2.1	3.7
Mfg.	2.2	2.6	2.4	0.8	−0.4
Nonfarm nonmfg.	1.3	2.0	1.0	0.6	−0.5
Mining	0.9	2.4	1.4	−4.0	−1.4
Construction	0.5	2.2	−0.8	−3.1	−2.5
Railroads	2.8	4.4	0.3	0.7	1.8
Nonrail transp.	1.1	0.8	2.4	0.9	−1.2
Communications	4.6	5.3	3.2	4.3	4.0
Public utilities	3.2	5.4	1.2	−0.9	−2.2
Trade	2.1	2.5	2.4	0.5	−0.7
Finance, insurance	0.5	1.1	0.3	−0.9	−1.3
Real estate	1.3	1.8	−0.1	1.2	−1.0
Services	0.2	0.4	−0.3	0.2	1.0

Source: American Productivity Center.

growth also slowed down markedly in all other industrialized member nations of the Organization of Economic Cooperation and Development after 1973.[3]

The productivity slowdown has generated much concern as to the causes and the outlook — whether the productivity trend has permanently slowed or whether the economy will return to the longer-term trend rate. Since the focus of this chapter is on industry productivity trends, we shall merely summarize briefly our views on these important questions, which have been dealt with at some length elsewhere.[4]

The causes of the slowdown are quantified within the framework of a Denison-type growth accounting model in table 10. As shown there, the rate of increase in real product per labor-hour decelerated by 2.4% between 1948–66 and 1973–78. The various causal factors identified in the table — which serves as a good introduction to the interindustry analysis presented later — accounted for the portions of the slowdown indicated in table 11.

TABLE 10
Sources of Growth in Real Gross Product, U.S. Domestic Business Economy, 1929–78

Source	1929–48	1948–66	1966–73	1973–78[a]	1980–90 (projected)
Average annual percentage rate of change					
Real gross product	2.6	3.9	3.5	2.4	3.4
Total factor input	0.3	1.1	1.9	1.6	1.8
Labor	0.3	0.4	1.4	1.3	1.3
Capital	0.3	2.8	3.3	2.3	3.2
Real product per unit of labor	2.3	3.5	2.1	1.1	2.1
Capital/labor substitution	–	0.7	0.5	0.3	0.5
Total factor productivity	2.3	2.8	1.6	0.8	1.6
Source of total factor productivity growth: Percentage point contribution					
Advances in knowledge	0.7	1.4	1.1	0.8	0.9
R&D stock	0.5	0.9	0.7	0.6	0.6
Informal	0.3	0.3	0.3	0.2	0.2
Rate of diffusion	–0.1	0.2	0.1	–	0.1
Changes in labor quality	0.8	0.6	0.4	0.7	1.0
Education and training	0.5	0.6	0.7	0.8	0.8
Health	0.3	0.1	0.1	0.1	0.1
Age/sex composition	–	–0.1	–0.4	–0.2	0.1
Changes in quality of land	–	–	–0.1	–0.2	–0.3
Resource reallocations	0.4	0.8	0.7	0.3	0.3
Labor	0.3	0.4	0.2	0.1	0.1
Capital	0.1	0.4	0.5	0.2	0.2
Volume changes	0.4	0.4	0.2	–0.1	0.4
Economies of scale	0.4	0.4	0.3	0.2	0.3
Intensity of demand	–	–	–0.1	–0.3	0.1
Net government impact	0.1	–	–0.1	–0.3	–0.2
Services to business	0.3	0.1	0.1	0.1	–
Regulations	–0.2	–0.1	–0.2	–0.4	–0.2
Actual/potential efficiency and n.e.c.[b]	–0.1	–0.4	–0.6	–0.4	–0.5

Source: John W. Kendrick, based in part on estimates by Edward F. Denison, *Accounting for United States Economic Growth, 1929–1969* (Washington, D.C.: Brookings Institution, 1974), and on his statement in *Special Study on Economic Change,* Hearings before the Joint Economic Committee of Congress, June 1978 (Washington, D.C., 1978).

Note: Dash (–): Zero or negligible.

[a] Preliminary.
[b] Not elsewhere classified.

TABLE 11
Contributing Factors to Sources of Growth

Factor	Percentage Points
Reduced growth of capital per unit of labor	0.4
Lower rate of technological progress	0.6
Change in labor quality and efficiency	−0.1
Deteriorating quality of natural resources	0.2
Less favorable resource reallocations	0.5
Lower growth of demand and output	0.5
Increased government regulation	0.3
Net impact of other factors	0
Total	2.4

Source: See table 9.

It should be stressed that the investment climate of the 1970s was much less favorable than in the earlier period due to accelerating inflation, which, exacerbated by the oil shock, eroded real profit margins; to greater economic instability; and to increased governmental intervention in the economy. Each of the factors listed, and others, had a differential impact by industry, however, as will be discussed shortly.

The outlook for productivity and economic growth in the 1980s appears to be better than for the 1970s. Since some of the forces depressing productivity in the 1970s played out, it would be possible to approach the previous secular trend-rate of productivity growth if positive policies to promote investment and productivity were adopted.[5] The policy initiatives of the Reagan administration and Congress make it appear quite probable that acceleration will occur in coming years.

The Industry Productivity Record

There was considerable dispersion in rates of productivity change among the thirty-one industries over the period 1948–79, as shown in the first column of table 12. Rates ranged from highs of 4.6% a year for communications and 3.7% for electrical machinery down to 0.4% for primary metals and 0.2% for services. The average deviation of the industry rates around the business sector average of 2.0% a year was 0.9%. About two-thirds of the industry groups fell in the 1.0% to 3.0% range, as shown in the frequency distribution in figure 5. No industry experienced an absolute decline in total factor productivity over the thirty-one-year period. The greater the degree of industry detail, the greater the degree of dispersion in productivity and the other variables. The last column shows that dispersion continued great in the 1979–81 subperiod, during which productivity declined in two-thirds of the industries.

TABLE 12
Rates of Change in Total Factor Productivity, U.S. Business Economy,
by Industry Group, 1948–81

Industry Group	1948–79	1948–53	1953–57	1957–60	1960–66	1966–69	1969–73	1973–79	1979–81
Private business economy	2.0	3.2	1.6	2.0	3.1	1.3	2.0	0.4	-0.4
Manufacturing	2.2	3.0	1.1	1.2	3.7	1.0	3.5	0.8	-0.4
Food	2.7	3.2	2.8	1.6	3.7	0.9	6.5	0.0	4.5
Tobacco	1.8	2.1	2.6	5.2	0.3	2.0	2.8	0.3	-7.0
Textiles	3.6	0.5	3.6	2.1	7.9	0.5	-4.6	3.7	-0.9
Apparel	2.6	2.4	1.3	2.3	2.2	0.8	4.4	3.8	1.2
Lumber	2.8	0.2	5.8	1.7	7.1	1.0	2.7	0.2	-2.9
Furniture	2.0	2.1	1.9	0.2	2.8	1.8	0.3	3.3	1.4
Paper	2.3	3.6	-0.2	2.1	2.7	3.2	5.3	0.0	-2.8
Printing	1.4	2.0	2.9	1.0	3.1	0.6	1.1	-1.1	1.5
Chemicals	3.4	1.9	4.7	3.0	4.9	2.7	6.2	1.1	-1.2
Petroleum	1.9	1.8	0.9	6.6	4.2	-2.5	6.0	-2.3	-8.0
Rubber	1.7	1.9	-2.0	5.9	3.4	2.5	1.9	-0.3	-0.2
Leather	1.2	-1.8	-0.2	2.7	3.2	-0.4	4.0	1.0	-0.7
Stone, clay, glass	1.4	2.4	0.6	1.5	2.3	1.3	1.4	0.1	0.6
Primary metals	0.4	2.9	-0.8	-4.1	3.3	-2.5	3.1	-1.9	-2.7
Fabricated metals	1.4	1.7	0.5	1.2	2.6	0.9	1.6	0.6	-0.4
Nonelec. mach.	1.3	2.3	-1.5	1.3	2.6	-0.1	2.9	0.8	1.3
Elec. mach.	3.7	4.3	2.3	3.2	5.6	3.6	2.9	3.2	1.0
Trans. equip.	2.5	4.9	0.4	2.0	4.3	0.7	4.3	0.3	-4.9
Instruments	2.8	4.3	2.3	3.3	3.7	3.4	1.5	1.1	0.5
Misc.	2.6	1.2	2.3	3.1	2.6	4.6	3.5	2.0	2.7
Nonfarm nonmfg.	1.3	2.2	1.3	1.8	2.2	0.9	1.0	0.1	-0.5
Mining	0.9	3.0	1.9	0.8	2.9	2.6	0.5	-4.0	-1.4
Construction	0.5	3.0	2.1	4.0	0.7	-0.5	-1.0	-3.1	-2.5
Rail transp.	2.8	3.0	3.0	4.1	6.8	1.4	-0.5	0.7	1.8
Nonrail transp.	1.1	-1.6	1.7	-0.1	2.6	1.7	2.9	0.9	-1.2
Communication	4.6	6.7	5.5	6.3	3.6	3.5	3.0	4.3	4.0
Public utilities	3.2	7.9	5.6	5.3	3.5	2.8	0.0	-0.9	-2.2
Trade	2.1	2.6	1.8	1.2	3.5	0.7	3.7	0.5	-0.7
Finance, insurance	0.5	2.2	2.5	-0.6	0.3	1.1	-0.4	-0.9	-1.3
Real estate	1.3	2.3	1.1	2.4	1.5	0.2	-0.2	1.2	-1.0
Services	0.2	0.6	-2.0	1.9	1.1	1.0	-1.3	0.2	1.0
Farming	3.5	5.5	2.9	4.0	3.2	4.0	3.0	2.1	3.7

Source: See table 9.

Dispersion in industry rates of change in output (real gross product) was even greater than in productivity, of course, ranging from just over and under 7% a year for communications and electrical machinery to low negative amounts for leather and leather products (mainly shoes) and railroad transportation (see table 13 and figure 5).

Rates of change in output per labor-hour 1948–79 were higher than rates for total factor productivity in all but one industry group, since real capital increased faster than labor in all except real estate. Rates ranged

TABLE 13
Rates of Change in Output (Real Gross Product), U.S. Business Economy,
by Industry Group, 1948–81

Industry Group	1948– 79	1948– 53	1953– 57	1957– 60	1960– 66	1966– 69	1969– 73	1973– 78	1979– 81
Private business economy	3.5	4.1	2.4	2.1	4.9	3.4	3.8	2.7	0.6
Manufacturing	3.6	5.8	1.0	0.8	6.8	2.8	4.1	2.1	−1.3
Food	2.7	3.4	2.3	1.3	3.9	1.4	5.5	2.6	3.4
Tobacco	2.1	1.8	2.5	5.3	0.9	2.1	3.7	0.6	1.7
Textiles	3.2	−0.6	1.1	1.3	9.6	1.5	5.3	2.0	−3.4
Apparel	3.0	3.4	0.4	2.6	4.9	0.8	5.3	2.4	0.0
Lumber	2.7	−2.2	1.4	0.9	8.1	1.8	6.0	1.8	−6.7
Furniture	3.2	3.2	1.7	0.9	5.9	2.8	2.7	3.0	0.1
Paper	4.1	6.2	1.9	3.8	5.2	5.8	5.6	1.2	−2.2
Printing	3.0	2.8	4.2	2.4	5.2	3.1	1.9	1.0	3.9
Chemicals	6.1	6.2	7.4	4.5	8.0	6.6	6.5	3.7	−0.3
Petroleum	3.6	4.9	2.5	5.8	4.1	−0.6	8.3	0.7	−5.4
Rubber	5.1	5.9	−0.6	6.6	9.1	7.8	6.0	1.8	−2.2
Leather	−0.2	−2.5	−1.2	1.4	4.0	−3.2	0.3	−1.1	−3.2
Stone, clay, glass	2.8	4.0	1.8	2.6	4.1	2.4	3.8	0.6	−3.0
Primary metals	1.1	5.3	−1.1	−6.3	6.1	−1.6	2.9	−1.7	−6.8
Fabricated metals	3.5	7.0	0.4	0.5	6.6	4.5	1.8	1.7	−3.9
Nonelec. mach.	3.7	5.6	−1.1	−0.6	8.1	1.7	4.4	3.8	1.9
Elec. mach.	6.8	11.1	2.1	5.8	11.2	5.9	3.6	5.0	2.1
Trans. equip.	4.8	15.4	−0.2	−2.1	8.8	2.6	2.8	1.9	−7.9
Instruments	6.0	11.8	1.8	4.8	7.6	6.7	3.1	4.9	2.7
Misc.	3.1	2.6	1.3	2.6	4.3	4.3	4.4	2.1	0.9
Nonfarm nonmfg.	3.6	3.5	3.2	3.2	4.4	3.7	3.8	3.0	1.4
Mining	2.0	1.6	3.2	−0.9	3.5	3.3	1.3	1.5	5.4
Construction	2.6	5.6	4.1	4.0	2.9	0.7	1.9	−0.5	−4.7
Rail transp.	−0.2	−1.1	−0.9	−2.8	4.5	−1.5	−2.8	0.4	−2.9
Nonrail transp.	2.8	−0.8	2.4	0.9	5.0	4.4	4.6	3.0	−4.2
Communication	7.3	7.2	6.2	5.6	7.3	8.8	7.6	7.8	7.9
Public utilities	5.9	9.7	7.2	6.8	5.5	7.0	4.5	2.4	1.4
Trade	3.8	3.8	3.6	2.8	4.9	3.6	5.0	2.7	−0.0
Finance, insurance	4.1	4.9	5.4	2.9	3.4	6.3	3.3	3.4	2.8
Real estate	3.1	2.9	2.5	3.7	3.9	2.2	3.0	3.1	0.2
Services	3.6	3.1	1.7	4.4	4.6	4.3	3.0	3.9	4.7
Farming	1.1	1.2	0.3	1.4	−0.4	1.7	2.0	2.0	−0.0

Source: See table 9.

from almost 6.0% for communications to 0.4% for real estate (see table 14 and figure 5).

The reconciliation item between output per unit of labor and output per unit of capital is capital per unit of labor. As shown in table 15, the latter variable increased by an average 2.1% a year 1948–79, which is approximately the difference between the 2.5% and 0.4% rates of increase in the labor and capital productivity ratios, respectively. Rates of increase in the capital / labor ratio ranged from 5.0% in communications to the sole

Number of industries

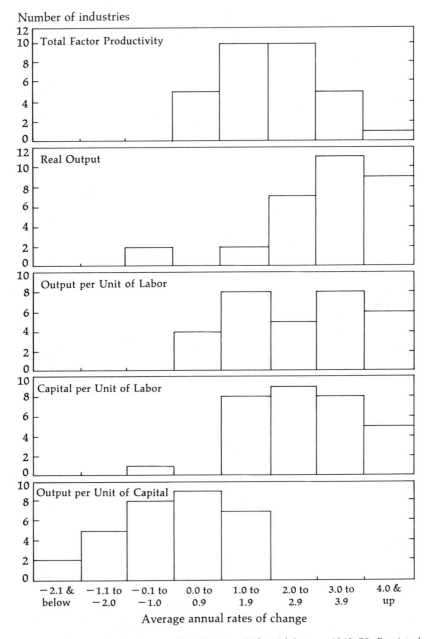

FIGURE 5.   Variable Frequencies for Thirty-one Industrial Sectors, 1948–79. Reprinted, with permission, from John W. Kendrick, *Interindustry Differences in Productivity Growth* (Washington, D.C.: American Enterprise Institute, 1983), p. 8.

TABLE 14
Rates of Change in Output per Unit of Labor, U.S. Business Economy,
by Industry Group, 1948–81

Industry Group	1948–79	1948–53	1953–57	1957–60	1960–66	1966–69	1969–73	1973–79	1979–81
Private business economy	2.5	3.7	2.3	2.6	3.6	1.8	2.6	0.8	0.5
Manufacturing	2.7	3.3	1.9	1.7	3.9	1.7	4.1	1.5	1.0
Food	3.1	3.6	3.2	1.7	3.9	1.3	7.1	0.6	5.0
Tobacco	3.7	3.9	3.9	6.6	2.3	4.3	4.7	2.6	−0.1
Textiles	4.4	2.4	5.5	2.8	7.9	0.9	5.0	4.5	−0.0
Apparel	2.8	2.4	1.4	2.2	2.3	1.2	4.7	4.3	1.5
Lumber	3.1	−0.8	5.8	1.5	7.7	1.6	3.3	1.5	0.0
Furniture	2.2	2.1	2.0	0.1	2.8	2.2	0.6	3.9	1.9
Paper	2.8	3.8	0.4	2.2	2.9	3.7	5.9	1.3	−1.0
Printing	1.5	1.8	2.5	1.1	3.4	1.1	1.7	−0.8	1.7
Chemicals	4.3	3.3	5.9	3.6	5.2	3.2	7.1	2.5	0.2
Petroleum	3.6	3.8	3.3	8.8	6.1	−0.2	6.8	−1.2	−4.9
Rubber	2.0	2.3	−1.5	6.6	3.0	2.9	2.2	−0.0	0.2
Leather	1.5	−1.6	0.0	2.7	3.3	0.0	4.7	1.6	−0.2
Stone, clay, glass	1.9	2.9	1.5	1.9	2.6	1.9	1.5	0.9	2.6
Primary metals	0.9	3.5	0.2	−2.9	3.2	−1.6	3.4	−1.4	−0.6
Fabricated metals	1.8	2.1	1.4	1.8	2.6	1.1	2.1	1.3	0.8
Nonelec. mach.	1.7	2.6	−0.9	1.7	2.6	−0.7	3.5	1.3	2.3
Elec. mach.	4.1	3.9	2.7	3.1	6.1	4.4	3.5	3.8	2.0
Trans. equip.	3.0	3.9	1.5	2.8	4.5	1.8	5.1	1.0	−1.8
Instruments	3.2	4.2	2.9	3.6	4.0	4.1	2.6	1.2	1.4
Misc.	3.0	2.8	3.9	2.8	2.1	5.3	3.6	2.2	4.1
Nonfarm nonmfg.	1.8	2.6	1.7	2.4	2.9	1.5	1.7	0.2	0.2
Mining	1.9	4.6	3.4	3.7	5.0	4.1	2.6	−5.2	−2.5
Construction	0.6	3.0	2.2	4.3	0.8	−0.4	−0.9	−3.0	−2.4
Rail transp.	3.3	3.5	3.6	5.2	7.3	2.0	−0.1	1.1	2.9
Nonrail transp.	1.5	−1.4	1.9	0.2	2.8	2.3	3.3	1.3	−0.1
Communication	5.9	7.0	6.2	7.7	5.2	4.8	4.9	5.8	5.5
Public utilities	4.9	9.5	6.9	6.5	4.8	4.8	2.7	0.6	−2.3
Trade	2.5	3.0	2.3	1.5	3.9	1.1	4.3	0.8	−0.1
Finance, insurance	1.0	2.1	2.5	−0.4	1.0	1.7	0.4	−0.1	−0.2
Real estate	0.4	1.1	0.0	2.0	2.6	−0.2	−1.1	−1.4	−0.9
Services	0.6	0.9	−1.8	2.5	2.0	2.1	−1.2	0.0	0.8
Farming	4.9	6.8	4.0	5.3	4.9	5.4	4.9	3.6	5.1

Source: See table 9.

negative of 0.9% a year in real estate. The frequency distribution can be seen in figure 1.

Finally, average rates of change in output per unit of capital ranged from 1.9% a year in lumber products and in electrical machinery to a negative 2.9% in finance and insurance (see table 16 and distribution in figure 5). Despite the growth of capital per unit of labor in almost all industries, savings were realized in capital per unit of output (the inverse of capital productivity) in more than half of the thirty-one industry groups.

Tables 12 through 16 indicate clearly that dispersions in rates of change

TABLE 15
Rates of Change in Capital per Unit of Labor, U.S. Business Economy,
by Industry Group, 1948–81

Industry Group	1948– 79	1948– 53	1953– 57	1957– 60	1960– 66	1966– 69	1969– 73	1973– 79	1979– 81
Private business economy	2.1	2.2	2.8	2.6	2.1	2.4	2.3	1.2	2.9
Manufacturing	2.4	1.6	4.3	2.2	0.6	3.3	2.4	3.1	5.4
Food	1.6	1.7	1.6	0.1	0.8	1.6	2.5	2.7	2.0
Tobacco	4.7	8.2	4.7	3.8	4.3	4.5	3.3	4.0	11.8
Textiles	4.7	14.6	8.5	3.1	0.1	2.1	1.9	3.2	3.7
Apparel	2.1	−0.3	1.2	0.0	1.8	6.1	3.2	3.6	2.7
Lumber	1.2	−5.7	−0.3	−0.7	3.7	3.7	2.4	4.7	9.0
Furniture	1.3	0.4	1.3	−0.8	−0.4	3.1	2.0	3.5	2.9
Paper	1.9	0.6	2.1	0.2	1.0	1.8	2.3	4.5	5.8
Printing	1.0	−1.4	−2.4	0.4	2.4	3.0	3.6	1.2	1.1
Chemicals	2.6	4.3	3.3	1.4	0.8	1.1	2.5	3.7	3.5
Petroleum	3.1	3.7	4.3	3.6	3.7	4.5	1.2	1.8	5.2
Rubber	1.3	1.9	2.8	2.5	−1.7	1.7	1.4	2.2	1.9
Leather	3.0	2.6	1.9	1.2	1.2	6.7	5.7	3.4	3.8
Stone, clay, glass	2.5	3.0	5.0	1.9	1.3	2.1	0.5	3.3	7.2
Primary metals	3.0	3.4	5.7	6.1	−0.2	3.6	1.8	2.8	8.7
Fabricated metals	3.0	3.5	6.2	3.9	0.3	1.4	3.2	3.7	6.1
Nonelec. mach.	2.7	2.7	4.1	3.3	−0.2	4.9	3.2	2.8	4.5
Elec. mach.	2.2	−3.4	2.7	0.5	3.6	5.7	4.1	2.9	5.0
Trans. equip.	2.1	−5.9	6.9	4.7	1.0	6.0	4.6	3.0	11.9
Instruments	1.9	−1.0	5.4	1.8	1.5	3.3	3.8	0.6	2.7
Misc.	2.6	10.7	7.4	−1.4	−2.4	3.3	1.0	1.1	6.7
Nonfarm nonmfg.	1.7	1.7	1.5	2.3	2.5	2.1	2.1	0.5	2.0
Mining	3.3	6.9	5.3	8.7	4.9	3.3	0.3	−3.0	−3.0
Construction	2.7	2.4	4.8	6.4	4.2	3.2	1.2	−0.8	1.0
Rail transp.	3.9	5.9	4.9	8.0	2.9	3.8	2.1	2.0	5.2
Nonrail transp.	2.4	2.9	2.3	2.3	1.5	4.6	2.6	2.1	5.9
Communication	5.0	4.8	6.7	8.7	5.2	3.4	4.6	3.2	3.0
Public utilities	3.8	5.7	4.4	3.4	2.7	3.7	4.8	2.7	−0.2
Trade	3.6	4.2	4.3	2.9	4.8	3.2	4.3	1.5	3.5
Finance, insurance	4.0	−0.9	0.2	3.5	7.7	4.9	7.2	5.0	6.5
Real estate	−0.9	−1.3	−1.3	−0.3	1.2	−0.5	−0.9	−2.9	0.1
Services	1.5	1.5	1.0	2.8	3.0	3.4	0.0	−0.5	−0.8
Farming	5.0	7.1	5.2	5.1	6.0	4.4	4.0	3.0	2.6

Source: See table 9.

in output, productivity ratios, and the capital / labor ratio were substantially higher in all of the seven subperiods than over the thirty-one-year period as a whole — more than 50% higher, on average. This reflects the considerable variability in rates of change of all the variables across the subperiods. Since the boundary years were peak business cycle years, the effect of the cycle was minimized, although some differences in ratios of actual to potential output in successive peak years do influence the subperiod rates of change, and differentially so by industry. But the variations primarily reflect the differences in the net impact of the noncyclical

TABLE 16
Rates of Change in Output per Unit of Capital, U.S. Business Economy,
by Industry Group, 1948–81

Industry Group	1948– 79	1948– 53	1953– 57	1957– 60	1960– 66	1966– 69	1969– 73	1973– 79	1979– 81
Private business economy	0.4	1.4	-0.5	-0.1	1.5	-0.5	0.3	-0.5	-2.3
Manufacturing	0.3	1.6	-2.2	-0.6	3.3	-1.5	1.6	-1.5	-4.2
Food	1.4	1.9	1.6	1.6	3.1	-0.3	4.5	-2.0	2.9
Tobacco	-0.9	-3.9	-0.7	2.8	-1.9	-0.2	1.4	-1.3	-10.6
Textiles	-0.3	-10.7	-2.8	-0.3	7.8	-1.2	3.0	1.2	-3.5
Apparel	0.6	2.7	0.2	2.2	0.5	-4.6	1.5	0.6	-1.2
Lumber	1.9	5.2	6.1	2.2	3.8	-2.0	0.9	-3.0	-8.2
Furniture	0.9	1.7	0.7	0.9	3.1	-1.0	-1.4	0.3	-1.0
Paper	0.9	3.2	-1.7	2.0	1.9	1.9	3.5	-3.1	-6.4
Printing	0.6	3.2	5.1	0.7	1.0	-1.9	-1.8	-2.1	0.6
Chemicals	1.7	-1.0	2.5	2.1	4.4	2.1	4.5	-1.1	-3.1
Petroleum	0.5	0.1	-0.9	5.0	2.3	-4.5	5.6	-3.0	-9.6
Rubber	0.6	0.4	-4.2	3.3	5.1	1.2	0.8	-2.0	-1.6
Leather	-1.5	-4.0	-1.9	1.5	2.1	-6.4	-1.0	-1.9	-3.9
Stone, clay, glass	-0.6	-0.1	-3.4	0.0	1.3	-0.1	1.0	-2.4	-4.3
Primary metals	-2.0	0.0	-5.1	-8.5	3.4	-5.1	1.6	-4.0	-8.5
Fabricated metals	-1.2	-1.4	-4.6	-2.0	2.3	-0.3	-1.1	-2.4	5.0
Nonelec. mach.	-0.9	-0.1	-4.8	-1.4	2.8	-4.0	0.2	-1.4	-2.1
Elec. mach.	1.9	7.5	-0.1	2.7	2.4	-1.2	-0.5	0.9	-2.9
Trans. equip.	0.9	10.4	-5.0	-1.8	3.5	-3.9	1.7	-1.9	-12.2
Instruments	1.2	5.3	-2.4	1.8	2.5	0.8	-1.2	0.7	-1.3
Misc.	0.4	-7.2	-3.3	4.3	4.6	2.0	2.6	1.1	-2.5
Nonfarm nonmfg.	0.1	0.9	0.1	0.1	0.4	-0.5	-0.4	-0.3	-1.8
Mining	-1.3	-2.1	-1.8	-4.6	0.1	0.8	0.3	-2.3	0.5
Construction	-2.1	0.6	-2.5	-2.0	-3.2	-3.5	-2.0	-2.3	-3.4
Rail transp.	-0.6	-2.2	-1.2	-2.6	4.3	-1.7	-2.2	-0.8	-2.2
Nonrail transp.	-1.0	-4.1	-0.3	-2.1	1.3	-2.2	0.7	-0.8	-5.6
Communication	0.9	2.3	-0.6	-0.8	0.0	1.4	0.3	2.5	2.4
Public utilities	1.0	3.6	2.4	3.1	2.1	1.0	-2.1	-2.0	-2.2
Trade	-1.1	-1.1	-1.9	-1.4	-0.9	-2.1	-0.1	-0.8	-3.5
Finance, insurance	-2.9	3.0	2.3	-3.9	-6.2	3.0	-6.3	-4.9	-6.3
Real estate	1.4	2.4	1.3	2.4	1.5	0.2	-0.1	1.5	-1.0
Services	-0.9	-0.6	-2.7	-0.3	-1.0	-1.3	-1.3	0.6	1.5
Farming	-0.1	-0.3	-1.1	0.2	-1.0	1.0	0.9	0.6	2.4

Source: See table 9.

causal factors, especially the rates of cost-reducing technological and organizational changes over the several subperiods.

More direct measures of the degree of variability of rates of change in output, the productivity ratios, and the capital / labor ratio are available. The average deviations of the subperiod rates of change from the average rate for total productivity and labor productivity in the business economy are both 0.7%; for output and capital productivity they are both 0.8%; and for the capital / labor ratio the average deviation is 1.2%. But the average deviations for the thirty-one industry groups are generally much higher, averaging more than twice as much as that for the business economy for all five variables. With respect to total factor productivity, variability is greatest for petroleum refining, primary metals, and public utilities. It is lowest for stone, clay, and glass products; fabricated metals; and real estate. Variability also differs among industries for the other variables.

The rankings of the thirty-one industries with respect to all five variables changed considerably from one subperiod to another. Variability of rankings with respect to total factor productivity is shown in table 17. It is lowest for fabricated metals, instruments, communications, and stone, clay, and glass. It is highest for petroleum refining, finance and insurance, and lumber. Communications, for example, which ranked number one over the entire period, was first only in one subperiod, 1973–79. It ranged between second and fourth in four subperiods, but was tenth and thirteenth in two. Electrical machinery, which ranked number two 1948–79, had ranks ranging from three to fourteen in the subperiods.

The Productivity-Price-Output Relation

Productivity increase is the opposite side of the cost-reduction coin. When total factor productivity rises, real factor costs per unit of output fall. If input prices were to remain constant, output prices would fall in proportion to the productivity advance. In an inflationary era such as the recent one, costs per unit of output rise by less than wage rates and other input prices to the extent of productivity growth. If profit margins were to maintain a constant ratio to costs, prices would also rise by less than input prices to the degree that productivity rises. In other words, productivity growth provides an offset to factor price increases with respect to unit costs and prices.

The labor productivity offset to rising average labor compensation per hour with respect to unit labor costs and prices in the U.S. business economy is shown in table 18. Note that since 1966 the productivity slowdown has been associated with accelerating increases in the price of labor, unit labor costs, and prices as measured by the implicit price deflator for gross business product. It would be possible also to show the extent to which increases in capital productivity had offset increases in the price of capital (including profits), as we have done elsewhere.[6] But for present purposes we merely note than nonlabor costs per unit of output had risen less than unit labor costs since 1966, reflecting in part some reduction in profit margins as prices have risen somewhat less than unit labor costs.

Our focus here is more on relative changes in productivity and prices by industry. Since we are dealing with real gross product and factor produc-

TABLE 17
Ranking of Total Factor Productivity Growth of Industry Groups,
U.S. Private Domestic Business Economy, 1948–79

Industry Group	1948– 79	1948– 53	1953– 57	1957– 60	1960– 66	1966– 69	1969– 73	1973– 79
Communications	1	2	3	2	10	4	13	1
Elec. mach.	2	6	13	10	4	3	14	5
Textiles	3	28	5	16	1	25	5	3
Farming	4	3	8	7	16	2	12	6
Chemicals	5	23	4	12	5	8	2	9
Public utilities	6	1	2	4	12	7	26	26
Lumber	7	29	1	20	2	17	18	20
Instruments	8	5	14	9	8	5	21	10
Railroads	9	10	6	6	3	14	29	14
Food	10	8	9	21	9	20	1	22
Apparel	11	14	20	15	26	21	6	2
Misc. mfg.	12	26	12	11	22	1	10	7
Transp. equip.	13	4	25	18	6	23	7	18
Paper	14	7	26	17	20	6	4	23
Trade	15	13	18	24	11	22	9	16
Furniture	16	20	16	28	19	12	25	4
Petroleum	17	24	22	1	7	31	3	29
Tobacco	18	19	10	5	30	11	17	17
Rubber	19	22	31	3	13	10	19	24
Fabricated Metals	20	25	24	25	24	19	20	15
Printing	21	21	7	26	17	24	23	27
Stone, glass, clay	22	15	23	22	25	15	22	21
Nonelec. mach.	23	17	29	23	24	27	15	13
Leather	24	31	27	13	15	28	8	11
Real estate	25	16	21	14	27	26	27	8
Nonrail transp.	26	30	19	29	21	13	16	12
Mining	27	9	17	27	18	9	24	31
Finance, insurance	28	18	11	30	31	16	9	16
Construction	29	11	15	8	29	29	30	30
Primary metals	30	12	28	31	14	30	11	28
Services	31	27	30	19	28	18	31	19

Source: See table 9.

TABLE 18
Productivity, Unit Costs, and Prices, U.S. Private Domestic Business Economy, 1948–81
(average annual percentage rates of change)

Year	Real Gross Product/ Hour	Labor Compensation/ Hour	Unit Labor Cost	Implicit Price Deflator
1948–66	3.2	5.0	1.8	1.8
1966–73	2.3	6.9	4.5	4.2
1973–79	0.8	8.9	8.1	7.6
1979–80	−0.3	10.0	10.3	9.2
1980–81	1.0	10.0	8.9	9.2

Source: U.S. Department of Labor, Bureau of Labor Statistics.

tivity by industry, the associated price indexes are the implicit price deflators for gross product originating in each industry. It should be noted that the implicit prices are not the selling prices of the industry outputs, but rather the weighted differences between the selling prices and the purchase prices of intermediate products (materials, supplies, and purchased services) consumed in production — since gross product (value added) is the value of output less intermediate purchases. Thus, changes in the implicit price deflators reflect changes not only in unit factor costs and in profit margins but also in unit costs of intermediate products. Unit intermediate costs, in turn, change with fluctuation in prices of the intermediate products and in their consumption per unit of output.

For these reasons the correlation between proportionate industry changes in total factor productivity and in the implicit price deflators 1948–79 is far from perfect. But it is negative, as would be expected, and is significant at the 0.01 level.[7] The relationship is closer for the thirty-one-year period than it is for the subperiods 1948–66 and 1966–79.

To the extent that the demand for goods is price-elastic, and if the effects of price elasticities are not outweighed by income elasticities working in the opposite direction, there should also be a negative correlation between the relative industry changes in prices and in outputs (reflecting relative changes in demand for the products of the various industries). This is indeed the case, but the correlation is closer when agriculture and the service sectors are left out because of offsetting income-elasticity effects. In the farming sector, not only is price elasticity of demand low, so is income elasticity. Therefore, despite good productivity and price performance, the demand for agricultural products has shown below-average increase over time. Despite poor productivity performance associated with relative price increases, output for finance, insurance, and services has risen quite strongly because of high income-elasticities of demand. But for the remaining twenty-seven industry groups, there is a significant negative correlation between proportionate changes in prices and in output.[8]

Given the negative correlations between relative industry changes in productivity and in prices, and between relative changes in prices and in output, it is clear that there should be a positive correlation between relative changes in productivity and in output 1948–79.[9] The coefficients of correlation are a bit lower but still significant in the two major subperiods. This reflects the fact that, in the short run, movements of prices and of unit costs may diverge significantly, whereas over longer periods their trends are almost parallel.

It should also be noted that the productivity-output relation is reciprocal, reflecting the effects of scale economies on productivity as well as the effects of productivity on scale of output working through prices. That is, industries with above-average productivity growth that experience above-average output growth due to declining relative prices also enjoy the advantage of better-than-average opportunities for economies of scale, which in turn reinforce the superior productivity performance. But it must also be mentioned that economies of scale do not occur automatically. Usually, investment is required to take advantage of the opportunities for greater specialization of personnel, plant, and equipment, which are opened up by the growth of volume.

Cause of Interindustry Differences in Productivity Growth Rates

The interindustry differences in productivity growth rates provide a handle for regression analysis of causal factors. Different industries probably have differing potentials for productivity advance, and the potentials may change at different stages of development of the industry and the broader economy. Nevertheless, multiple-regression analyses have established that industry measures of most of the causal forces discussed earlier can explain most of the interindustry differences in rates of change in total factor productivity or in output per unit of labor input.[10]

A list of the independent variables used in the various regression analyses follows. Each of the variables has proved significant in one or more of the analyses, but not all of them in the same regression. Because of intercorrelation among certain of the explanatory variables, some of the candidates are significant in certain combinations (usually when the inter-correlated variables are omitted) and not in others. For example, the R&D ratio and average education of workers are correlated, so one or the other — but not both — emerges as significant in the multiple regressions.

Rate of change in real capital per unit of labor
Rate of change of output (or of input)
(−) Cyclical variability of output *
Ratio of R&D outlay (total, or privately funded) to sales
   (or to value added)
Ratio to sales of R&D embodied in intermediate product purchases
Ratio to sales of R&D embodied in capital goods purchases
Average education of workers
Average age of workers
Proportion of females in work force
(−) Rate of change in proportion of females
(−) Ratio of union members to total employment
Rate of growth of unionization ratio

*(−) indicates a negative relationship. The other variables are positively related to the dependent variable.

(−)   Percentage of labor-days idled due to work stoppages
      Layoff rate
(−)   "Quit" rate
      Concentration ratio (weighted average of percentages of sales
        accounted for by four largest firms in component industries)
(−)   Changes in concentration ratio

Another volume could be written discussing and interpreting the regression equations, but here only a few general comments will have to suffice. First, the listed variables relate to all the groups of causal forces used in the growth accounting exercise, with a few exceptions. The "resource reallocation" grouping does not apply to an interindustry analysis, except to the extent that there were intraindustry resource shifts (which we did not measure). To the extent that there are shifts among firms or establishments within an industry, one would assume that competition would result in the relative growth of units with above-average productivity gains and the relative decline and eventual disappearance of the least progressive firms. None of the variables relates to governmental impact, much of which is generalized, and we did not have measures of those that have a differential impact by industry. Since 1970 the impact of regulations has increased substantially and has affected industries to different degrees, but industry-specific measures were not available. Finally, the declining average quality of natural resources relates mainly to the mineral industries, which were not included in the regression analyses.

With respect to scale effects, the use of rates of change in output could produce spurious results, since errors in the output measure would affect the productivity measure in the same direction, a bias that would not apply to use of input growth rates. Further, the strong positive correlation between industry rates of change in output and in productivity reflects a reciprocal relationship. That is, within the industry sector, relative productivity changes are negatively correlated with relative price changes, which, in turn, are negatively correlated with relative changes in sales and output. But the fact that the output-productivity correlation is stronger than that obtained through the relative productivity-price-output relationship suggests the presence of economies of scale.

As far as technological advance is concerned, it is highly significant that the R&D performed by suppliers and purchased through producer goods affects an industry's productivity growth more than does internal R&D. Moreover, privately financed R&D performed by the firm has more effect than that which is government financed.

Notably, of the variables reflecting labor efficiency, two show a cyclical as well as a cross-sectional relationship to productivity change. In the latter phase of expansions, as layoff rates fall and "quit" rates rise, productivity advance slows. The opposite occurs in the latter phase of contractions. As pointed out many years ago by Wesley C. Mitchell, the movements of productivity are intimately related to the cost-price relationship over the business cycle and are thus an important part of its explanation.[11] The slowing of productivity in latter expansion means an acceleration of unit labor costs, which eventually press against prices, reducing profit margins. The opposite sequence occurs in the latter part of contractions.

A number of potentially important variables could not be tested due to lack of data on an industry basis; for example, average age of fixed capital, average work experience of employees, and intensity of formal and/or on-the-job training.

Growth accounting has not been as fully applied at the industry level as at the aggregate business-sector level. In the United States, Jorgenson and Gollop have gone part of the way by estimating for fifty-one industries the increases in "quality" of labor and capital inputs associated with relative shifts in the composition of the inputs. They found that the quality of inputs increased in all industries and accounted for a significant portion of productivity growth in the businsss economy as a whole.[12]

Companies with productivity measures often use them as a basis for analyzing the reasons for change. Beyond variables that can be quantified (such as the growth of capital per worker), the knowledge of executives in various areas concerning specific technological factors (such as the installation of new equipment in a particular plant or the state of labor relations) can be consulted. In the case study that follows, after describing the performance of the companies involved, we point up some of the causal forces behind the record.

A Case Study: The Bell System

In the competitive sector of the economy, company productivity estimates are usually confidential, so that we cannot use actual data to illustrate company/industry comparisons in that sector. In regulated industries, however, regulatory bodies have become increasingly concerned with the productivity performance of the firms under their jurisdictions, and some have sought to use the regulatory authority in such a way as to promote productivity growth. This concern, combined with the interest of company managers in tracking their productivity record, has led to the spread of productivity measurement among firms in the transportation, communications, electric and gas utilities, and other regulated industries. The productivity estimates frequently become part of the public record in connection with regulatory or other legal proceedings.

Some years ago John Kendrick helped the American Telephone & Telegraph (AT&T) Company set up productivity measurement systems for both the Western Electric Company, manufacturing arm of AT&T, and the Bell Operating Companies (BOCs). In the fall of 1981 he testified concerning their productivity performance in comparison with that of their own industries and the business economy as a whole for the Justice Department antitrust case against AT&T. The following descriptive analysis is drawn from the proceedings of that case.

Comparison of table 19 with the earlier tables indicates that both the operating companies as a whole and Western Electric have increased their productivity at a faster rate 1948–79 than their industry groups, and much faster than the total business economy (see figure 6). Total factor productivity in Bell operations grew at an average annual rate of 4.9% 1948–79, compared with 4.6% for the communications industry. The differential was greater for real product per unit of labor: 6.5% versus 5.9%. Real capital investment per unit of labor grew a bit less rapidly in the operating companies than in communications, and the output/capital ratio grew more rapidly: 1.8% compared with 0.9% a year. Output (real product) itself increased by 0.6% a year more in Bell operations than in the industry.

TABLE 19

Rates of Change in Output, Inputs, and Productivity Ratios, Bell Operating Companies and Western Electric Company, 1948–79

	1948–79	1948–53	1953–57	1957–60	1960–66	1966–69	1969–73	1973–79
Bell Operating Companies								
Output (real product)	7.9	7.2	7.7	7.4	7.7	9.3	7.6	8.4
Inputs								
Total	2.8	2.1	3.0	−1.0	3.6	4.5	4.7	2.5
Labor	1.3	1.4	2.5	−2.9	1.9	3.5	1.9	0.7
Capital	6.0	7.1	6.5	6.8	5.6	5.7	7.2	4.1
Productivity								
Total	4.9	5.0	4.5	8.5	4.0	4.6	2.8	5.8
Labor	6.5	5.7	5.1	10.4	5.7	5.7	5.6	7.6
Capital	1.8	0.1	1.1	0.6	2.0	3.5	0.4	4.2
Capital (labor ratio)	4.6	5.6	3.9	9.8	3.6	2.1	5.2	3.3
Western Electric Company								
Output (real product)	7.9	3.5	14.2	4.1	10.4	9.0	8.5	6.2
Inputs								
Total	2.1	−4.0	9.1	−0.1	5.5	4.1	4.1	−1.7
Labor	1.0	−5.0	9.1	−2.2	5.1	3.7	2.1	−3.3
Capital	5.2	0.9	9.3	7.8	7.0	5.2	8.9	1.0
Productivity								
Total	5.7	7.8	4.7	4.2	4.6	4.7	4.2	8.0
Labor	6.8	8.9	4.7	6.4	5.1	5.1	6.2	9.8
Capital	2.5	2.6	4.4	−3.4	3.2	3.6	−0.4	5.2
Capital (labor ratio)	4.2	6.1	0.2	10.1	1.8	1.5	6.7	4.4

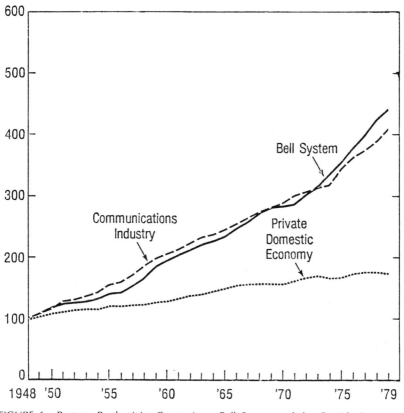

FIGURE 6. Postwar Productivity Comparison: Bell System and the Outside Economy (index numbers: 1948 = 100)

Over the subperiods the variability of output growth was a bit less for Bell operations than for the industry. The average deviations of subperiod rates of growth of total factor productivity were the same, averaging out a greater variability in the labor productivity rates and a lesser variability in the capital productivity rates.

Western Electric's total factor productivity averaged 5.7% a year, compared with 3.7% for the electrical machinery industry (see figure 7). The differential between growth rates of output per unit of labor input was greater — 2.7 percentage points — due to a much faster rate of growth of real capital investment per unit of labor input in the company than in the industry: 4.2% compared with 2.2%, on average.

The variability of Western Electric's output growth over the several subperiods has been much greater than that of Bell operations, reflecting the greater volatility and irregularity in growth of demand for capital goods than for telecommunications services. But the variability in subperiod rates of change in Western Electric's productivity ratios has

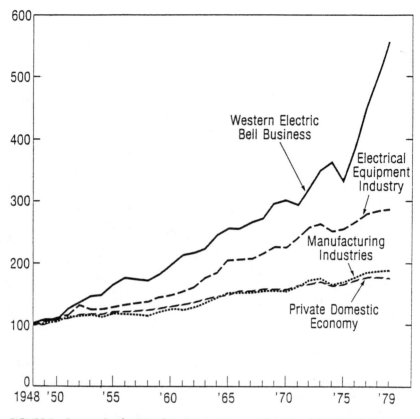

FIGURE 7.   Postwar Productivity Comparison: Western Electric and the Outside Economy
(index numbers: 1948 = 100)

been only somewhat greater, indicating considerable success on the part of management in adjusting growth rates of inputs to those of demand and output. Nevertheless, the variability of Western Electric's growth in total factor productivity and labor productivity was greater than that experienced by the electrical machinery industry as a whole.

In the case of Bell operations, superior productivity performance made it possible for average prices (rates) charged by the telephone companies to rise at an average annual rate of only 1.2% a year between 1948 and 1979, compared with trend rates of increase in average prices of the communications industry of 1.7% and in the implicit price deflator for the gross private domestic product of 3.2% a year (see figure 8). As already noted, the favorable productivity and price performance was associated with trend rates of growth of real gross product for Bell operations of 7.9% a year, compared with 7.3% for the communications industry and 3.6% for the private domestic economy.

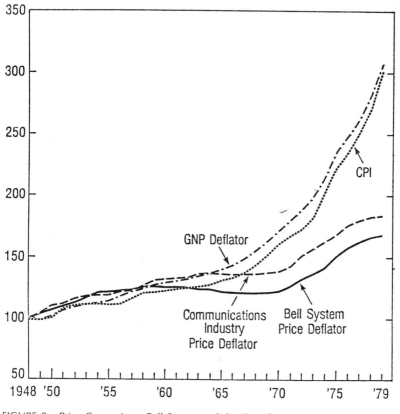

FIGURE 8.   Price Comparison: Bell System and the Outside Economy (index numbers: 1948 = 100)

Western Electric's outstanding productivity performance was associated with a trend rate of increase in its prices of 1.1% a year, compared with 2.5% for the electrical equipment industry, 2.9% for industrial commodities, and 3.2% for the private domestic economy (see figure 9). The low rate of increase in Western Electric's prices contributed to its 7.9% a year average growth of real product, compared with 6.8% for the electrical equipment industry and 3.5% and 3.6%, respectively, for all manufacturing and the private domestic economy. The relative decline in Western Electric's prices helped hold down the growth of the rate bases of the Bell telephone companies. This, together with the advantageous productivity and price performance of the companies, resulted in great savings to their customers compared with what their outlays would have been if the Bell System productivity performance had been no better than that of the business economy as a whole.

With respect to reasons for the Bell System growth of real product per

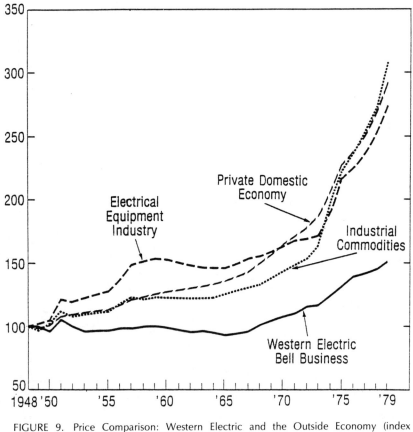

FIGURE 9.   Price Comparison: Western Electric and the Outside Economy (index numbers: 1948 = 100)

unit of labor input, the statistics that were presented in table 19 make it possible to quantify the contribution of capital / labor substitution. This variable is the rate of increase in capital per unit of labor weighted by the capital share of gross factor income in the base period. It equals the difference between the rates of growth of total factor input and labor input, or, alternatively, the difference between the growth rates of labor productivity and of total factor productivity. For Bell operations it amounted to 1.5% between 1948 and 1979, and for Western it was 0.9 percentage point. Capital / labor substitution thus accounted for almost 20% of the rate of growth of real product per unit of labor for the two entities combined.

These numbers understate the importance of tangible capital formation to productivity growth, since new plants and equipment bring cost-reducing technological innovations. It is our judgment, and that of most productivity analysts, that, over the long run, technological advance is the most important contributor to the growth of productivity. Underlying technological progress are two crucial types of intangible investment. The first is outlay for engineering and R&D, which produce the inventions that become innovations once management makes the decisions to implement them. The other is education and training, required not only to educate scientists, engineers, and business administrators who are responsible for the inventions and innovations, but also to train the work force to operate the increasingly complex technology. What do the data show regarding the Bell System's intangible investments?

In 1979 the Bell Operating Companies spent $519 million on R&D as defined by the National Science Foundation. This outlay represented 1.4% of the BOCs gross product, considerably more than is spent by most non-manufacturing firms. More importantly, Western Electric spent $687 million. This was 11.8% of its gross product originating from Bell business, and compared with 6.7% for all manufacturing companies. The reason for the relatively much higher outlay by Western is that its R&D is directed not only toward improving its own productivity, but also toward improving the design of its apparatus and equipment in order to increase the productivity and quality of service of the system as a whole. The $1.2 billion spent by both entities for R&D represented 2.7% of their combined gross products, which compares with a 2.3% ratio to GNP of total R&D outlay in the economy as a whole.

Most investment in education is financed by individuals and state and local governments and is completed by the time young people enter the labor force. Over the decades the amount of "human capital" per worker due to education has been increasing, and the Bell System, along with other firms, has benefited from the trend. But the Bell companies and Western Electric additionally provide formal training and retraining programs for both management and nonsupervisory employees for up to several months. The companies provide tuition refunds for college-level programs pursued by employees. In 1979 the cost of these educational and training programs amounted to over $1.5 billion, even more than was spent on R&D. This does not include the cost of informal on-the-job training, which is difficult to estimate. Additionally, in 1979 the Bell System spent over $75 million on medical, health, and safety programs, which are also a form of intangible investment.

Management has the responsibility not only for making the innovations and associated investments to improve technology but for operating efficiently under given technologies. The Bell System has a sophisticated set of measures to keep track of labor efficiency and of the quality of service in relation to engineering or statistical standards and norms. This helps ensure that the potential benefits of technological advance will be realized in terms of unit real cost reductions.

It is widely believed that increases in output make possible economies of scale, which enhance productivity gains. If so, such economies, which come from increasing specialization of people, machines, and plants and from spreading overhead costs over more units of output, could have been significant for the Bell System, whose output grew much faster than the real GNP. But for companies as large as those that compose the Bell System, it is questionable whether further economies automatically result from increases in scale of operation. In any case, management must make the decisions to take advantage of the opportunities that may arise and provide for necessary investments as well as for the continuing reorganization of production and support functions that growth entails.

The economies that may become possible as a result of the growth in a company's capacity and output should not be confused with changes in productivity associated with short-term changes in the rate of utilization of capacity. There is a significant positive correlation between year-to-year percentage changes in output and in productivity of both the Bell System and Western Electric, especially the latter. When demand and production fall below the most efficient rate of utilization of capacity, this has a depressing effect on productivity. Conversely, an output increase toward the range of the most efficient rate of utilization of a given capacity tends to augment the secular productivity advance — but this is a short-term phenomenon. When existing capacity has fully been utilized, plant, equipment, and inventory must be expanded if rising output is to continue to be associated with advancing productivity.

Following the court-ordered breakup of AT&T in January 1984, it will be interesting to see if the operating telephone companies, consolidated to seven in number, and Western Electric will have as good a productivity performance as the historical record has shown.

III

PROMOTING
COMPANY
PRODUCTIVITY

10

Company Productivity Programs: The State of the Art

As a result of the publicity surrounding the need for productivity improvement in recent years, most organizations claim to be aggressively attacking the problem. Almost as many claim to have a *formal* productivity improvement program. In fact, in the last five years many types of productivity programs with various renditions of "key elements" have become almost as commonplace as safety programs, energy programs, and so on. The problem remains, however, that many of the programs are ineffective. Very simply stated, the major problem with many company productivity improvement programs in the United States today is that they lack direction and priority and are not supported by a formalized company policy or position on productivity. Despite an awareness of the productivity issue and a sense of need for productivity improvement programs, many company programs are sporadic, short-lived, and can better be characterized as the "campaign of the month"; focus on cost cutting without considering more positive strategies; are not linked to adequate measurement systems; and do not focus on employees as the key resource for effecting change.

Current Practice

Today's company productivity improvement programs can be described in one of seven ways:

Broad-brush, Corporate-level Measures

Productivity is usually defined by some very broad ratio, such as sales per employee or sales to pay, which every business unit or profit center in the corporation can understand. In most cases, ratios like these are tracked over time, and often corporate targets for improvement are set. Less frequently, the corporate sales per employee or sales to pay goal is parceled out to the operating units and individual improvement targets set.

Obviously, pros and cons accompany this approach to a productivity improvement program. On the positive side, appropriate measures tend to bring productivity to the surface as an issue for the corporation; are easily understood and accepted conceptually as productivity measures reflecting outputs and inputs; are simple to compute and are based on data that are readily available; and can easily be computed for other companies from such data sources as annual reports, 10-Ks, or the Fortune 500 listing. On the negative side, such broad ratios can be affected by factors such as inflation, changes in product / service mix, inventory policy, subcontracting, accounting policy, and the like — any of which can give a false productivity reading; do not explicitly reflect the impact of other factors like capital, materials, and energy; assume that all labor inputs are equal; and oftentimes are difficult for people throughout the organization to relate to because most organization members cannot directly affect the ratios.

Grass Roots Approach: Plant by Plant, Department by Department

As opposed to the corporate-level measures program, the grass roots approach is characterized by few or many efforts in individual units throughout the corporation. Usually, no continuity or common theme drives the productivity efforts of the units; rather, each unit acts on an individual basis.

Industrial Engineering Orientation

Based on the historical industrial engineering principles or standards, time and motion studies, and labor efficiency, the industrial-engineering orientation unfortunately has become associated with concepts such as "work harder," "work faster," and "speed up," which have given the industrial engineering discipline a bad name in some circles.

Cost Reduction

Another fairly traditional approach to productivity programs, from the opposite side of the coin, is cost reduction. Explicit targets and measures are set relative to the costs associated with inputs to the productivity equation. Cost-reduction programs are broadly applicable to all input factors — labor, capital, materials, and energy. They are affected by changes in the prices, as well as the quantities, of the inputs.

Human Resource Focus

The theory behind the human resource focus, epitomized by "quality of work life" programs, is that a happy, satisfied employee will respond productively. Thus, the activities designed to motivate people draw heavily upon behavioral science techniques. Other factors, such as capital, materials, and technology, are viewed as less significant leverage points for productivity improvement.

Incentive-based Approach

Tangible incentives (usually money) directly related to labor productivity characterize the incentive-based approach. The most common programs are gain-sharing plans like Scanlon, Rucker, and Improshare, all of which find the company sharing financial gains with employees based upon some predetermined formula and goal. Broader profit-sharing programs are more widespread but are less directly related to productivity improvement than are the gain-sharing plans.

Combination of Approaches

For all practical purposes, few so-called productivity programs embody only one approach; the more successful programs skillfully blend all the approaches. Over time, in fact, a combination and adaptation of approaches in any one corporation will become the norm for working on productivity.

Elements for Success

Following are the eight elements that today characterize the efforts of those organizations with successful productivity improvement programs.

Top Management Commitment and Explicit Involvement

It goes without saying that top management support is important to any corporatewide initiative, be it safety, energy, human relations, or even the United Way campaign. The same holds true for a productivity initiative, only more so. Productivity is more than a program. It is an attitude, a philosophy, a state of mind, and is exemplified by the role and model of the top management group. In short, top management must make productivity a natural, but explicit, part of the operating philosophy of the organization.

The following examples illustrate top management commitment and involvement:

- Recently a major Fortune 500 company built its entire annual report around the theme of productivity. Commentaries on capital spending, safety, energy, employee ideas, research, and marketing were all presented from a productivity perspective.

This in and of itself does not improve productivity, but it does exhibit explicit commitment and involvement. Top management has publicly gone on record with the shareholders and the employees to state that productivity is, and will continue to be, a prime motive governing their actions and decisions.

- A major Fortune 100 corporation recently issued the following consensus statement from its senior management: "Productivity is a state of mind — a corporate culture — that takes time to transform. It must first be appreciated and cultivated from the top down. . . . It involves all of us — worker, middle management, and top management. . . ."

Formalized Company Policy or Position on Productivity

Regardless of whether a company is centralized or decentralized, it is essential to a successful productivity improvement effort that a formalized company policy or position on productivity be in place. It is just as important a policy as are those on return to shareholders, customer service, innovation, risk taking, ecology, corporate citizenship, and the like. The Berwick Group, a Boston-based management consulting firm, reported findings from a survey of executives at seventy companies about why productivity improvement efforts fail. The overwhelming response (70%) was that the "lack of a coherent, consistent, and company-wide strategy for improving productivity is the main reason why such efforts fail."

The company policy / position on productivity is the basis for addressing productivity as a strategic issue. The policy / position statement sets the tone and the sanction for productivity as a way of life throughout the corporation and its operating units. The following excerpts on productivity are drawn from actual company operating policies or principles:

- The company "will, through both traditional and innovative methods, improve productivity . . . in all operations for the benefit of our customers, employees, and shareholders and to ensure the successful continuation of our business."

- "It is recognized that continual improvement in productivity, during periods of an inflationary economy, is mandatory if we are to sustain real growth."

- "We seek to maximize our productivity at all levels through the proper use of capital, material, technology, and people. Productivity is a primary factor in our ability to achieve our financial and business goals."

Productivity Organization

Structure for the improvement effort is vital. Although there is no single best way to organize for improvement, it is important to specify the key individuals, committees, and task forces. Degrees of formality vary from company to company and in large part are determined by the centralized or decentralized nature of operations. Apart from individuals, two structural components historically have proven effective in most successful improvement efforts. They are the productivity steering committee (the policy group) and the productivity council (or task force).

Productivity Steering Committee

Composed of leading line and staff executives, the productivity steering committee is an independent forum for periodically reviewing the company position and policy on productivity improvement. The committee has the latitude to address itself to any area of productivity, whether it be labor, capital, materials, energy, or systems at any level within any component, division, or group of the company. The committee, with the approval of the president and chief executive officer, has the authorization to direct the implementation of changes or revisions in the company productivity improvement program.

The primary role of the productivity steering committee is twofold:
1. serve as a forum for exchanging ideas and initiating programs
2. monitor company policy to ensure that changes are not counterproductive in the long run and do not have a negative impact on productivity

Productivity Council

Representatives from each operating division / component / department and major staff group of the organization comprise the productivity council. Each member of this council is the productivity program coordinator for his or her respective division / component / department or staff group. The council meets periodically and has the following broad objectives:
*   to stimulate, solicit, and disseminate productivity improvement ideas
*   to coordinate good practices
*   to evaluate specific goals, plans, programs, results, and problems
*   to monitor, update, or recommend revision of the company position on productivity
*   to serve as a catalyst for the efforts of divisions / components / departments and assure consistency of effort

The company productivity steering committee serves as the advisory and approval body for the activities of the productivity council.

Productivity Coordination

Successful companywide productivity improvement efforts are characterized by good coordination of the individual unit programs with overall corporate policy, strategy, and goals. The position of "productivity coordinator" is now commonly found in many firms. Among the Fortune 500 companies having formal productivity programs, positions like productivity manager, director of productivity services, and vice-president for productivity, are quite commonplace.

The organization's productivity coordinator usually reports to top management. This person spends time communicating with unit / division / plant managers on productivity questions, conducting meetings and seminars on the subject, preparing and disseminating productivity improvement materials and ideas, establishing and coordinating the work of productivity councils / committees, and preparing studies of productivity trends throughout industry and within the company. Periodically, the productivity coordinator works with unit / division / plant managers on their plans and progress in improving productivity. Regularly, the coordinator works with a wide variety of middle managers on specific techniques that are or might be utilized to boost productivity.

The productivity coordinator's principal duties include:

- initiating and maintaining effective productivity awareness and communications programs
- serving as an adviser and consultant to operating units regarding their individual productivity programs
- monitoring the key factors contributing to low productivity and developing and recommending corrective actions
- maintaining liaison with productivity centers and other outside organizations having a productivity interest
- collecting and analyzing data relative to national, international, and industry trends as well as interfirm and intrafirm comparisons, and highlighting potential problems
- ensuring that appropriate education and training in productivity improvement is accomplished throughout the company
- identifying, compiling, and cataloging a repertoire of productivity improvement techniques that can be referred to and drawn upon by the operating units

Further, the productivity coordinator usually serves as chairperson of the organization's productivity council and member / secretary of the productivity steering committee as specified earlier.

People / Quality of Work Life Orientation

It is universal in those productivity improvement efforts deemed to be successful that positive employee relations and good quality of work life are viewed as integral parts of the overall plan. Regardless of whether the organization is labor intensive or capital intensive, product-oriented or service-oriented, people are the common denominator.

Here are some examples from selected successful improvement programs to illustrate the point.

- Excerpts from one company's productivity policy: "As part of our principal strategy, we will:
    - Design job assignments and work environments with an understanding and awareness of the importance of fostering productivity.
    - Promote effective two-way communication between employees at all levels to understand better the problems and concerns that affect productivity.
    - Employ programs that will motivate employees to produce products and provide services more effectively and efficiently."

- Beatrice Foods Company, headquartered in Chicago, addresses directly the people and productivity issue in its productivity philosophy: "At Beatrice, our people are the strength of our productivity effort. They help us use our resources more efficiently and effectively. This means working smarter with our tools, our capital, and our human resources. . . . The most important factor in improving productivity is the positive attitude of the management team. This attitude is important for developing ways to reduce costs, compete effectively and ease the pressures of inflation. . . ."

- Robert J. Day, president and chief operating officer of the United States Gypsum Company, stated in USG's 1980 annual report, "The key to the Company's productivity record is the innovation and ingenuity of our employees. . . ."

One or More Formalized Employee Involvement Technique

As stated, successful productivity improvement efforts are characterized by an active concern for the issue of quality of work life in the organization. The principal approach to improving quality of work life of those organizations with successful productivity programs is employee involvement, which includes a variety of approaches to interpersonal and organizational ways of working.

In successful productivity improvement efforts, one or more formalized employee involvement techniques is in place and is an explicit part of the program, and helps employees identify more fully with the goals of the enterprise.

- Beech Aircraft Corporation in Wichita, Kansas, has an employee suggestion program with more than 90% of the employees eligible for awards. This technique is not only designed to involve employees, but it *is* the productivity improvement program at Beech Aircraft. Beech Aircraft management believes that the suggestion system approach to getting employees involved and improving productivity has paid off. The company feels that for every award dollar spent there has been a four-dollar return.

- Honeywell, Inc., headquartered in Minneapolis, Minnesota, uses a variety of employee involvement techniques throughout its many worldwide locations, including suggestion programs, quality circles, management by objectives, team building, job enrichment, and many other approaches to employee communication and feedback. Particularly noteworthy are the results achieved by Honeywell through the use of employee suggestion programs throughout the corporation. The National Association of Suggestion Systems (N.A.S.S.) ranks Honeywell's program as one of the most successful in the country; Honeywell has received national awards for the excellence of its systems for seven years in a row. In 1979, Honeywell received 221 suggestions per 100 eligible employees, far above the national average of 15 suggestions per 100 employees. Also in 1979, Honeywell had an employee participation rate of 46%, more than double the N.A.S.S. average of 20%. Finally, Honeywell awarded 49% of its suggestions received in 1979, compared to the national average of 24% reported by N.A.S.S.

- Tektronix, Inc., located in Beaverton, Oregon, is a manufacturer of high technology electronic equipment. Tektronix's program is called "Tek Circles" and is a variation of the quality circle concept. Tek Circles stresses the team approach to problem solving and productivity improvement. Eighty percent of the ideas for improvement at Tektronix have come from circles. It is a time-tried and proven program. In its first five years of operation more than 1,500 employees and managers were trained in problem-solving techniques. Through the Tek Circles program 2,122 improvements have been implemented for a savings of over $2.13 million.

Measurement

The one factor that characterizes virtually every so-called productivity improvement program is measurement. Unfortunately, many companies get sidetracked by the measurement issue because they cannot agree on such questions as where to measure, which input factors to track, and how to integrate with financial analyses. Unsuccessful productivity programs can be distinguished in this regard because management is so busy trying to resolve the measurement questions that they never get around to addressing the improvements.

The best advice is to keep it simple at first and let the measurement systems and the productivity improvements grow together. It must be remembered the productivity measurement is not the primary target; merely measuring productivity is not going to improve it. But measurement is essential, since several important aspects of a well-rounded improvement effort are covered. The following list summarizes the benefits of measurement, as discussed in earlier chapters.

- Productivity measures help to heighten awareness. They combine outputs and inputs into meaningful relationships and help define and communicate to employees what is meant by productivity change.

- Productivity measures provide the basis for tracking trends and rates of improvement. They can be viewed as "health" indicators that tell the organization about its progress in achieving primary goals. In this regard they sometimes can be regarded as early warning indicators useful in spotting problems not readily apparent from financial analyses.

- Productivity measures serve as planning tools. It is becoming increasingly important that organizations consider the productivity impact of their investment, acquisition, and capital expansion decisions. In short, productivity measures are important to making productivity an integral part of the planning process.

- Productivity measures, obviously, permit one company to compare itself with others or with its industry on levels and rates of productivity growth. Many industry and trade associations are now generating productivity data and some are sponsoring inter-firm comparisons, as noted in chapter 8.

- The most important reason why an organization needs productivity measures rests in the fact that financial ratios can often obscure the truth behind an organization's performance. An organization may be achieving targeted profit margins in the short run and yet have declining productivity. Unless this is spotted through productivity measurement, the organization may never arrive at the real solution, which is to focus on productivity, sacrifice margins in the short run, and survive in the long run.

Top-down Program of Stimulation and Awareness

It goes without saying that the best ideas for improvement often come from the bottom — that nobody knows more about the improvements that need to be made or the changes that should take place than the people who are doing the work. However, the stimulation and impetus for improvement has to start at the top and filter down through the organization. It begins in the office of the chief executive. Programs of top management education and awareness must address at minimum the basic principles of productivity, and how these principles can be incorporated in the corporate strategies and programs; the importance of productivity to performance; the relationship between productivity and quality of work life; productivity measurement; human resource strategies for productivity improvement; and the possible courses of action for addressing productivity / quality of work life issues and opportunities.

Productivity awareness and education must continually cycle and recycle through the organization between top and bottom. Films, video tapes, speeches, training programs, productivity newsletters, packaged motivational programs, advertising, and the like may be appropriate.

- Caterpillar Tractor Company prepared a film entitled "Genius at Work," which features the real productivity "geniuses" — Caterpillar's own employees.

- The southwestern region of Ohio Bell prepared a video tape series that took a futuristic look at the Bell System. The film was entitled "What Killed the Bell System?" and was intended to be a dose of future shock. In the film the Bell System is about to be nationalized by Congress. Internal strife within Bell has caused the system to collapse: it takes six months to get a telephone installed; management complains of sloppy work, waste, and theft; workers complain about the incompetency of their supervisors; the public reviles the entire system. The video tape series was shown to craftsmen, supervisors, and managers and was followed by intense dialogue and analysis. All of the participants realized that *they* could possibly kill the Bell System. This approach was effective for Ohio Bell because it created a climate in which all employees were anxious to discuss their job problems and the barriers that prevented them from doing a better job.

- Productivity handbooks / pamphlets have been prepared by many companies including Honeywell, Sperry, Beatrice Foods, Southern California Edison, McDonald's, the Norton Company, National Semiconductor, and others.

More than ever, productivity improvement is a challenge and an opportunity as well as the key to the long-term survival of the private free-enterprise system. Yet in spite of past efforts, there is still much uncertainty about how to start, unrealistic expectations for a prescriptive productivity program, and too low a priority given to the issue in explicit terms within many organizations.

11

Productivity Improvement Programs: A New Look and an Emerging Pattern for Success

Managers have learned a lot from the productivity program efforts of the 1970s. Repeated experiences have revealed the mistakes and pitfalls, as well as the approaches to take in the future, relative to launching and running productivity improvement efforts. In this chapter we will first summarize the mistakes and pitfalls that can easily be encountered and then discuss an "Emerging Pattern for Success," which should help reshape thinking on the elements of a formal productivity improvement program.

Common Mistakes in Productivity Programs

Mandate from Top Management

Frequently, a mandate or edict from the top is used to launch a productivity improvement effort, resulting in a situation far less desirable than that which existed before anything was initiated. C. Jackson Grayson, Jr., chairman of the APC, recently cited the following example:

> About a year ago, the president of a major oil company issued a brief but firm edict reminding his top managers of the importance of productivity and directing them to take appropriate actions. He did not specify the actions, but he did name a deadline. After a few months, they were to report back to him on what actions they had taken and what results they were seeing. This edict was taken very seriously by those who reported to him and few questions were asked.
>
> An outside productivity expert called in by one of the company's operating divisions reported: "The people in the division told us, 'We have to have a program in 30 days!' When we said it couldn't be done in 30 days they were almost frantic. The atmosphere was irrational. They pleaded for us to promise them something in 30 days."

Despite words of caution from their consultants, the company's managers plunged ahead in many different directions. There was no coordination, no planning, no training, and a good deal of time was wasted at all levels. After a few months, things returned to normal, but the experience left a bad taste. Today, when anyone mentions productivity improvement, company executives there tend to wince.[1]

Unclear Rationale for Productivity Improvement

Hardly anybody will contest the basic concept of improving productivity. Likewise, energy conservation and safety are not arguable. The problem is that some organizations do not pause long enough to reach a consensus as to why they want to improve productivity.

What is the rationale for the productivity improvement effort — to remain competitive? To cope with rising costs? We have found companies whose managements really were not sure in explicit terms just what a productivity improvement effort was going to do for them. Productivity improvement should become a strategic issue and an integral part of ongoing operations. Without a thorough understanding of what needs to be accomplished and why, the improvement effort will lose meaning.

Weak Commitment from the Top

For any effort to succeed, the company needs to feel the involvement of the chief executive officer (CEO). Although expected to delegate the details to others, of course, the CEO cannot slough off responsibility. His or her interest and involvement must be viewed by all as genuine and indelible, not just as a temporary enthusiasm to be humored. Top management also must demonstrate its interest by providing continued, enthusiastic support. Without this, subordinates' efforts will migrate to areas that seem to interest "the boss" more.

Such inspiration and enthusiasm of top management must be converted to thorough and ongoing support for, commitment to, and involvement in the effort. One example of weak commitment occurred recently when a consumer goods company engaged a productivity consultant after receiving extensive criticism regarding its poor performance. The productivity expert conducted a week-long formal program to generate productivity improvement ideas and to motivate line managers to communicate effectively the productivity message. On the last day of the program, the CEO was scheduled to address the group and offer some encouraging words about the productivity improvement effort. Unfortunately, an unenthusiastic "staffer" substituted for the CEO and proceeded to play down the achievements and play up the long hours that the managers had spent on the program. He ended his talk with the words, "Thank God it's

Friday." In a few minutes this lackluster assistant to the CEO had destroyed the program before it had begun.

The "Appoint-a-Coordinator" Trap

The staff level and reputation of the person put in charge of the productivity improvement effort immediately signals how seriously others are expected to take the matter. In too many cases a so-called junior executive is delegated the job of coordinating the productivity improvement effort. This is especially true when little, if any, thought, definition, planning, and special training have been provided before that person was put in charge.

Strange as it may seem, many times the productivity coordinator does not have access to the necessary staff and resources to carry on the effort. It is equally important that he or she have the necessary "clout" to impress others in the organization with the importance of productivity improvement. Without the proper respect and reputation, it is usually not long before other managers are humoring the productivity coordinator as little more than a one-person crusade armed with a slide show and a flip chart.

The Measurement Hang-up

One of the elements to be addressed early on is productivity measurement, which defines productivity within the organization and gauges the progress of the effort. The pitfall to be avoided, however, is having productivity measurement become the ultimate goal. Too many times we have seen organizations spend an inordinate amount of time developing measures, formulas, computer programs, and simulations, and neglecting to *get on with the improvements!*

The best advice is to keep it simple in the beginning and let the productivity measurement program grow and evolve naturally with other elements of the overall improvement effort. Application of the principles in this handbook will eventually result in multipurpose measures with many uses.

"Program" Approach versus Organizational Change Effort

At the root of another problem is the widely held belief that productivity improvement is just another company program, along with the annual savings bond drive or the United Way campaign. This approach immediately places productivity in the wrong frame of reference. Even the word *program* may suggest a finite beginning and end — definitely not the case with a productivity improvement effort. What we are really talking about is an organizational change effort — adopting new roles, new approaches, maybe even new styles of managing and supervising. A productivity improvement effort may be characterized by numerous programs, all of which are designed to support the effort as appropriate.

There is a strong tendency in U.S. companies to emphasize neatly packaged programs that achieve quick, easily measurable results. Such programs begin with slogans and paycheck stuffers and end when the mercury bursts through the top of the pledge goal thermometer. Productivity improvement does not lend itself to this kind of approach.

Failure to "Take the Pulse" of the Organization

Often we find organizations failing to ask the basic question, Are we really ready to start a productivity improvement effort? They sometimes plunge ahead with communications, policies, and actions that backfire simply because management did not take the time to assess organizational awareness and attitudes toward the productivity issue. Recently, a well-known company was attempting to start a productivity improvement program while the members of the collective bargaining unit were on strike — the issue, unreasonable workloads and low pay in certain functional areas.

Good intentions are not enough. They must be timed properly to ensure success. Some key questions that ought to be asked to help "take the pulse" include:

- Are management / employee / union relations in the company such that none of the parties would view negatively a desire to tackle head-on the pressing issue of productivity improvement?
- Does the company have a positive rating in working conditions, pay levels, company policy and administration, and job security?
- Is top management willing to share with employees at all levels the economic benefits that can be derived from improvements in productivity?
- Is the company's accounting system "healthy" and flexible enough to accept changes required to effectively portray productivity data?
- Is top management willing to listen to the employees?
- Does top management believe that the company's performance depends substantially on the efforts of its human resources?

Responsibilities Not Clear

Frequently, organizations think that all they have to do is appoint a productivity coordinator, assign responsibility, give proper authority to the coordinator, and "eureka!" — productivity improvement will result. Obviously, this is not true. The productivity coordinator does play a principal role as the overall catalyst for the effort, but the ultimate responsibility for coordination and action rests with key managers throughout the organization.

Specific functions, involving both line and staff, must be assigned throughout the organization. Many organizations flounder simply because productivity is not high enough on the priority list, usually because responsibilities for coordination and action have not been made clear throughout the organization. To tackle the problems of unclear responsibility, the management team must come to grips with several major productivity planning issues. It needs to ask:

- Why do we want to work on productivity improvement?
- Who is responsible for productivity presently?
- How do we shift productivity from an implicit to an explicit responsibility?
- What is the normal way of injecting a new emphasis into an organization?
- What incentive is there for anyone to work on productivity?
- How do we incorporate the productivity effort into our overall business plan?

Fascination with Techniques

The last major mistake or pitfall companies might encounter in launching a productivity improvement program is what is called the "technique" syndrome — companies grab a packaged program or a tangible technique to satisfy their interest and enthusiasm for starting a productivity improvement program.

Not too long ago we heard the story of three chief executives who had met for lunch to discuss various aspects of their respective businesses. In the course of their discussion, the topic of productivity came up and each related what was being done in his organization. Quality circles were mentioned (as invariably they are in situations like this), and each chief executive had something to say. The first described how his quality circle program had grown from fifteen to fifty-two circles over the past twelve months. The second chief executive discussed how his company was piloting quality circles in two white-collar areas, one in accounting and one in the design engineering group. The third chief executive could say only that he did not have any quality circles in his organization. The postscript of the story is that a few days later, a quality circle consultant was called into the third organization to conduct facilitator training.

Suggestion programs, quality circles, gain-sharing plans, employee involvement programs, capital improvements, methods improvements, and so on will all improve productivity if the situation in the organization is conducive, the timing is right, and the technique is properly administered. What worked well for one company may be a disaster for another. So if somebody comes around selling "green pills" designed to improve productivity — beware! Top management really needs to know the situation first so that it is in the best position to make an intelligent decision about which way to proceed and what techniques to use.

Planning a Productivity Improvement Effort

The most important point to remember when working on productivity is that it is not just "another program," in the usual sense of the phrase. Productivity improvement needs to be viewed as a continuous, iterative, orderly process. In order to adopt and adapt a productivity perspective and make it a part of organizational culture requires an understanding of the "Sequence for Productivity Success": awareness / education, strategic planning, assessment, implementation, and evaluation / refinement. These major phases of the process typically are executed in sequence, although they may overlap and recycle as the organization works on productivity improvement. Each phase can represent a major step in making productivity improvement a natural part of organizational functioning.

Awareness / Education

Understanding and believing that the productivity issue is real and needs to be addressed at the firm and organizational level underlies the first step in the process. Commitment by organization members to "make it happen" depends upon the levels of awareness and acceptance of the issues. Awareness / education starts at the top of the organization, and in and of itself is a never-ending process. General identification and communication of internal productivity issues is vital for raising the level of awareness and commitment of top management and chief decision-makers.

The awareness phase constantly cycles throughout the organization to ensure that the importance of productivity is understood at all levels among employees. The messages involved in the phase are:
- the need for productivity and quality of work life improvement
- the expected benefits for both the organization and its members from improvements in productivity
- information on what is already being done about productivity in the organization
- education on process and techniques for achieving improvements in productivity quality of work life

A thorough understanding and acceptance of the several roles of the members of the organization relative to productivity awareness are also part of the process:
- *top management* must become aware of productivity and quality of work life issues and ensure that the organization understands

the importance of productivity improvement. At this stage of the process top management needs to think about the appropriate priority for productivity and establish a climate of continuity for productivity emphasis.

- *middle managers* as well need to become aware of productivity and quality of work life issues. Additionally, middle management's prime responsibility is to design and carry out the systems to communicate and support the awareness messages.
- *first-line supervisors and foremen,* in addition to becoming aware of productivity and quality of work life issues, provide the link between the organization's goals and the people who are producing. On a day-to-day basis they provide continuity for the productivity emphasis.
- *employees,* like management and supervisors, become aware of the productivity and quality of work life issues. In the awareness phase, employees need to know that their role in productivity improvement is to communicate upward, to make suggestions individually or as members of problem-solving groups, and to understand the relationship of job performance to productivity.

Strategic Planning

Unfortunately, many organizations, having accepted the productivity challenge, by-pass the most critical step — strategic planning. This phase is intended to prevent the productivity improvement effort from becoming another "program," or, worse yet, from not being consistent with the mission, goals, and operating philosophies of the organization. This stage of the improvement process is critical because it is through strategic planning that a productivity perspective gets incorporated into the philosophy and character of the organization.

Strategic planning for productivity usually involves the following members of top management: chief executive officer, chief operating officer, executive committee or top management team, and productivity coordinator. Frequently, a productivity adviser from outside the organization is involved with top management in the early stages of the awareness and strategic planning phases to facilitate the process and lend expert opinion and commentary to the deliberations.

Strategic planning for productivity involves answering questions like:
- Why work to improve productivity?
- What are the levels of awareness throughout the organization?
- How involved will top management become?
- Is productivity improvement implicit or explicit?
- What reinforces improved performance?
- What is the normal way of injecting a new emphasis into the organization?

- What can we learn from past history — successes and failures?
- How should we organize for improvement?
- What are our leverage points?
- How should we measure improvement?
- What are management and employee attitudes?
- What do we want to be in 1990 . . . 2000?

Once armed with answers to these and other productivity planning issues, an organization will be in a better position to choose rationally the best course of action. The outcome of the strategic planning phase is a sound framework and structure for the improvement effort. But in order to set the stage for assessment, top management must now be committed philosophically and strategically to productivity improvement, a commitment that is visibly communicated and demonstrated. Such support is demonstrated by a written policy or position on productivity and quality of work life, which, in effect, sanctions a productivity perspective for the organization. In this way, a productivity perspective can become an integral part of the planning and budgeting process, from which will emerge a long-term strategy for productivity improvement.

Assessment

After strategic planning, the organization should be in position realistically to consider its strengths and weaknesses as well as the barriers to improvement, and objectively to evaluate opportunities. The assessment phase is a continuation of the process begun with strategic planning but involves a more detailed, structured look at operations to identify: relative potential for improvement in different areas (human resources, capital, materials and energy, and technology); leadership style implications; significant individuals in the organization; organization and structure of the productivity effort; goals of the productivity effort; and improvement approach and plans for implementation.

Again, *process* is the primary consideration in conducting an effective assessment. The assessment approach chosen usually depends upon the situation and can take the form of audits, structured diagnostics, functional analyses, survey techniques, informal observations, operations analyses, structured brainstorming, or a combination of techniques.

In short, the objective is to address opportunities across the broad perspectives of labor, capital, materials, and technology. The process yields organizational commitment to workable plans that capitalize on the most significant opportunities. Most successful improvement efforts have focused on each of seven principal elements:

- *assets* — the effectiveness with which an organization utilizes its human, material, capital, and technological resources and the systems, procedures, and practices that affect their utilization

- *goals* — the impact of organizational objectives, both officially stated and unofficially pursued, that establishes expectations for performance and serves to direct employees' efforts
- *rewards and recognition* — the impact of the reward system, both financial and nonfinancial, and its effectiveness in encouraging desired behavior on the part of employees
- *communication* — the degree to which employees have the information necessary to perform their jobs efficiently, and the effectiveness of top-down, bottom-up, and sideways communication
- *measurement and analysis* — the accuracy and coverage of existing productivity measures, and the existence of adequate analytical data to facilitate management decision-making and goal setting
- *employee participation* — the avenues available for employees to contribute to the decision-making process, and the degree to which management seeks and encourages ideas from employees
- *organization and leadership* — the impact of various management practices, and the effectiveness with which various organizational components interact

Implementation

The implementation phase is the active phase. Unfortunately, too many organizations jump right to action without addressing the planning or assessment issues, resulting in "false starts," misdirection, incorrect technique, or "just another program." The organization that has proceeded logically through the first phases is now in a much improved position to take action and achieve results. Ideally, as the organization begins the implementation phase, organization members are now aware of the productivity and quality of work life issues; top management support and commitment has been secured; target areas for improvement have been identified; the productivity organization has been set up; productivity objectives have been established; and a satisfactory approach has been selected and plans laid out, including involvement of workers at all levels.

The organization is ready to conduct the necessary training and indoctrination, apply/install the approach in target areas, coordinate the effort, and maintain communications/publicity as appropriate. More specifically, approaches to productivity improvement that can be accomplished as a joint labor-management effort include the following: quality improvement and zero-defects programs; recovery and salvage of materials; energy conservation; improved use, maintenance, and repair of equipment; job redesign — simplification or enrichment; reduced labor turnover, absenteeism, tardiness, overtime, and unproductive time; improved health and safety; planning of training programs; design of tools or products; and organization of work and office or plant layout.[2]

Regardless of the approach selected, there needs to be appropriate training of all involved individuals.

- *functional managers* need to be taught what impact the selected approach will have on their operations. Will it require policy or procedure modifications? Will their active participation be required? How?

- *foremen / first-line supervisors* need to be given a thorough understanding of every detail of the selected approach. They will have the major responsibility for answering the questions, maintaining the ongoing effort, and training employees. They should know if the selected approach will affect their scheduling and assignment methods and what they will gain from it.

- *union officers / committee members / stewards* need to be carefully shown the potential benefits to employees of the selected approach. Proper training of this group will eliminate serious problems later. They must be shown how productivity improvements can be realized without raising questions of job security among their members.

- *employees* must be trained ultimately for any approach to be successful. They need to know how it will improve productivity; what they'll gain from it; what will be expected. Industrial engineering training, for example, can help workers participate in job redesign to promote efficiency.

In short, the successful implementation of the productivity improvement effort happens by enlisting the participation and support of others, communicating effectively what needs to be done, and initiating and operating the effort.

Evaluation / Refinement

The evaluation/refinement phase of the productivity improvement process is the time to measure, analyze, document, report, publicize, recognize, and reward results of efforts.

Naturally, evaluation and refinement should be ongoing and not occur at only one point in time. Such activities include: documenting the progress of the improvement effort — measuring results and analyzing findings to determine what worked, what failed, and why; reporting results and recommendations to top managers and decision makers; modifying failing or marginal efforts; and diffusing successful efforts by publicizing results and building on the successes. All evaluations basically take the form of a comparison whether it be a planned versus actual comparison, a time trend, a before-and-after approach, or a comparison with a control group or activity.

During evaluation and refinement, important questions need to be asked: Were the objectives met? Do the results reflect the desired changes?

What were the specific improvements? Did the effort pay off in terms of net gains? How were employee attitudes affected? Where do approaches need to be modified? Where is there opportunity to capitalize further on the successes? Most important, to whom are the successes attributable, and how should they be rewarded?

The keys to successful evaluation and refinement require specific emphasis upon:

- clearly defined program goals, objectives, and targets
- representative measures of performance at all levels of the organization
- accurate and complete data
- isolation of extraneous influences, such as concurrent program changes, major disturbances in the organizational environment, and business conditions
- most important, timely and appropriate reward and recognition for those who have contributed to the effort and have effected change

A Final Note

An accepted and adapted sequence for productivity success emphasizing strategic planning and assessment makes the task of choosing and implementing actions more rational. Significant gains may not come from working harder or better; doing things *differently* may be the answer. Employee involvement really pays off when innovational ideas are generated. After all, productivity growth over the long run largely reflects cost-reducing technological and organizational innovations.

The action guidelines are clear:

- commitment and involvement need to become major management goals.
- organizations need to structure an explicit approach to productivity improvement.
- long-term strategies for results must evolve to cover aspects such as opportunity identification, goals, measures, rewards, participation, education, and assignment of responsibilities.
- productivity needs to become a part of each organization's regular business plan and budget.

Peter Drucker states that "productivity is the first test of management's competence." By meeting more fully one of the most important challenges and opportunities of the times, business can turn around the productivity slowdown.

IV
APPENDIXES

Contents

Appendix A

CASE STUDIES: COMPANY PRODUCTIVITY MEASUREMENT SYSTEMS

CASE 1:
TOTAL PRODUCTIVITY MEASUREMENT AT THE MIDEAST MANUFACTURING COMPANY

For many years the economist in this large manufacturing company had been estimating the physical volume of sales as an aid to market analysis. The series had also been related to labor-hours for comparison with output per labor-hour in the industry and as a means for projecting labor requirements in connection with long-term sales forecasts.

Interestingly enough, it was in the industrial relations department that the work was carried further in an attempt to measure total productivity. It was felt that knowledge of total productivity would provide an important background for establishing company wage objectives. It would make possible a determination of the effect of any given wage increase on prices and profit margins.

After development of the measures, the head of the industrial relations department explained them to other management people and pointed out additional possible uses, such as interplant or department comparisons, short-range budgeting, and longer-term projections. He found much interest in the concept and measure of total productivity, but the estimation work continued as part of industrial relations research.

Cases 1 and 2 are reprinted, with permission, from John W. Kendrick and Daniel Creamer, *Measuring Company Productivity: Handbook with Case Studies,* 2nd ed. (New York: The Conference Board, 1965). The names of the companies were changed in that volume to preserve confidentiality. The data have not been updated, since the purpose of the cases is chiefly to illustrate methodology.

Output

The output measure was taken as the deflated value of "net sales and other operating revenue." Dividend and interest income from portfolio holdings of stocks and bonds was, of course, excluded. Instead of adjusting net sales for the estimated value of the change in semifinished and finished goods inventories, the company decided to adopt the alternative procedure of excluding from variable inputs the amounts attributable to production for inventory. The rationale was that productivity measures based on sales are more closely related to estimates of investment return. In practice, productivity estimates based either on sales or production will be very similar if the inputs are estimated consistently.

A price deflator for sales had been prepared for many years by the corporate economist. Because of the large number of products, a representative sample of products and product groups is used to approximate price changes in all the various divisions and departments and in the company as a whole. Prices and dollar sales for all products are available in company records. Each item chosen as representative is specific with reference to grade and type, f.o.b. pricing point, lot size, and order quantity bracket. Quoted prices by detailed specifications are used in preference to average realized price (dollar sales divided by quantities), since the latter is affected by changes in intraproduct mix and sales patterns.

Prices are sampled monthly and are weighted by quantities sold in each month. Relatives are computed for each product group, first using January of each year as a base, and then each year's index is chained into the base period 1947–49. The index numbers for each product group are combined into broader indexes for sections, divisions, etc., through direct weighting by current-period value weights.

The chain index procedure has the advantage of permitting prices of new products to be incorporated into the index each year. The use of current (variable) weights in the price index computations is consistent with the desired objective of obtaining a real sales measure with fixed price weights through deflation.

Labor Input

The basic procedure for estimating labor input was to estimate total labor compensation allocable to production of goods sold and to deflate by an index of average hourly compensation. Total compensation was obtained as the sum of wages and salaries as published in the simplified operating statement, as benefit costs (including those not in payrolls), and as payments to unemployment compensation and old age and survivors' insurance funds. Compensation of force-account construction workers was excluded, since the value of their product was capitalized and thus was not included in sales. Finally, a deduction was made for the portion of labor compensation estimated to be embodied in the increase in inventories of semifinished and finished goods. Since inventories are priced at cost on the books, the latter adjustment was made by calculating the labor cost as a percentage of the estimated total cost of labor, materials, and services in total production, and applying this percentage to the estimated change in inventories.

The derivation of the index of average hourly compensation starts with data on production-worker hours actually worked, which were available from accounting records. Average annual hours worked by nonproduction workers were taken as standard hours (2,080), less paid vacations, holidays, and sick leave. The last adjustment was based on partial personnel records on disability experience and is subject to some margin of error. Labor-hours were obtained as the product of employment and average hours worked by salaried employees. Since it was not feasible to separate construction-worker hours from the total, an average hourly compensation series was obtained as the quotient of total compensation and labor-hours, and the index numbers of this series were used to deflate total compensation, less that of construction workers.

It was recognized that the current product of workers engaged in long-range R&D is not included in current year's sales, but owing to the difficulty of segregating the total earnings of this type of employee they were not excluded from the labor input estimates.

It should be noted that the average hourly labor compensation deflator would be influenced by the shift of workers from lower- to higher-paying occupational specialties. This probably results in some upward bias in the deflator, downward bias in labor input, and upward bias in the derived productivity estimates. It would be preferable if the deflator could have been made up as a weighted average of average hourly earnings of each of the more important specialties, or occupational classes, of workers. Even a distinction between production and nonproduction workers would have been useful, in view of the increasing relative importance of the latter.

Purchased Materials and Services

Aggregate current dollar purchases of materials and services had to be estimated as a residual. From the operating statement estimates of "cost of goods sold; selling, general, and administrative expenses; and other operating charges," labor compensation and state income taxes were deducted, leaving materials and services. Federal income taxes and depreciation had already been excluded. This residual was considered a good approximation to material and service costs on a production basis after an allowance for the cost of materials portion of inventory change. Property taxes and other indirect taxes were left in on the grounds that these could be considered as a payment for governmental services to the business.

To reconvert to a sales basis, the portion of inventory change allocable to materials (estimated as described earlier) was added to the residual. The next step was to break down the purchases by certain categories to make them more amenable to deflation. From the central purchasing section it was possible to secure estimates of purchased materials net of construction materials which are to be excluded from input. Separate estimates of containers, supplies, freight, and power, which were to be deflated separately, were deducted from the central purchasing section total. From the purchases of operating materials, so derived, was subtracted an estimate of change in raw materials inventory in order to obtain an estimate of operating materials consumed (for which a ready-made price deflator was available).

Subtraction of the central purchasing section estimate from the total gave another residual. It was possible to identify and estimate roughly the major components: advertising expenses, facilities rentals, and general property taxes. The final minor residual represented, in effect, the statistical discrepancy between direct estimates of purchased materials and services and those estimated indirectly from the operating statement, as described.

The price deflator for the most important element, that of operating materials consumed, was a weighted average of prices of all the quantitatively significant types of materials used. Some of these price series were based on average annual market prices as reported in trade journals. But if the prices paid by the company differed significantly from quoted prices, then average prices actually paid were computed from the records of the central purchasing section.

Fixed weights were used, based on the relative dollar expenditure for each type of purchased material, but the weights changed every few years. Ideally, weights should vary each year, but a revision every three years or so probably avoided major distortion.

For containers, supplies, and purchased power, the appropriate components of the Bureau of Labor Statistics (BLS) producer price index were used. A freight rate index was compiled based on Interstate Commerce Commission general freight rate increases. A composite index of advertising rates was compiled by the advertising section from trade sources. Facilities rentals were deflated by the BLS index of machinery and motive product prices. Finally, general property tax payments were deflated by the Commerce Department price index for state and local government purchases; an alternative to this procedure would have been to extrapolate base-period tax payments by the real value of taxable property.

Capital Input

The basic method here was to estimate the total value of capital assets in constant dollars and the capital "input" by applying the base-period gross rate of return on invested capital at replacement value to the real stock estimate. The real stocks were estimated in terms of the type shown on the balance sheet, of which fixed investment in plants and equipment was by far the most important (see table A.1).

Cash, marketable short-term securities, and deferred charges were deflated by a composite "cash use" index. This represents an index of the prices of the expense categories for which reserves might be expended: labor compensation, materials and services, and construction. Deflators for the first two items have been described; for construction, the *Engineering News Record* (ENR) index of construction costs was used. Weights were based on the relative importance of the several categories of expenses in successive periods.

Accounts receivable were deflated by the sales-price index. Raw materials inventories were deflated by the index of purchased materials prices. Semifinished and finished goods inventories were broken down into the labor and purchased materials components as described earlier, and each was deflated by the corresponding price index.

In the case of permanent investment, the treasurer's section maintains a "perpetual inventory" of all items of plant and equipment in use. A card is kept on each item throughout its useful life, showing the acquisition cost. In each year, the replacement value of all fixed assets in use is calculated by multiplying the original cost of each item by the ENR index of construction costs in the current year, with the year of acquisition set at 100.0. Gross permanent assets in constant dollars can then be computed by deflating the total replacement cost by the ENR index with 1947–49 as 100.0.

A perpetual inventory system is most advantageous for estimating capital stock. A defect of the estimates, however, lies in the use of the ENR index for conversion of all fixed assets to replacement and constant prices. This index has gone up considerably more than the average price of machinery and equipment as measured by the BLS indexes for this category. The ENR index also probably overstates the increase in plant construction costs per unit, since it is a weighted average of construction wage rates and materials prices, without allowance for the effect of productivity advance.

It would have been preferable if the company could have estimated from its own records annual price changes of the types of equipment it purchased, using comparable items from one year to the next — or even have used a composite of the relevant BLS machinery items. For construction, an index of building costs per square foot of floor space for com-

TABLE A.1
Balance Sheet (in current and constant $) and Capital Input (in constant $) of
Mideast Manufacturing Company, 1947 and 1957 ($ in thousands)

Item	1947			1957		
	Current $	Price Deflator (1947-49 = 100)	Constant $ (A ÷ B)	Current $	Price Deflator	Constant $ (D ÷ E)
	(A)	(B)	(C)	(D)	(E)	(F)
Cash, securities, and deferred charges	64,300	96.2	66,840	118,100	137.9	85,642
Accounts receivable	20,667	94.9	21,778	53,567	106.2	50,440
Inventories: raw materials	15,533	100.0	15,533	28,100	108.9	25,803
Semifinished and finished goods	22,367	96.1	23,275	58,700	137.7	42.629
Gross permanent investment (plant and equipment)	405,200	95.3	425,184	914,567	142.0	644,061
Total gross investment (1 + 2 + 3 + 4 + 5)	528,067	95.6	552,610	1,173,034	138.2	848,575
Capital input[a]			87,312			134,075

[a] Total gross investment in constant dollars multiplied by 15.8%, which represents the average 1947–49 rate of return of operating income before taxes and depreciation allowances on the replacement value of total gross investment.

parable type structures would probably be better than the usual type of "construction cost" index such as the ENR.

Some offset to the probable upward bias of the ENR index as representative of the price of plant and equipment was provided by an upward adjustment to this index made by the treasurer in the early postwar years, because of the presumed decreased efficiency and higher cost of construction. This adjustment was gradually eliminated between 1948 and 1954, so that the adjusted index shows less increase after 1947 than the straight ENR index.

A few words should also be said about the company's use of gross rather than net fixed assets. This was justified on the grounds that maintenance activity has always been kept at a high level in this company, so that productivity of capital assets remains high until they are actually replaced. Nevertheless, creeping obsolescence does gradually reduce the ability of aging assets to contribute to net revenue even if their operating efficiency remains high. It was our opinion that real net asset value is a better measure of capital stock and input from this point of view.

Likewise, whereas the company includes depreciation allowances as part of the return on capital, an alternative is to include depreciation as part of intermediate input. Real depreciation allowance could be computed as part of the perpetual inventory calculation of capital stocks.

The Productivity Ratios

It is apparent from summary table A.2 that total productivity, by taking account of nonlabor inputs (all of which rose more than labor input) increased substantially less than gross output per labor-hour — that is, it increased 39%, compared with 90% over the decade.

If intermediate (materials and services) inputs are deducted from both gross output and input to obtain a measure of "total factor productivity," the increase is 84%, compared with the 39% increase in total productivity, owing to the materials saving achieved over the period. Net output per labor-hour, however, shows a still larger increase — 111% — because capital per worker increased substantially over the period.

The total factor productivity measure indicates the change in efficiency in use of the basic labor and capital factors associated with the industry. It is comparable with total productivity at the national level, as based on real product estimates, which are the sum of real product or value added in all

TABLE A.2
Productivity Summary of Mideast Manufacturing Company, 1947 and 1957
($ in thousands)

	1947			1957			
						Constant $	
Item	Current $	Price Index (1947-49 = 100)	Constant $ (A ÷ B)	Current $	Price Index (1947-49 = 100)	(Millions) (D ÷ E)	(Index 1947 = 100) (F ÷ C)
	(A)	(B)	(C)	(D)	(E)	(F)	(G)
Output							
Net sales and other operating revenue	265,167	94.9	279,417	666,567	106.2	627,653	224.6
Inputs							
Labor (excluding construction)	81,367	93.3	87,210	190,400	183.9	103,535	118.7
Materials consumption	86,133	100.0	86,133	183,767	108.9	168,748	195.9
Services	26,600	92.5	27,676	62,567	140.5	44,532	160.9
Capital (gross of depreciation)			87,267			134,300	153.9
Total (2 + 3 + 4 + 5)			288,286			451,115	156.5
Total productivity (index, 1F ÷ 6F)							139.1
Addenda							
Net output (1 − 3 − 4)			165,608			414,373	250.2
Factor input (2 + 5)			174,477			237,835	136.3
Total factor productivity (8 ÷ 9)							183.6
Net output per labor-hour (8 ÷ 2)							210.8

the firms and industries of the economy. The total productivity measure is better suited for analysis of changes in costs and prices of the company's products.

CASE 2:
TOTAL FACTOR PRODUCTIVITY MEASUREMENT AT A DURABLE GOODS MANUFACTURING COMPANY

This company is a large, multiplant manufacturer of a variety of complex products. Interest in total factor productivity measurement developed originally in the course of analyzing the consistency of the various segments of a long-term corporate forecast. A rough productivity framework was developed for this purpose, which also proved useful in appraising the implications, both national and corporate, of the productivity guidelines proposed by the Council of Economic Advisers. Out of this evolved a decision to construct a total factor productivity series for the company covering the entire postwar period. These data were then used to develop long-term trends of company productivity. Both the historical data and the basic framework have been used to estimate the impact on the company of current developments and emerging trends, both within and outside the company. These uses are discussed further in the final paragraphs of this description.

The project was undertaken in the economics section of the corporation, and the procedures recommended in the first edition of the National Industrial Conference Board booklet *Measuring Company Productivity* were adhered to very closely.

The development of a total factor productivity measure required the calculation of a time series for the volume of output, the volume of labor input, and the volume of capital input. For most of these elements, this involved taking value data from accounting records and converting them into series expressed in constant prices. The study covered the years since 1948, and all data were restated in terms of 1961 prices. The year 1961 was chosen as the base period partly because prices of a recent year would be more meaningful in the discussion, but mainly to satisfy criteria that the base period be one in which production was at a high level and the rate of return on investment relatively normal.

Table A.3 illustrates the computation of this productivity series, and the methodology is described in the following sections.

TABLE A.3
Computation of Total Factor Productivity, at 1961 Prices ($ and hours in millions)

Line No.	1961 ($)	1962 ($)	1963 ($)
1. Gross output (sales + manufactured plant + change in inventory)	200.0	220.0	235.0
2. Intermediate materials and services (including depreciation and taxes other than Social Security and income)	100.0	110.0	117.5
3. Value added (output for the productivity measure)	100.0	110.0	117.5
4. Labor input	25 hours at $2.80/hour } 70.0	26 hours at $2.80/hour } 72.8	27 hours at $2.80/hour } 75.6
5. Capital	20%ª × avg. investment of $150.0 } 30.0	20%ª × avg. investment of $162.5 } 32.5	20%ª × avg. investment of $171.0 } 34.2
6. Total input (line 4 + line 5)	100.0	105.3	109.8
7. Productivity increase (line 3 − line 6) (cumulative)	–	4.7 7.7	
8. Total factor productivity $\{\frac{\text{line 3}}{\text{line 6}} \times 100\}$	100.0	104.5	107.0
9. Partial productivity measures Output per unit of labor input $\{\frac{\text{line 3}}{\text{line 4}}\}$	1.429	1.511	1.554
10. Index (1961 = 100)	100.0	105.7	108.8
11. Output per unit of capital input $\{\frac{\text{line 3}}{\text{line 5}}\}$	3.333	3.385	3.436
12. Index (1961 = 100)	100.0	101.6	103.1

ª 1961 rate of return on average investment before income taxes.

The Measure of Output

The concept of output used in the study was "value added," or "income created within the firm." Value added refers to that portion of the value of production which is the direct result of the company's contribution to the market value of its production. There are essentially two steps in the determination of value added. First, sales *plus* manufactured plant,* *plus* the change in "in-process" and completed inventories *yields* gross output.

* The term *manufactured plant* refers to the company's internal effort expended on the construction, installation, and associated design of plant and equipment.

Then, gross output *minus* the sum of purchased materials and services (adjusted for the change in raw material inventories), depreciation, and taxes (other than social security and those based on income) *yields* value added. Depreciation was excluded from value added, since depreciation charges can be considered a time payment for machinery or structures purchased from the rest of the economy.

To develop this output measure, the accounting data for each of the above elements had to be restated in 1961 prices. The adjustment for price change was made, as follows:

1. *Sales* — sales by major product categories were adjusted by internal sales price indexes already available.
2. *Inventory change* — the percentage change in inventory volume during each year was obtained from inventory data available for the beginning and end of each year, valued at constant standard cost. These annual percentage changes were linked together to form an inventory-volume index. This was applied to the book value of inventories in 1961 to yield a constant price inventory series, from which the inventory change in constant prices was calculated.
3. *Manufactured plant* — a composite price index based on the BLS Producer Price Indexes for metalworking machinery and equipment, general purpose machinery and equipment, and electrical machinery and equipment was used to restate these data in constant prices.
4. *Depreciation expense* — these data in 1961 prices were obtained as a by-product of the restatement of net plant investment (which is described later, in the section on capital input).
5. *Materials and services purchased* — purchase price indexes were already available for a significant portion of total purchases. The BLS Producer Price Index for all commodities, other than farm products and foods, was used to restate all purchases not covered by internal indexes.
6. *Taxes (other than income and social security)* — the proportion that these taxes were of gross output in 1961 was applied to gross output in 1961 prices in each of the other years to obtain for that year the constant dollar series for these taxes.

The various series expressed in 1961 prices were then used to derive value added in 1961 prices.

The Measure of Labor Input

Total labor-hours worked by all employees in the company in each year formed the labor input series. These physical volume data were already available from company records. No deflation process was necessary. No weighting of labor-hours by skills was required, since analysis of the data indicated that no overall change in the average skill level had occurred during the period of the study.

The Measure of Capital Input

The capital input measure essentially represents the company's average annual net investment expressed in 1961 prices. Average annual net investment for each year is a thirteen-period average of month-end data. The restatement of the accounting data into constant prices was done separately for plant investment, merchandise investment, and all other investment.

1. *Plant investment* — The plant accounts include land, buildings, machinery, furniture, fixtures, and small tools. The values in the land account were not restated in constant prices. For each year from 1947 through 1961 the depreciable portion at year-end of each of the other five components of gross plant was arrayed by years of acquisition. Price factors were applied to the yearly acquisitions to obtain the 1961 dollar equivalent of each component.

   Separate price indexes were used for each plant account: the ENR Building Cost Index for the building account and the composite machinery index (described in connection with the restatement of the cost of manufacturing plant) for the machinery and small tool accounts.

   For furniture and fixtures a composite of two BLS producer price indexes was used. This composite was made up of the indexes for (1) commercial furniture and (2) office and store machinery and equipment.

   Manufactured plant "in-process," defense emergency plant (each deflated by the above-mentioned price factors for the year of acquisition) and war emergency plant (deflated by an average of the price factors for 1941 to 1945) were added to the data on depreciable plant in 1961 prices to obtain aggregate gross plant in constant dollars at the end of each year.

   Once there was a series for total gross plant in 1961 prices at year-end for each plant account, the next step was to utilize these data to obtain net plant investment. The fixed-period amortization method used by the company to depreciate furniture, fixtures, and small tools made it possible to derive net investment in constant prices for these two accounts directly from the series on gross investment at constant prices.

For buildings and machinery a more elaborate procedure was required. Gross additions to each account for each year were restated in 1961 prices, using the same price factors utilized in restating gross investment by year of acquisition. For each year, the annual depreciation charge in 1961 prices was computed by applying to average gross plant in constant prices, obtained by averaging beginning and end-of-year investment, that year's ratio of actual depreciation charges to average gross plant valued at original cost.

For the year 1960 a special study, made for other purposes, provided an estimate of the depreciation reserve on December 31, 1960, by year of plant acquisition. For December 31, 1960, the depreciation reserve for each component of plant was restated in 1961 prices, using the price factors previously applied to gross plant by year of acquisition. The December 31, 1960, depreciation reserve in constant prices was deducted from the December 31, 1960, gross plant in constant prices to obtain net plant in constant prices. To estimate net plant for the other year-end periods, the net plant data in constant prices for the end of 1960 were adjusted by the constant dollar gross additions and depreciation charges for each year back to 1947 and forward to the present.

The net plant data for the various plant accounts were then added together to provide two series, one at original cost and one in 1961 prices. Since these two series represented year-end data, a two-period moving average of each was taken to provide the annual average series. The ratio of the constant price series to the original cost series provided a price factor for each year, which was applied to the net plant portion of average annual investment in that year to restate it in 1961 prices.

2. *Merchandise investment* — From the data developed to restate inventory change in 1961 prices, described earlier, it was possible to derive an inventory price index for ends of years. A two-period moving average was computed to provide an index, with 1961 equal to 100, which was divided into the merchandise portion of average investment to arrive at a series in 1961 prices.

3. *Other investment* — An implicit price deflator, obtained by dividing sales in current prices by sales in 1961 prices, was used to restate other investment into 1961 prices. This deflator was selected because much of the other investment represents such items as accounts receivable and cash on hand, which would be appropriately restated by using the overall price movement of products and services sold.

Combining Labor and Capital into a Total Factor Input Measure

The labor and capital input series described earlier were combined, using the 1961 average compensation cost (including all fringe benefits) per labor-hour worked as the weight for the labor-hours worked series and the 1961 pretax rate of return for the weight of the average net investment series.

Derivation of Productivity Measures

For the year 1961 (the base period) the combined factor inputs are equal to value added. In all other years, however, they differ from value added, and this difference is a measure of productivity change. The total factor productivity series was computed by dividing output (value added) in 1961 prices by total factor inputs also in 1961 prices. This yielded a total factor productivity index, with 1961 = 100. Table A.3 illustrates these procedures.

Uses

The uses to which this material has been put can be classified into two broad categories — those dealing with the distribution of productivity increases and those dealing with the "production function."

1. *Distribution of productivity increases* — table A.4 illustrates the computation of the distribution of the productivity increase for 1962. It starts out with 1962 values at 1961 prices taken from table A.3. The spread of $4.7 million between value added and factor inputs is the productivity increase available for distribution. A comparison of 1962 results valued at 1961 prices with 1962 results valued at 1962 prices indicates what distribution actually was made:

To customers as a ½% price cut	$1.00
To suppliers as a 1% increase in purchase prices	1.00
To employees as a 3% increase in wages and fringes	2.20
To stockholders as a higher rate of return on average investment	.24
To the federal government as taxes on the higher rate of return	.26
Total	$4.70

Thus, productivity measurement provides a useful framework for

TABLE A.4
Distribution of Productivity Increase, 1962

Line No.	Value at 1961 Prices ($)	Value at 1962 Prices ($)	Change	
			$	%
	(A)	(B)	(C = B−A)	
1. Gross output	220.0	219.0	− 1.0	− ½
2. Intermediate materials and services	110.0	111.0	+ 1.0	+ 1
3. Value added (line 1 − line 2)	110.0	108.0	− 2.0	
4. Labor input	72.8	75.0	+ 2.2	+ 3
5. Capital input	32.5	33.0	+ .5	+ 1¼
6. Federal income tax	16.9	17.2		
7. Net profit	15.6	15.8		
8. Total input (line 4 + line 5)	105.3	108.0	+ 2.7	
9. Productivity increase (line 3 − line 8)	4.7	0	− 4.7	

analyzing changes in the company's cost structure. Although the tax rate was unchanged from 1961 to 1962 in the data shown in table A.4, this same approach can be used to study the impact on the company of changing tax rates. Similarly, the line for "Intermediate materials and services" can be split up in order to permit separate analyses of depreciation, material content of production, and other purchased materials and services. This framework was also useful in appraising the Council of Economic Advisers' productivity guideposts for wage and price policy in terms of actual operating data. It makes clear that the guideposts involve simplifying assumptions about capital-output ratios, depreciation rates, and replacement costs of capital investment.

2. *Production function* — the production function implied in table A.3 can be utilized in long-term forecasting of company operations. The employment implications of a long-term sales forecast provide an illustration of this type of use, and table A.5 contains a sample of such a computation. Once the matrix has been developed to provide a range of forecasts, separate statistical studies can be made to help determine the most reasonable set of assumptions. For instance, correlation studies relating changes in business volume to changes in total factor and partial productivity measures can be used in selecting the most appropriate rate of change in output per unit of labor input. Similarly, long-term trends fitted to historical data on hours worked per employee can be used to select the most likely level for this variable in the forecast year.

Innumerable variations and combinations of these two approaches are possible, and they can be applied to total inputs, or the labor and capital

TABLE A.5
Estimate of 1971 Employment Based on a Productivity Model

Let:

X = Employment
P = Intermediate materials and services divided by gross output
G = Gross output
H = Hours worked per employee per year (in millions)
R = Annual % increase in output per unit of labor input
n = Number of years from 1961 to forecast year
W = 1961 employee compensation per hour worked = 2.8
L = 1961 labor input divided by 1961 value added = .7

Then:

$$X = \frac{(L)(G)(1-P)}{(1+R)(H)(W)} = \frac{.7G(1-P)}{2.8(H)(1+R)^n} = \frac{G(1-P)}{4H(1+R)^n}$$

If, for example, gross output in 1971 is given as $360 million, a matrix of employment estimates involving various assumptions about the other variables can be constructed as follows:

Estimated 1971 Employment Assuming:

Hours Worked/ Employee/ Year	Annual Rate of Increase Output/ Unit of Labor Input (%)	Intermediate Materials and Services as % of Production		
		48%	50%	52%
2,000	5	14,365	13,813	13,261
	4	15,808	15,200	14,592
	3	17,411	16,742	16,073
1,900	5	15,122	14,540	13,958
	4	16,640	16,000	15,360
	3	18,328	17,623	16,918
1,800	5	15,962	15,348	14,734
	4	17,565	16,889	16,214
	3	19,347	18,602	17,858

inputs separately. The framework lends itself to other analyses, such as the impact of product-mix changes on the relationahip between value added and gross output.

CASE 3:
PLANTWIDE PRODUCTIVITY MEASUREMENT AT GENERAL FOODS CORPORATION

What do Super Sugar Crisp, Maxwell House Coffee, Open Pit Barbecue Sauce, Minute Rice, Jello Pudding, Gravy Train Dog Food, and Tang Beverage Mix all have in common?

Yes, they are all edible and, yes, they are all manufactured and distributed by General Foods (GF) Corporation, a $5 billion plus multinational corporation that operates around the world to provide food products of all types for practically any occasion. But another, perhaps more interesting common feature of these food items is that they are all subject to the same yardstick for measuring the efficiency by which they are produced. They are all covered by GF Plantwide Productivity Measurement Program (PPMP).

Program Development

In 1975 the corporate management addressed itself to the question:

Can we measure on a total plant basis how effectively a plant uses the resources made available to it in the form of materials, labor, and capital in turning out production? If we can, how should we do it?

A group composed of cost accountants, industrial engineers, and manufacturing operations employees was formed to address this basic question. The result of their investigation was a PPMP.

The principal feature of the PPMP is the computation of a productivity index (PI) for each plant. The PI for a year is the ratio of the productivity during that year and the productivity during a base, i.e., the current-year productivity, divided by the base-year productivity. It indicates the plant's productivity improvement from year to year. Tested in 1975 on two large plants (one capital intensive and the other labor intensive) the PI is presently being computed at twenty of the thirty-four major plants at GF, with more plants being added each year.

GF employs close to fifty thousand men and women at more than one hundred locations in sixteen different countries. Every shopping day consumers purchase some 23 million packages of GF products. In producing these products for the marketplace GF has for many years maintained an objective of being the low cost producer in the food industry. The PI has become a valuable indicator of the company's progress toward that goal.

Description of PI

The PI for an individual plant portrays the overall management effectiveness at the plant. Since productivity is defined as output divided by input, the productivity index is the ratio of output and input with both factors adjusted for inflation. The output (the numerator of the productivity calculation) is conceptually the cost value that should have been added by converting raw and packaging materials into finished goods if plant operations were carried out at base-year efficiency levels. It is, therefore, the value (in base-year dollars) added to the raw materials that are put into the production process.

The input (denominator of the productivity calculation) is the amount of effort and resources expressed in base-year dollars used to achieve the output. The input elements that combine to form the total input amount include:

- direct labor,
- service labor — maintenance, quality control, etc.,
- administration and clerical manpower,
- purchased services and supplies,
- raw and packing materials lost in production,
- energy,
- depreciation, property taxes, insurance, and
- cost of capital — investment in land, buildings, machinery and equipment, inventories.

All of these elements add to the value of the raw materials being processed. Therefore, the value of the product equals the value of the raw materials plus the value of these input elements.

Since both the output data and the input data are converted to base-year dollars, the productivity index becomes a simple ratio of (1) the current productivity (output / input) stated in base-dollar terms and (2) the base-year productivity (output / input for the base). The base-year PI, of course, equals 1.0, since the base-year productivity figure would be divided by itself. If the productivity index for years subsequent to the base year is greater than 1.0, the productivity (output / input) for that year exceeded the base-year productivity. Similarly, productivity deteriorated for the year if the PI for the year is less than 1.0.

The PI is a total factor productivity index, that is, it includes all inputs that contribute to output. Many PIs focus on one input, the most common being labor productivity, which commonly represents the production output (say, revenues or units produced) divided by the labor input (such as labor-hours, number of employees, or even labor cost). Limiting the number of inputs, however, reduces the information conveyed by such partial PIs. For example, a firm's labor productivity may be increasing while its capital productivity is decreasing and unless the two are viewed together, the net effect on the firm's profits cannot be computed.

Because GF takes into account all input factors that add to the value of raw materials, its PI reflects the net of productivity increases and decreases; that is, if labor productivity increases while capital productivity decreases by the same amount, the net effect on the PI is zero (assuming equal weighting of labor and capital). Since the inclusion of an input amount is dependent on whether the input is associated with the product output, the following explanation addresses first the output and then the input elements associated with the output elements.

Measuring Output: Base Year

To demonstrate the method of computing the PI, assume that a product requires two inputs — labor (including overhead and associated costs) and raw materials. To compute the output, GF determines for labor and materials the cost of a unit of output during the base year. For example, assume the following data:

Cost Elements	Base-Year Cost ($)
Labor cost / unit of output	0.24
Materials-lost cost / unit of output	0.20

GF receives this type of data from its cost accounting system for each product. Basically, GF is interested in representing the output as the value added to the raw materials that are put into the production process. For example, how much more valuable is a pound of processed and canned coffee than a pound of raw coffee beans ready for processing? Notice that GF employs a materials-lost measurement for productivity measurement as opposed to a materials-used approach. There are two primary reasons for employing this approach:

- Materials lost represents the cost reduction opportunity at the plants. The purchasing of materials and the related price management is not a plant function but is carried out at the corporate level.
- Using materials lost reduces the impact of raw materials cost on the PI. Raw materials represent a high proportion of the cost of GF products. Changes in total materials cost caused by the volatility of commodity prices would distort the PI. Moreover, if materials-consumed data were included in the output figure, they would have to be eliminated in order to arrive at value added.

Since GF's cost accounting system generates a materials-lost figure, the data are readily available. An example of this lost-cost approach is as follows: Assume that during the base period 200,000 pounds of raw materials were lost while the plant was producing 500,000 cases of a finished product. If the base-year purchase price of the raw materials was $0.50, the total cost of lost raw material would equal $100,000 (200,000 × $0.50) and the unit cost would equal $0.20 / case. On the labor side of this example, assume that one employee making $12.00 an hour (including all overhead and related costs) produced 50 cases of product an hour (or $0.24 / case) during the base year. Therefore, 500,000 cases would require a total labor cost of $120,000 (500,000 × $0.24). If all of the raw material had found its way to the can, the value added to the raw material would equal the amount of labor necessary for processing (excluding, for this example, capital costs). However, when raw material is lost in production, the finished value must increase to reflect the value of the loss. Therefore, the value added (output) during the base year is $220,000 ($100,000 in lost raw material cost and $120,000 in labor cost).

Measuring Input: Base Year

In the example cited, the inputs into the plant are raw materials and labor. As with the calculation of output, the materials input is represented by raw materials lost in production, which was given in the example as 200,000 pounds at $0.50 a pound or $100,000. The labor input portion is also identical to the output calculation ($120,000), since all labor input contributes directly to the value added to the raw material. The capital factor is not included in the calculation of the base-year PI, since the capital productivity equals the difference in the current cost of capital and the cost of capital during the base year (making this difference zero when computing the base-period capital productivity). Therefore, the input total is also $220,000 ($100,000 for materials lost, $120,000 for labor, and zero for capital) and the PI for the base period is 1.0 ($220,000 of output ÷ $220,00 of input). The PI is 1.0, of course, because the methods used to calculate both the value added to the raw materials (output) and the total value of the input elements are essentially the same.

Measuring Output: Current Year

The PI for a year subsequent to the base year is computed by using current-year volume at base-year prices.* For example, if 600,000 cases of product were produced during the current year, using 10,800 labor-hours, the output (value added) would be $264,000 − $120,000 in raw material (600,000 × $0.20 / case) and $144,000 in labor (600,000 × $0.24 / case). Again, notice the prices used in computing the value added are base-year prices ($0.20 / case for raw materials and $0.24 / case for labor). The only variable, therefore, in the output calculation for the current year is the production volume.

Measuring Input: Current Year

In computing the input (denominator) for the current-year PI, the current-year volume of input elements is used along with the base-period prices (purchase cost) of those inputs. In the example cited, assume that during the current year 190,000 pounds of raw material were lost in production and that it took 10,800 labor-hours to produce the 600,000 cases. The total input value (at base-year prices) for the current year would be

---

*If base-year prices are not available, current-year prices are reduced by price deflators to estimate base-year prices. Although this technique is not preferable to using actual base-year prices, it is sometimes necessary — especially with pooled cost areas, such as overhead and administration.

$224,600 — $95,000 for raw materials (190,000 units × $0.50/unit), $129,600 for labor (10,800 hours × $12.00/hour), and no change in the cost of capital.

The PI for the current year is, therefore, $264,000/$224,600 or 1.18. This calculation and the preceding steps are summarized in table A.6.

The reason for using materials lost in production rather than materials used in production should be apparent from the data in table A.6. Notice how the materials portion of the total PI has a somewhat lesser weight than the labor portion. Had the materials calculation considered materials used instead of materials lost, the materials would have had a much greater weight than labor in the total PI calculation, with the danger that a disproportionate cost reduction effort might be directed by the plant to materials rather than to labor and materials equally.

One of the principal advantages of this method of calculating the PI is its ability to absorb without distortion the effect of changes in product mix. For example, as shown in table A.7, the plant produces three prod-

TABLE A.6
Calculation of Productivity Index

Output	Base Year			Current Year		
	Total Cost ($)	Units Produced	Cost/ Unit ($)	Base-Year Cost/($)	Units Produced	Total Cost ($)
Material (lost)	100,000	500,000	0.20	0.20	600,000	120,000
Labor	120,000	500,000	0.24	0.24	600,000	144,000
Total	220,000					264,000

Input	Base Year			Current Year		
	Units of Input	Purchase Cost/Unit ($)	Cost of Input ($)	Base-Year Purchase Cost/Unit ($)	Units of Input	Cost, Base-Year Prices ($)
Material (lost)	200,000	0.50	100,000	0.50	190,000	95,000
Labor	10,000	12.00	120,000	12.00	10,800	129,600
Total			220,000			224,600

Base-Year PI	Current-Year PI
$\dfrac{\text{Output}}{\text{Input}} = \dfrac{\$220,000}{\$220,000} = 1.0$	Material PI $= \dfrac{\$120,000}{\$\ 95,000} = 1.26$
	Labor PI $= \dfrac{\$144,000}{\$129,600} = 1.11$
	Total Factor PI $= \dfrac{\$264,000}{\$224,600} = 1.18$

Source: American Productivity Center.

TABLE A.7
Raw Materials Lost in Production, Product Mix Example, Fiscal 1973–75

Output	Standard Units Produced			1973 Cost/ Standard Unit ($)	Output: Value Added ($)		
	1973	1974	1975		1973	1974	1975
A	1,000	3,000	10,000	1.00	1,000	3,000	10,000
B	2,000	2,000	0	5.00	10,000	10,000	0
C	3,000	1,000	0	10.00	30,000	10,000	0
Total					41,000	23,000	10,000

Input	Qty. Lost in Production			Base-Year Purchase, Standard Unit ($)	Input, Base-Year Prices ($)		
	1973	1974	1975		1973	1974	1975
A	2,000	6,000	24,000	0.50	1,000	3,000	12,000
B	4,000	4,000	0	2.50	10,000	10,000	0
C	6,000	2,000	0	5.00	30,000	10,000	0
Total					41,000	23,000	12,000
Partial Productivity Index: raw materials lost in production					1.00	1.00	0.83

Source: See table A.6.

ucts in unequal proportion from year to year. In spite of the change in product mix, however, the 1974 PI is still 1.0 (with 1973 as the base year), and in 1975 the PI of 0.83 reflects a reduction in materials productivity (a greater percentage of materials are lost) and not the effect of a shift in product mix.

Translating PIs into Cost-Reduction Targets

Table A.8 displays the basic data for computing the PI for six years, including the base year 1973 and a projected PI for 1978. In addition to the two basic elements (labor and materials) the data include a line for packaging materials. Notice further that the cost of capital factor is contained only among the inputs and there only as a change in the cost of capital from the base year. The production volume figures are included to permit an analysis of the PI as a function of the throughput of the plant.

The data from table A.8 provides some initial insight into why the productivity of the plant has fluctuated. For example, it appears that volume reductions have had the significant negative impact on the absorption of fixed costs. In this respect the plant should be more responsive to volume declines in incurring fixed costs. It also appears that the unfavorable trend in variable cost productivity (primarily labor) is partially a result of low

TABLE A.8
Productivity Results of Plant A ($ in million)

	1973	1974	1975	1976	1977	1978a
Output						
Raw materials lost in production	42.6	41.9	33.2	39.8	35.5	35.3
Packing materials lost in production	0.3	0.3	0.3	0.3	0.3	0.3
Labor & overhead	25.4	25.5	19.2	22.7	19.9	19.4
Total output	68.3	67.7	52.7	62.8	55.7	55.0
Input						
Raw materials lost in production	42.6	41.0	32.4	37.9	34.2	32.7
Packing materials lost in production	0.3	0.3	0.3	0.4	0.3	0.3
Labor & overhead	25.4	25.3	26.2	28.1	25.3	25.9
Increase in cost of capital	–	–	0.4	(0.9)	(1.0)	(1.4)
Total input	68.3	66.6	59.3	65.5	58.8	57.5
Productivity index (output + input)	1.000	1.017	0.888	0.958	0.947	0.956
Volume (millions of units)	18.1	17.6	14.5	16.2	13.5	12.5

Source: See table A.6.

Note: Parentheses signify negative value.

a Projected PI.

TABLE A.9
Impact of 1978 Cost-Reduction Program, Plant A ($ in thousands)

Project Title and Description	Annual Net Savings (1978 $)	Annual Net Savings (1973 $)	Cost of Capital (1973 $)	Change in Plant Input ($)
Equipment replacement	3492	1088	78	1010
Reduced raw material losses	1700	527	69	458
Energy conservation	250	24	–	24
Crewing	350	241	–	241
Reformulation	1043	717	–	717
Other opportunities	161	111	–	111
Total plant	6996	2708	147	2561

1978 productivity index: 0.956
Revised 1978 index if all cost reduction is achieved: 1.001

Source: See table A.6.

volume. The reduced raw material shrinkage and reduced cost of capital have been the brightest spots over the last six years. Finally, it will take a reduction in input costs of $7.5 million (or 13% of the $57.5 million) to attain a target index of 1.10 in 1978.

As suggested by the mention of a target index, another benefit of the GF PI calculation is that it permits the computation of a "bottom-line" cost-reduction figure, which can be associated with a particular PI and

TABLE A.10
Productivity Results of Plant B ($ in millions)

	1973	1974	1975	1976	1977 L/E	1978 Plan
Output						
Raw materials lost in production	22.7	22.6	20.5	23.8	24.6	23.2
Packing materials lost in production	0.2	0.2	0.2	0.2	0.2	0.2
Labor & overhead	11.4	12.0	10.9	12.6	12.7	12.1
Total output	34.3	34.8	31.6	36.6	37.5	35.5
Input						
Raw materials lost in production	22.7	22.2	19.9	22.3	22.2	21.3
Packing materials lost in production	0.2	0.2	0.2	0.2	0.2	0.2
Labor & overhead	11.4	11.3	10.9	11.9	12.1	11.9
Increase in cost of capital	0	(0.4)	(0.3)	(0.8)	(0.9)	(1.1)
Total input	34.3	33.3	30.7	33.6	33.6	32.3
Productivity index (output ÷ input)	1.000	1.045	1.029	1.090	1.112	1.098
Volume (millions of units)	18.5	18.7	17.1	19.9	19.9	19.0

Source: See table A.6.

Note: Parentheses signify negative value.

which can be given a plant manager as a cost-reduction target. For example, if Plant A (table A.8) were to establish a PI objective of 1.0 for the year 1978, it would need to reduce its input cost by $2.5 million, since the value added (output) in 1978 is expected to be $55 million and the input is expected to be $57.5 million. Table A.9 depicts the plant manager's plan to realize the cost reductions necessary to reach a target PI of 1.0. A similar analysis can be used to verify the statement above that a $7.5 million reduction in input is needed to attain a target index of 1.10.

Another example of the productivity trend for a plant is given in table A.10. In this case, Plant B appears to have experienced a positive change in productivity over the years, with a few dips due to volume reduction. The primary improvements are in the area of raw material yield and, to a lesser extent, in labor productivity. There are not significant unfavorable trends. Table A.11 outlines how the manager of Plant B anticipates raising the PI to 1.123 by saving $720,000, i.e., by reducing the inputs by that amount.

Application of PI at Division Level

The PI calculation is not restricted to use at the plant level. It can also usefully be employed at the division level, where the plant PIs are aggregated into a divisional PI. These data are reflected in table A.12 in the

TABLE A.11
Impact of 1978 Cost-Reduction Program, Plant B ($ in thousands)

Project Title and Description	Annual Net Savings (1978 $)	Annual Net Savings (1973 $)	Cost of Capital (1973 $)	Change in Plant Input ($)
Packing material specification changes	80	49	(8)	41
New blending system	45	24	(11)	13
Vacuum pump	20	7	(1)	6
Recirculate cooling water to vacuum pumps	13	4	(2)	2
Agglomerator	20	7	(2)	5
2 lb. lid applicator	30	19	(2)	17
New scale – can line no. 1	120	37	(9)	28
Yield improvement of 1.0% on product X	670	214	–	214
Yield improvement of 0.8% on product Y	232	74	–	74
Yield improvement of 0.2% on product Z	134	43	–	43
Sewer connection charge not needed	200	138	–	138
Reduce efficiency loss on processing equipment to 4.0%	150	103	–	103
Other opportunities	86	36	–	36
Total plant	1800	755	(35)	720

1978 productivity index: 1.098
1978 index if all cost reduction is achieved: 1.123

Source: See table A.6.

Note: Parentheses signify negative value.

same format as the individual plant data, and as with the plant data, the division data can provide valuable insights on divisional operations. For example, the primary reason for the maintenance of the divisional PI at the base-year level is that improved raw material yields and reduced capital investment have offset the drop in labor productivity and the underabsorption of fixed overhead over the years. Reduced volume and its resultant unfavorable effect on fixed cost absorption has been the single most negative factor.

Just as the plants can have PI targets translated into cost-reduction targets, so can divisions establish cost-reduction objectives, as shown in table A.13. For example, assuming that a division's objective is to achieve a PI of 1.10 in 1978 and 1.20 in 1983, each plant must make some significant progress in reducing its level of input. The following table shows for each plant and division the required reduction in input:

TABLE A.12
Divisional Productivity Measurement ($ in millions)

	1973	1974	1975	1976	1977 L/E	1978 Plan
Output						
Raw materials lost in production	121.3	122.1	107.3	116.5	102.4	96.5
Packaging materials lost in production	1.0	1.1	1.0	1.0	0.9	0.8
Labor & overhead – plants	79.3	83.6	72.4	78.6	68.5	64.5
Labor and overhead – div. HQ operations	2.2	2.3	2.0	2.2	1.9	1.8
Total output	203.8	209.1	182.7	198.3	173.7	163.6
Input						
Raw materials lost in production	121.3	119.6	104.6	112.6	97.2	89.5
Packaging materials lost in production	1.0	1.0	0.9	1.1	0.9	0.8
Labor & overhead – plants	79.3	82.5	83.0	87.3	78.9	77.8
Labor and overhead – div. HQ operations	2.2	1.6	1.5	1.6	1.9	1.9
Increase (decrease) in cost of capital over base year – plants	–	(0.7)	0.4	(3.1)	(3.4)	(4.7)
Increase (decrease) in cost of capital over base year – div. HQ operations	–	(0.5)	(1.0)	(2.0)	(1.2)	(2.0)
Total input	203.8	203.5	189.4	197.5	174.3	163.3
Productivity index (output ÷ input)	1.000	1.027	0.964	1.004	0.997	1.002

Source: See table A.6.

Note: Parentheses signify negative value.

Plant	*1978 Cost Reduction ($000)*	*1983 Cost Reduction ($000)*
A	7,526	11,692
B	58	2,749
C	7,573	11,661
D	541	1,412
Total for division	15,698	27,514

Role of PPMP at GF

The primary purpose of the PPMP is to assist in meeting the company's continuing goal of being the low cost producer in the food industry. Some of the uses of the PPMP include:

TABLE A.13
Divisional Summary of Plant Productivity Index Impact of 1978 Cost-Reduction Program
($ in thousands)

Plant	Annual Net Savings (1978 $)	Annual Net Savings (1973 $)	Less Cost of Capital (1978 $)	$ Change in Plant Input
A	6,996	2,708	147	2,561
B	1,800	755	35	720
C	4,301	2,373	28	2,345
D	414	219	29	190
Total division	13,511	6,055	239	5,816

	1978 Index before C/R	Index Change Due to C/R	Revised Index Incl. C/R
A	0.956	0.045	1.001
B	1.098	0.025	1.123
C	0.953	0.041	0.994
D	1.093	0.013	1.106
Total all plants (incl. div. HQ)	1.002	0.037	1.039

Source: See table A.6.

- to permit analyses of operations by cost element (raw materials, labor, and capital)
- to motivate the plant managers in achieving cost reduction
- to provide a common measure among plants and among divisions
- to permit the measuring of the effects of cost-reduction programs
- to provide a basis for long-range and short-range planning to include facilities planning
- to identify areas of potential improvement
- to permit the evaluation of various engineering techniques for cost reduction
- to highlight areas (by subelement) of potential improvement

As with any good system, the PPMP is constantly being studied and refined. As more plants participate in the system, it is likely to gain in acceptance companywide. The motivation provided by the individual plant productivity indexes is sufficient by itself to justify the system. However, the additional uses of the system in planning and analysis have made the PPMP a very valuable management tool.

GF has realized that as world food problems grow, members of the food industry will be under increasing pressure to process and distribute food products using the most efficient methods available. Its management believes that in the PPMP it has a meaningful measure of its progress toward optimum efficiency in the manufacturing process. Its general-purpose design permits application of the system to the myriad food products already processed by GF as well as to future products. Its design simplicity also allows for translating PIs into specific cost reductions, that is, into a language that plant managers understand and to which they respond. The PPMP, therefore, combines the attributes of a useful and flexible tool for corporate management with an understandable and accepted measure for the plant employee.

Appendix B

CASE STUDIES: COMPANY PRODUCTIVITY
IMPROVEMENT PROGRAMS

CASE 1:
SOLAR TURBINES INTERNATIONAL:
QUALITY CIRCLES GENERATE SAVINGS,
IMPROVE QUALITY OF WORK LIFE

Solar Turbines International is aware of the tangible and intangible benefits resulting from quality circles. For every problem solved, Solar recognized a marked savings. Quality of work life improved, generating receptivity to new ideas by employees and management. Solar's future plans are to continue expanding quality circles, due to strong top management support and employee cooperation.

Organizational Background

Solar Turbines International is an operating group of International Harvester Company [1] and is recognized to be the leading manufacturer of 1,200 and 4,000 HP gas turbine-driven compressor, pump, and generator packages. Solar has five manufacturing and overhaul plants located around the world. Three plants are in San Diego, with three thousand employees, and the remaining plants and facilities employ nine hundred people worldwide. The company had sales of $350 million in 1979 and expects a significant increase in 1980.

Approximately seventeen hundred of Solar's employees belong to one of three labor unions: International Association of Machinists, International Union of Operating Engineers (Welders), and the International

Brotherhood of Electrical Workers. The quality circle program has not been a negotiable item, and the unions have not objected to the development of the circles.

History and Development of the Program

In the spring of 1974, the management of Solar conducted an employee opinion survey in preparation for the next year's contract negotiations. The companywide survey of employees' opinions revealed that employees at all levels wanted more challenging work. They wanted to be more involved in planning policies, procedures, and methods. They also wanted productivity improvement as a way to increase their wages.

Department supervisors, with the help of a facilitator, asked for volunteers from the hourly work force to form employee task teams to study the issues that were identified in the survey. Out of approximately 2,200 hourly employees, 232 volunteered and 56 of these volunteers were selected and divided into six teams. They met after work and received overtime pay for the meeting time. The teams produced a lengthy check list of suggestions and complaints. Corrective action was taken by the teams and/or management on most of the suggestions. Monthly "rap sessions" were initiated to improve communications between management and other employees. Two departments were selected to test these informal rap sessions with groups consisting of ten appointed employees from the same work area.

The employee task teams demonstrated to management that the hourly work force wanted to be involved. However, the full benefits of the teams were not realized because only a small percentage of employees were involved.

In 1975 Solar experienced a four-month strike by the IAM. Management realized the severity of its communications problems, as evidenced by low management credibility and poor rapport between first-line supervisors and hourly workers.

Before the strike was over, management decided on two corrective actions. First, a new approach to supervisory training was implemented, which stressed human relations and communications. Second, monthly departmental meetings were instituted during which foremen could announce new policies and products and developments outside of manufacturing, and employees could express their ideas and concerns.

In early 1976, a quality assurance task force (composed of the vice-president of manufacturing with a cross section of people in the company from engineering, finance, and human resources) was formed to study and make recommendations on how Solar could improve the quality of its products and reduce costs. This task force studied all aspects of the company's operations, including the company's quality situation and reputation, by visiting customer sites around the world. It appeared that employee attitudes toward quality had changed as Solar moved from government (aerospace) work, which had tight quality control, to commercial industry, which had less restricted quality requirements. After six months, the task force concluded that one major challenge was to improve employee attitudes toward quality. All employees, from salesmen to engineers to shop-floor workers, needed to recognize the importance of quality.

One member of the task force had read how Lockheed's quality circle program had successfully changed employee attitudes through involvement. Two separate plant-line management teams were sent to Lockheed to observe and make recommendations. Both teams were enthusiastic supporters of quality circles and recommended their implementation at Solar. However, some of the plant managers were skeptical and had different ideas on how to run a circle.

In 1977, after much deliberation, the decision was made to run a pilot program. Two "formal"quality circles were established in one manufacturing plant and two "informal" groups in another. The formal circles hired an experienced quality circle consultant and carefully followed the Japanese mode. This involved voluntary participation, training for the group leaders and participants, the support of a facilitator, and formal presentations to management.

In the informal groups, supervisors volunteered to participate, but all employees in the department were expected to participate. The informal meetings turned into "gripe sessions" with little employee contribution on problem solving. Without training, the supervisor conducted these groups for the purpose of identifying and resolving employee problems.

After six months the pilot program ended and the "formal" quality circle approach was selected because of its very apparent advantages. The advantages were a formalized problem-solving effort, ability to solve problems quickly, effective documentation, more efficient flow of information, and employee cooperation.

Description of the Program

The manager of quality human factors is the program manager for quality circles. He reports to the manager of total quality assurance, who in turn reports to the vice-president of technical operations.

The initial training of circle leaders and participants is conducted by Solar's two full-time facilitators. Additional responsibilities of the facilitators are coordinating the initial formation of circles, coaching the leaders after circles have been implemented, attending all circle meetings, monitoring the effectiveness of each circle, consulting with the organization on how to support the efforts, and coordinating quality circle information throughout the organization.

Quality circles at Solar are led by first-line supervisors who volunteer for the program. They receive two days of training. The first day covers the quality circle process. Attendees learn about formalized brainstorming, data gathering, cause and effect analysis, and how to use Pareto charts, histograms, and control charts. They also learn how to make economic evaluations and develop their solutions for oral presentation to management. The second day deals with group motivation and how to make circles effective.

Duties of the leaders include taking part in their participants' training sessions; keeping the circles in process; contacting other departments and support personnel whenever necessary; promoting circle participation and involvement; developing the human resources of the circle; and planning and participating in the meetings. Facilitators meet with the leaders prior to each circle meeting to insure planning for meetings. After the meeting, the facilitator provides the leader with a feedback sheet, which serves as a behavior change tool and a documentation of the leader's skills.

Most circles consist of about ten members. Solar originally held eight, one-hour training sessions once a week for circle members, but management discovered that one-day, off-site sessions were more effective. They give employees the feeling that they are involved in a unique experience and permit them to get more quickly involved in problem solving. Facilitators conduct the training and provide the same basic information on the circle process that the leaders receive.

Circle participation is voluntary and members are allowed to drop out if they wish. However, positive, effective members feel a commitment to attend and participate in circle activities, understand and use the quality circle process, and focus on facts and data rather than on opinion.

Circles meet once a week during regular working hours and participants do not receive any extra compensation. When the first and second shifts meet together and employees must come in early to attend a meeting, they receive overtime pay.

The first step in every circle is the identification of problems. This is done by brainstorming. Each circle member is given the opportunity to suggest a problem; no ideas are rejected or criticized. When all ideas have been listed on a chart or blackboard, they are arranged in order of priority and work begins on the most important one. Solar circles usually work on more than one problem at a time so that if there are delays on one project, members can continue to work on another.

Once the problems have been identified, the team must make a more complete analysis and determine what data are needed. This is usually done through Pareto or cause and effect analysis. The facilitator retrieves data from other departments whenever a team requires them.

When a circle has developed recommendations for resolving a problem, it is ready to present them to management. Several circle members participate in the presentation, which is made to the level of managers whose approval is necessary for implementation.

Solar carefully documents the activities and results of its quality circles. Minutes are generally kept for each circle meeting. The facilitators record the activities and progress of each circle in preparation for a quality report. The overall effectiveness of the program is monitored by the steering committee, consisting of the vice-president of manufacturing, the director of total quality assurance, the manager of training and development, the three plant managers, and the facilitators.

Solar's tracking system records the number of projects started and completed, the average number of circle labor-hours needed to complete a project, the average number of working days between the completion date and the implementation date, the average estimated value of the change per project, and a verification of improvements made by the change. Documentation is also maintained on circle effectiveness, leader effectiveness, member participation, organization support, and return on investment.

Results

Solar estimates that the total cost of the program for the first year and a half was $79,000. This includes the salary of the manager of quality human factors, who works half-time on quality circles; the salaries of two full-time facilitators; consulting fees, supplies, and materials; travel; the cost of time spent in meetings; and the cost of support personnel contributing to circle projects.

The annual estimated value of the problems resolved during the first year and a half was $90,000. Each problem required an average of eight, one-hour meetings and each solution saved approximately $7,500.

One problem solved involved the planning process for a CENTAUR eighth-stage compressor disc at Solar's Harbor Drive Plant. The number of operations was reduced by the circle from nine to three, and an operation was eliminated that was previously performed outside. The first year's net savings came to $8,400 after a nonrecurring cost of sixty-five labor-hours. Although the problem did not originate as a quality issue, the company has realized fewer rejections, a benefit assumed to be due to the major reduction in set-ups, and the fact that the parts will be machined on higher precision NC equipment versus the manual equipment.

At the Kearny Mesa Plant, the analysis on one project indicated that the electrical assembly department did not have a sufficient number of company-supplied tools. After spending forty-four labor-hours analyzing worker delay times and making a $2,200 investment in additional tools, annual savings amounted to $31,700.

Solar believes that tangible benefits are not the critical considerations in supporting quality circles, and that there have been important intangible savings. These include general quality of work life, improved cooperation within the circle and department on time-saving techniques, more employee receptivity to the profit improvement actions of management, a greater understanding of the complexity of business on the part of participating employees, and an improved training program for supervisors.

Two circles have ceased to operate. The cause for these terminations is not obvious. However, the influence of the leaders and organization support were contributing factors. In one case, the leader's style was so contrary to a participative approach that the circle never made it through the eight weeks of training. In addition, there were some allegations that upcoming contract negotiations had an impact on member participation.

The second situation involved a circle that was one and a half years old. Over time, the leader strayed from the circle techniques and process. Although the leader was coached and confronted by the facilitator and program manager, little change occurred. The net result was that meetings were held with little involvement or participation by the members; thus, the circle chose to disband. Another factor that should be considered is that the leader felt that the company was slow in responding to suggested changes, thus she and the circle lost faith in its ability to be effective.

Future Plans

Solar plans to expand the number of circles in fiscal 1980 from twenty to forty, including new circles in finance, human resources, and sales. With this expansion, the company expects to complete sixty to eighty projects in 1980 for a net annual savings, after fixed and variable costs, of over $1 million.

Solar's top management strongly supports the circle concept. They view it as a management style that should become a way of life and a means of contributing to the quality of work life. However, change comes slowly and particularly changes with managers considering this participative approach as an alternative to their autocratic or laissez-faire styles.

Other Programs

Solar has an hourly employee suggestion program, which is kept completely separate from quality circles. There is also an annual company picnic, an active recreation association, and periodic presentations to employees by all three plant managers at strategic times of the year, such as Christmas.

CASE 2:
CONTROL DATA CORPORATION: INVOLVEMENT TEAMS IMPROVE WORKER-MANAGEMENT RELATIONS, EMPLOYEE PERFORMANCE

Involvement teams at Control Data have been very successful, growing from one pilot team at the end of 1977 to forty teams in mid-1980. The program offers employees the opportunity to deal with work-related problems and concerns through brainstorming and problem-solving.

Organizational Background

Control Data Corporation is a publicly owned corporation occupied in the application of its computing technology, financial resources, and consulting services. The organization has two main activities: the computer business and financial services. There are roughly 58,000 employees in forty-seven countries. In 1979 the corporate earnings were $124 million. Roughly two-thirds of this figure was generated by the computer business, the arm of Control Data with which this case is concerned.

Control Data is essentially a nonunionized organization. None of the areas now employing the involvement team program is unionized. Overall management style has been aggressive, providing an authoritative, rather than participative, atmosphere.

History and Development of the Program

Top-level management interest in production programs, cost reduction, and team development resulted in the initial 1977 discussions of a possible quality circles program. There was a desire to utilize more efficiently the human resources within the company.

Management decided to proceed with the establishment of a pilot team in December 1977. Another pilot team was begun in July 1978 at a second plant. Both of these teams were involved in manufacturing. In the establishment of these two teams, employees were given a general introduction to the concept of quality circles, after which some employees volunteered to participate as team members. Two managers were selected and trained to serve as team leaders for these initial groups. All training was, and is still, conducted by internal trainers. These two pilot teams were successful. Thus, in November 1978, management decided to support the creation of more teams and the development of more extensive leader and management training.

Description of the Program

An involvement team is a small group of employees (average of ten members) who do similar work. The team members voluntarily meet weekly on company time, to review problems and concerns related to their work in an attempt to discover solutions to the problems. Areas considered in these meetings include productivity, quality, and communications. Areas that are not addressed by teams are those of salaries and benefits, hiring and firing policies, and personalities. The team recommends solutions to management, implementing solutions themselves if possible.

Each team has a leader who is a manager, trained during a two-day session. The team leaders are trained in involvement techniques by the team administrators. Team leaders in turn train the team members in goal setting, brainstorming, etc. These people are responsible for the operation of their teams.

There are currently two involvement team administrators working with the program, one full-time and one part-time. These two people have a wide range of responsibilities. They develop necessary training materials and conduct training and orientation sessions for team leaders. They also work closely with the steering committee, maintain records, and serve as the interface between the teams and other company organizations.

The largest division of Control Data, which has approximately half of the teams, also has a steering committee, composed of the division management personnel. The committee's function involves administrative decisions and general direction of the program. It is concerned with such issues as how many teams should be established, where they should be established, etc.

Management support is demonstrated through provision of time, space, and materials necessary for team meetings. Support also takes the form of encouraging employees to attend scheduled team activities. The management responds to team requests and solutions expediently, implementing approved solutions and providing detailed explanations for denial of requests. A manager may also suggest problems for team consideration.

Direct costs of the involvement team program have not been documented. However, the involvement team manager works full-time as involvement team administrator. There is also a half-time administrator in the largest division. In addition, there is the expense of the training notebooks and other training materials. But these costs are considered minimal by the company when compared with the benefits of the program.

No differences in production are noticed as a result of the work time lost in the weekly team meetings. Therefore, there is no apparent cost to the company here.

Results

There has been no formal evaluation of the program, but rather it is judged on the basis of the general well-being of the organization. There has been no attempt to gather statistical results because it is considered very difficult to determine what portion of improvements is attributable to involvement teams and what to other aspects of the company "people development" orientation.

Every six months a review meeting is held between management and employees involved in the program. At this meeting highlights and progress of the past months are reviewed.

Benefits reported by Control Data's management include improved management-worker relations, improved communication, increased productivity, higher quality work, and improved employee performance. The employees are enjoying the opportunity of self-expression, problem solving, and seeing action taken as a result of their suggestions. Employees are enthusiastic and take pride in being recognized. They feel they have considerable control over the quality and efficiency of their work.

Future Plans

Control Data has no definition of how far the involvement teams program may reach. There is a long-range focus on developing teams and learning from experiences. Two or three teams are being added each month in a variety of areas including professional, clerical, payroll, test areas, etc. There is an aim to gain broad experience and perspective from these varied groups. Future plans also include development of involvement teams in some of the unionized areas of the corporation.

CASE 3:
MORSE BORG-WARNER:
RUCKER/SCANLON HYBRID REDUCES
EMPLOYEE GRIEVANCES AND TURNOVER,
INCREASES PRODUCTIVITY

The program at Morse Borg-Warner is unique because it utilizes a
Rucker Plan bonus formula and Scanlon Plan committee, suggestion, and
participation systems. Originally implemented as a traditional Rucker
Plan, it evolved over a period of about a year into its current hybrid
nature.

Organizational Background

In 1978 Borg-Warner employed 54,800 people in the United States,
Canada, and twenty other countries on six continents. The corporation is
divided into five business areas: (1) air conditioning and building products,
(2) chemicals and plastics, (3) financial services, (4) industrial and steel
products, and (5) transportation equipment. Net sales in 1979 were $2.6
billion and net income was $116 million. The corporation is ranked in the
top quartile of the Fortune 500.

The plant on which this case study focuses is the gearing division of
Morse Borg-Warner located in Denver, Colorado. This division has
approximately 325 employees on three shifts and is involved in the design
and manufacture of gears, gear boxes, and industrial speed reducers. The
plant's net sales in 1979 were $17 million. The factory utilizes conventional
and nonconventional metalworking equipment. Workers are represented
by the International Association of Machinists.

History and Development of the Program

By 1976 Borg-Warner Corporation had recognized the need for
improved productivity. During 1976, the Denver plant had a major strike,
which accentuated the need for reinvolvement of employees in order to get
operations back to normal. In response to these recognized needs, the division manager and industrial relations manager initiated the search for an
appropriate productivity improvement and employee involvement program.

A joint study group was formulated at Morse in early 1977. The group consisted of four union stewards (including the chief steward) and three management individuals (the division manager, industrial relations manager, and controller). They examined various types of programs — work measurement, individual incentives, and group incentives. The committee decided a group incentive program would be most appropriate because it would create the opportunity to build a team in the plant. Another advantage of the group program was that it offered broader coverage with more employees involved. After studying various group incentive programs, the committee felt a Rucker Plan would be most compatible with Borg-Warner's accounting procedure, since the bonus formula is based on allowed compensation versus actual compensation. A year later, in March 1978, the study group submitted to top management its recommendation to adopt a Rucker Plan. It recommended beginning the program with a Rucker bonus formula and the standard Rucker method of committee structure, later moving into a Scanlon Plan committee structure. A synopsis of the group's recommendations was published in the plant's monthly newsletter in April 1978, and top management's final approval of the program was obtained.

Thus, in May 1978, the productivity sharing program was introduced with a slide presentation to all employees by the outside Rucker consultant. At this time booklets describing the bonus calculation were distributed. Seventeen productivity representatives and their alternates were selected and oriented to serve on productivity improvement committees. The productivity sharing program formally began in June 1978.

The productivity improvement committees' objective was to solicit ideas and suggestions from employees. Although there were idea forms with which to gather employee input, no formal method of processing ideas existed. Facilitation of idea discussion and action was the function of the central idea coordinator.

In the last quarter of 1978, management began to discuss the Scanlon committee structure with the productivity representatives and supervisors. During the second quarter of 1979 an outside Scanlon consultant came to Morse to assist in training supervisors, productivity representatives, and managers. He also assisted in establishing the two-tier, production committee / screening committee structure. An orientation session was held for all employees on the Scanlon committee structure and suggestion system.

Description of the Program

Morse Borg-Warner's productivity sharing program has become a hybrid program. Originally based on the Rucker Plan and its principles, it now includes the Scanlon Plan suggestion system and employee involvement through committees. The objectives of the program are greater participation of employees in the improvement of productivity and quality of work life and the sharing of increased profits.

Bonus

The employee bonus calculation is a traditional Rucker formula with a Rucker Production Standard of 45.31%, based on the financial figures of 1973–75 and 1977. The year 1976 was omitted from the base period due to the abnormalities of business caused by the strike. Rucker calculations often vary in terms of the method of determining the sales value of output. At Morse Borg-Warner it is determined by calculating net sales plus or minus product inventory change.

The bonus is distributed in a monthly check separate from the regular payroll check. Each month one-third of the employees' bonus pool is placed in reserve to help cover periods of low profits. Any balance left in reserve at the end of the year is distributed to all participants in separate bonus checks.

Committee Structure and Suggestions

The Scanlon influence is evidenced in the structure of employee involvement. The plant has sixteen departmental production committees, typically consisting of four people (one supervisor, two elected employee representatives, and an area union steward). The productivity representatives promote the suggestion system and encourage fellow employees to submit suggestions. Production committees meet at least once monthly on company time to review pending suggestions and new ones that have been submitted to the representatives. Suggestions are evaluated based upon their value and the cost of implementation.

Individuals or teams are appointed to investigate each suggestion to determine its values and costs. Departmental production committees have four options. They may (1) implement the suggestion if its implementation cost is three hundred dollars or below, (2) reject the suggestion with an explanation to the originator, (3) refer the suggestion to the screening committee, or (4) refer the suggestion to the recommendation committee. A suggestion is referred to the screening committee if it is an appealed suggestion, if implementation cost is over three hundred dollars, or if its implementation would affect other departments. If a production committee feels the suggestion needs further investigation before referral to the screening committee, the suggestion is passed to the recommendation committee.

There is one screening committee composed of twenty-six people for the plant. There is a representative from each of the production committees, the chief union steward, and thirteen management individuals (including the division manager). The division manager chairs this committee.

The committee meets bimonthly: once at the end of each month to process suggestions and once at the beginning of each month to learn the results of the bonus calculation. The screening committee evaluates the merits and costs of all suggestions referred to it by the production committees, either accepting or rejecting them.

The screening committee members are the first employees each month to learn if there is a bonus and its size. They discuss the plant's financial performance for the previous month, as well as what factors were primarily responsible for the month's bonus outcome.

Morse recently established the eleven-member recommendation committee, which consists of every department manager and the productivity coordinator. The committee has a dual purpose of routing suggestions to appropriate individuals for investigation and following up investigations to ensure timely handling of suggestions. This committee is currently investigating and recommending action on a backlog of suggestions that had accumulated. The recommendation committee does not make implementation decisions, but merely makes recommendations to production or steering committees based on investigation.

In addition to these three committees, there is a productivity, training, and safety coordinator. The coordinator facilitates the functioning of the program, attending every production committee meeting in this capacity. This person is also involved in planning and conducting the training and safety programs in the plant.

The suggestion form developed by the organization is a mechanism for valuable documentation of each suggestion. The form includes the following information: name of the suggester, the suggester's support for implementation, when the suggestion was investigated, who investigated, conclusions of the investigation, when it was referred to the screening committee, screening committee comments, when it was implemented or rejected, etc. Through maintenance of these forms, the status of a suggestion is available at any time.

Problems

Problems have been identified in each area of the program. As a result, management has recognized and responded to the need for continual maintenance of the various facets of its productivity sharing program.

First, Morse has learned that the suggestion portion of the program does not function smoothly when suggestions are not handled in a timely manner. In the past, it was not uncommon for production committees to seek out individual investigators in order to learn the status of suggestions.

Often suggestions were not investigated because they had been assigned to an inappropriate person. Slow response tended to decrease employee initiative to submit more suggestions. In response to this problem, management proposed to the screening committee that a new entity be added: the recommendation committee. The committee has not existed long enough to prove itself to be an effective solution to this problem.

Next, Morse has found that maintaining employee involvement and awareness levels is important. When participants lose sight of the importance of their involvement they begin to cut corners, evidenced by not keeping employees informed of the status of their suggestions, untimely handling of suggestions, and a general ambivalence. There are a variety of activities to cope with this need. The orientation materials for productivity representatives and production committee chairpeople has just been revised and improved. In addition, approximately an hour of each new employee's orientation program is spent with the productivity coordinator, who explains the productivity sharing program in detail. The monthly newsletter is another vehicle that aids in increasing employees' awareness of the program and their impact on it. Bonus results and other program-related information is reported here. Bulletin boards throughout the plant keep employees informed of business statistics and conditions, departmental and plant productivity levels, and the general performance of the company and how its employees contribute to that performance. There are plans for a new bulletin board recognizing a suggestion / employee. The purpose of the bulletin board will be better to acquaint employees with one another and individual suggestions.

Finally, management points out that measuring and publicizing the productivity of departments or shifts carries the risk of creating unhealthy competition within the plant. To offset this side effect, Morse Borg-Warner places great emphasis on the performance of the entire plant through the means already mentioned and through monthly departmental meetings.

Results

Management at Morse cites five indicators of the program's success, although it carefully points out that the program is not the only impacting force in these areas. The areas monitored are: grievances and labor relations; turnover, absenteeism; the productivity index; and the Rucker bonus.

In the first area, the company typically averaged ten to twelve grievances per quarter prior to the implementation of the Rucker Plan. From April to December of 1979 grievances were down to an average of six per quarter. During the first half of 1980, the rate was even lower, five per quarter. In addition, the grievances which *are* filed are settled in their initial stages. When Morse realized the need for a reduced work week for the summer (1980), management discussed this need and all of the reasons with union representatives and employees. Although there was regret on the part of all involved that business conditions required a reduced work week, the proposition was positively received by employees.

The company has seen a significant decline in turnover. The rate is currently holding at 2.0–2.5% per month. Turnover in the general Denver area is approximately 4%, which was the level in the Morse Borg-Warner plant prior to initiation of the program. Earlier, between the years 1973 and 1975, the plant averaged turnover in excess of 10%. Absenteeism figures have likewise improved. Absenteeism is currently 3.3–3.5% per month, down from 4.0–4.5% per month prior to the program. These improvements indicate increased employee satisfaction, probably due in part to activities of the productivity sharing program.

Morse measures direct labor productivity monthly by a formula of efficiency times utilization. Productivity in the plant was up to 56% from 49% during the period of October 1978 through October 1979.

The final, and perhaps the most obvious, indicator of the program's success is the Rucker bonus level. From the program's inception through October 1979 there were very few bonuses. In fact, the bonus was usually negative. From November 1979 through May 1980 there have been positive bonus results in six out of the seven months and a zero bonus in the seventh month. During this period bonuses have ranged from 1% to 15% of employees' pay, with an average payout of 5.3%.

Future Plans

Morse Borg-Warner has specific plans for the future in differing stages of progress. These plans fall into three separate areas: economic awareness; production committee effectiveness; and possible incorporation of some quality circle concepts.

There are plans to increase more fully employees' economic awareness of the business system in which the company operates and their role in the company's success. The intention is to accomplish this through means already mentioned: bulletin boards, "department of the month," "suggestion of the month," training, etc.

Management hopes to improve the effectiveness of the production committees by responding to skill needs of supervisors and productivity representatives. Plans for training sessions in problem-solving and decision-making are being formulated. The desire is to help this group of personnel become "team builders" in a participative environment.

Finally, plant management is beginning to consider exploring the use of some quality circle concepts and techniques. They see these as natural complements to the existing involvement of their employees.

CASE 4:
PRODUCTIVITY IMPROVEMENT
AT TENNECO, INC.

In late 1979, Tenneco, Inc., decided to conduct experiments aimed at improving productivity and quality of work life. On several occasions we had worked with people at the American Productivity Center in Houston and we became aware of a situation that interested us. As a new initiative, the APC's Custom Services department was getting ready to launch a major project at the plant level of a client company in the processing industry. The APC was interested in conducting similar projects with other clients in other industries. We ultimately reached an agreement with the APC and with executives from our Tenneco Automotive Division that we would conduct a project in one or more of our Walker Manufacturing Company plants. Walker manufactures exhaust systems, lifting equipment, and other automotive components, and they have several similar plants in different geographical areas.

Aberdeen, Mississippi, was the site of the first of Tenneco's productivity improvement projects. We had no commitments beyond the first project, but soon after it was completed we made plans for a second project in Greenville, Texas. Both are Walker plants, manufacturing mufflers and exhaust pipes. Together, they offered somewhat contrasting conditions. Aberdeen is one of Walker's older plants. It is unionized, with a highly experienced, relatively stable work force. Plant efficiency, a measure of direct hours earned compared to standard hours, was approaching 100%. Direct to indirect ratios, cost of quality, variance to budget, and other measures placed Aberdeen at or near the top of comparative plant performance indices.

The Greenville, Texas, plant had been in operation less than five years. Overall plant performance was still relatively low. Plant efficiency by comparison was at about 90%. Other contrasting features included their non-union status and a relatively inexperienced work force at all levels.

The framework for these projects, developed by the APC, is called "Productivity Focus." Focus examines how the organization functions in seven key areas that are thought to significantly impact productivity and quality of work life. The seven areas are illustrated in figure B.1.

Contributed by Max E. Zent; reprinted, with permission, from *The Texas Business Executive,* Spring 1981.

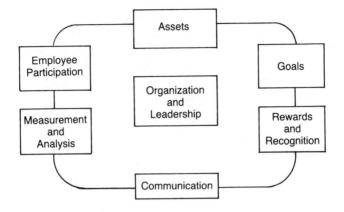

Assets
The effectiveness with which an organization utilizes its human, material, capital and technological assets is fundamental to the productivity equation.

Goals
Productivity goals are necessary to support and reflect the productivity/quality of work life emphasis of the organization and to establish expectations for change and improvement.

Rewards and Recognition
Processes that encourage and reward employees for working cooperatively toward productivity improvement reinforce the behavior the organization is seeking.

Communication
Through effective communication, an organization can clarify its goals and expectations for productivity improvement, provide performance feedback, recognize contributions, obtain ideas for improvements and identify barriers to productivity and quality of work life.

Measurement and Analysis
The measurement of productivity is essential to both understanding and improving productivity and is the basis for performance feedback relative to productivity goals.

Employee Participation
To the degree that employees are involved, contribute their ideas and efforts toward improvements and experience pride in the organization's accomplishments, both productivity and quality of work life are enhanced.

Organization and Leadership
At the hub of productivity improvement are leadership and organization causing things to happen.

FIGURE B.1.   Productivity Focus

Each project was carried out in six distinct steps. The sequencing of steps and the approximate number of days to complete each step is illustrated in figure B.2. Because the process and framework for each plant project was essentially the same, the description that follows is generally applicable to both plants.

The Initial Visit

The first step of each project was a meeting between the project team, the plant manager, and the plant manager's boss. We had previously familiarized ourselves about the key people in the plant – their specific roles and backgrounds, general plant history, and overall plant performance. But we were there to clarify expectations – theirs and ours – evaluate whether or not conditions seemed suitable to proceed, and complete some of the planning that required their involvement.

Relative to clarifying expectations, we discussed and described all phases of the ensuing project. One main objective was to establish a trust relationship with the plant manager and his staff, and we were particularly concerned that they view the project as theirs, not Walker's or Tenneco's, but theirs – they were in charge, they owned the project including all of the information that would flow out of the project. There was one exception, a Catch-22 situation.

On the one hand we did not want the information from the study, specifically our findings, to go to anyone other than the plant manager and his staff. We reasoned that if we could make that promise we would have better access to sensitive but important information and certainly a more comfortable situation for the plant manager. On the other hand, our own framework was built on premises such as, "If you expect change to take place in an organization it requires a clear measurement and analysis of current conditions, goals for preferred conditions, rewards and recognition for improvement, etc." Hence, we believed that there was relatively little real opportunity to improve productivity and quality of work life in the plant unless the plant manager discussed our findings with his boss and they agreed to goals and strategies for improvement. Accordingly, we built that condition into our expectations with the plant manager and his boss, programming it to occur within a month following the conclusion of the project.

During our initial plant visit we were prepared tactfully to abort the project if we noted any unusual apprehension or any other condition that might risk our success. We insisted that the plant manager have the same right. In both plants we seemed mutually excited about getting on with it.

The main planning activity involving the plant manager and his staff was to select the employees who would be interviewed. For several

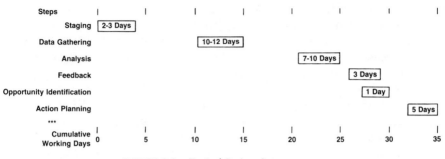

FIGURE B.2. Typical Project Steps

reasons — time required, volume of information generated, and the law of diminishing returns — we did not want to interview more than sixty to seventy people (out of the five hundred at Aberdeen and three hundred at Greenville). It was therefore essential that we had total agreement that those selected were a representative cross section of the entire organization. We sought a representative distribution by age, experience, sex, race, shift, etc.

Data Gathering

It took a week after our initial visit to finalize our plans for data gathering. This included scheduling interviews, fine-tuning interview strategies and logistical preparations. The plant needed time also to plan and prepare for us so that we would not be unnecessarily disruptive to normal production requirements.

In cooperation with the plant manager our project leader conducted several brief meetings with the work force before we started interviewing. They explained the whos, whys, and hows of the project and asked for cooperation and participation from the work force. One of our main concerns was to get the points across to the work force that we were interested in trying to improve both productivity and quality of work life; we represented an attitude of "work smarter," not "speed up" or "sweat shop," and we were neither promanagement nor prolabor. These were facts — all of them — but understandably we had to prove it to a few skeptics by our actions. Fortunately, in both projects, the work force seemed to fully trust us after a few interviews were completed. In fact, we got utmost cooperation. The sincere interest most workers demonstrated to us in wanting to help improve productivity in their plant reassured us we were doing the right thing in sponsoring these projects.

The average interview lasted about ninety minutes and many lasted two hours, some even more. By design, our interviews were open-ended and nonleading. For example, we asked people, "How do you know when you are doing a good job?" By following their response wherever it took us, we learned if and how their productivity was measured, whether or not they had productivity improvement goals, how their performance was rewarded, what got in their way of doing better, etc.

Only three of five of us on the project team did the interviewing. We could each interview four employees per day. At the end of each interviewing day, we had twelve scenarios to share with one another. Pieces of information started fitting together like watching a Polaroid picture gradually develop before our eyes. We took notes constantly during the interviews, except in about 5% of them, where it became obvious that our note taking was inhibiting the openness of the interviewee. We reassured everyone at both the beginning and the conclusion of the interview that confidentiality would be maintained, and we were careful never to violate that confidence.

By the time we began the Greenville project, we had developed a written survey that paralleled our employee interviews. So, in our second project, we administered the survey to all employees who had not been interviewed. As a consequence, every employee had some means of participating in the project and we had a cross check on some of our findings.

The two people on our team who were not involved in the general interviewing concentrated on operational analyses in the industrial engineering, production control, accounting, and manufacturing engineering functions. We all participated in these and other functional analyses after most of the interviews were completed. Collectively, we examined several major areas that included:
- work standards
- production scheduling
- inventory control
- quality control
- maintenance systems
- energy management
- the management information system

For the most part, our operational analyses were conducted jointly with key people from each respective area.

Data Analysis

In reality, analysis began prior to the initial visit at the plant and continued throughout the project, but the formal analysis took place back in our Houston offices over several days immediately following data gathering. Given the large volume of data we had collected, our task was one of both analysis and synthesis aimed at separating the significant from the trivial.

There were many positive factors among our findings at both plants, but our concentration turned to findings that needed improvement. Findings were sorted into the seven areas illustrated by the Productivity Focus model (see figure B.1). In each plant, we ended up with two to five findings each in goals, rewards and recognition, communication, employee participation, etc.

Feedback of Findings

Findings were disclosed first to the plant manager and second to his immediate staff. Feedback involving the staff was carefully structured over a period of three consecutive days to ensure clarity, in-depth discussion, individual viewpoints of agreement, expansions of data, and adequate reflection time. The process aimed at establishing staff ownership of the findings and commitment to action.

The whole process of feedback was delicate and toughest on the plant manager. After all, he felt the total burden of responsibility for all findings, whereas an individual department head could escape any direct barrage on the majority of the findings.

Identification of Major Opportunities

To the casual observer, it would probably seem as if major opportunities to improve productivity and quality of work life were already identified — just correct each finding. Actually, many of the findings were related and needed to be integrated and consolidated for effective management response. This step was largely in the hands of plant management. In each plant what had begun as about thirty findings resulted in about a dozen opportunity areas.

Action Planning

The group had to decide on which opportunities to tackle first. Criteria for selection were established and several opportunity areas were then selected for action planning. Teams were formed to begin the task. In many cases, employees with special knowledge from various levels of the organization were asked to help form the team.

Each team reviewed the findings related to their opportunity area, then worked their way through the project planning process illustrated in figure B.3. Later, each team's plan was reviewed by the plant manager and his staff for approval to implement.

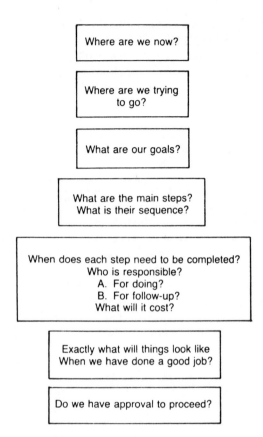

FIGURE B.3.   Project Planning Process

Evaluation

Having described the framework and process of these two plant projects, let me anticipate and respond to some obvious questions:

— *What are the results of these projects? Have they had a payoff?*

We think that these projects have been profitable for us and we will be doing more of them. So far, we have seen the biggest improvement at Aberdeen. Aberdeen's plant efficiency has improved about 5% since the project concluded in the spring of 1980. Walker equates that to about $75,000 for 1980. Cost of quality, a composite of scrap, rework, and quality control administrative costs, improved by about $100,000 for the year. In addition, Aberdeen ended the year with a $320,000 favorable variance to their controllable burden budget, representing a significant change over the previous year. Greenville has shown some improvement in all of these areas also, but at this point it is less dramatic. Because of various changes in production volumes and product mix that have occurred at both plants we cannot clearly attribute the plant improvements to these projects other than noting that the changes began occurring with the timing of the projects. We will continue a measurement effort for several months.

— What are some examples of findings?

Because of the confidentiality commitment previously alluded to, we do not disclose actual findings from these two studies. For an idea of what a finding might look like, however, here are some surrogates:

- Excessive employee turnover exists and the problem is not being addressed.
- Numerous hourly employees believe that malingering and violation of work rules are too often tolerated.
- The merit pay system, adequately designed, is inconsistent in practice.
- The process required to obtain needed repair parts, tools, and materials is viewed as unnecessarily cumbersome and creates excessive downtime.

— Can an organization conduct a study of this type without an outside agent?

We explored this question with management at both plants. They were unanimous in their opinion that the project could not be carried out by plant personnel nor by Walker headquarters because employees would not be as candid with "insiders." The more remote, the better.

They thought it might be done effectively by a trained staff from their Tenneco Automotive Division headquarters but preferred still more "distance," either Tenneco Inc. or an outside consulting group. So, the answer to this question is "probably not," but it depends on how "outside" inside can be, and what kind of trust there is with the specific people involved.

— What are the conclusions or implications noteworthy for other firms — large or small?

Hopefully, there are several. First let me state that our findings and the corresponding action requirements were significantly different at each plant. That reinforced our hypothesis that if you seek a total approach to improving productivity, start with a diagnostic study. It is unreasonable and foolhardy to take prescriptive action without first examining current conditions.

A diagnostic study, however, may not need to be as comprehensive as ours. If you sense a deficiency in one specific focus area it may be sufficient to evaluate just that area, but do not totally ignore the interdependent influence of the other areas.

Second, an outside look at your organization may be helpful. It can add objectivity and perhaps extract information not readily available to insiders. As Tommy Gates, the Aberdeen plant manager, expressed, "Management of an organization too often receives information that is filtered and colored by what someone thinks they would like to hear."

Third, we believe that the average worker cares about plant performance and will contribute useful ideas toward improving productivity.

Finally, the productivity focus model is a good conceptual tool for managing productivity. Certain principles seem intuitive: People do that which they are measured against and for which they are rewarded; goals should be based on measurements and analyses; and employees should be involved in the life of the organization through communication and feedback and participation in decisions affecting their work. Perhaps most important is the principle that someone must provide the organizational clout and leadership to make things happen — concepts are in the model; results come only from execution.

Appendix C

MULTI-INPUT PRODUCTIVITY INDEXES FOR THE U.S. BUSINESS ECONOMY, BY SECTOR AND INDUSTRY GROUP

For several decades the Agriculture Department has prepared and published annual estimates of total productivity in the farm sector of the U.S. economy.[1] Until April 1983, the Labor Department confined its productivity estimates for the U.S. business economy by sector[2] as well as by industry[3] to the partial, output-per-labor-hour type of measure. The need for broader total, or "multiple-input," productivity measures on a regular basis had been emphasized by recommendations contained in reports prepared by the Joint Economic Committee, the General Accounting Office, and a panel of the National Academy of Sciences,[4] that the Labor Department expand its measures.

Since 1980 the APC has sponsored the preparation and publication of multi-input productivity indexes for the U.S. business economy, by sector, on an annual and quarterly basis, parallel to the sector labor productivity estimates published by the Labor Department. In addition, the APC publishes annual estimates for thirty-one industry groups, which are consistent with the broader sector measures. These series were the basis for the discussion and analysis contained in chapter 9. Since 1983, the Labor Department has been experimenting with broader measures for industries as well as sectors.

The concepts and methodology underlying the estimates are basically those developed by John W. Kendrick in his volumes for the National Bureau of Economic Research, as updated in 1980 in collaboration with Elliot S. Grossman in *Productivity in the United States: Trends and Cycles.*[5] Dr. Grossman is maintaining the series quarterly for the APC, incorporating the several revisions required to make them consistent with the Labor Department series. He has prepared a detailed description of methodology and sources of data for the subscribers to the APC series,[6] which provided the basis for the following summary.[7] We also provide

TABLE C.1
Indexes of Real Output, Inputs, and Productivity Ratios: Business Economy (1977 = 100.0)

Year	Output and Inputs				Productivity Ratios			
	Real Output	Labor Input	Capital Input	Total Factor Input	Total Factor Productivity	Output per Unit Labor	Output per Unit Capital	Capital-Labor Ratio
1948	37.2	80.7	41.4	68.0	54.6	46.0	89.8	51.3
1949	36.5	78.1	42.1	66.4	54.9	46.7	86.6	54.0
1950	39.8	78.9	43.5	67.5	59.0	50.4	91.5	55.1
1951	42.1	81.3	45.0	69.5	60.6	51.8	93.6	55.3
1952	43.5	81.4	46.1	69.9	62.2	53.5	94.4	56.6
1953	45.4	82.2	47.1	70.8	64.1	55.2	96.3	57.3
1954	44.6	79.5	48.1	69.3	64.3	56.1	92.6	60.6
1955	48.1	82.5	49.8	71.9	66.9	58.3	96.5	60.4
1956	49.3	83.7	51.3	73.2	67.4	58.9	96.1	61.3
1957	49.8	82.5	52.8	72.8	68.4	60.4	94.4	64.0
1958	49.0	78.8	53.8	70.6	69.5	62.3	91.2	68.3
1959	52.6	81.9	55.3	73.2	71.9	64.3	95.1	67.6
1960	53.5	82.0	56.7	73.8	72.5	65.2	94.2	69.2
1961	54.4	80.8	58.1	73.4	74.1	67.3	93.6	71.9
1962	57.4	82.1	59.9	74.8	76.7	69.9	95.8	73.0
1963	59.9	82.6	61.7	75.8	79.1	72.5	97.1	74.7
1964	63.5	83.9	63.8	77.4	82.0	75.6	99.4	76.0
1965	67.8	86.6	66.4	80.0	84.8	78.3	102.2	76.6
1966	71.5	88.6	69.3	82.3	86.9	80.7	103.2	78.2
1967	73.1	88.6	71.9	83.1	88.0	82.5	101.7	81.2
1968	76.8	90.1	74.7	85.0	90.3	85.3	102.9	82.9
1969	79.0	92.5	77.7	87.6	90.2	85.5	101.7	84.0
1970	78.4	91.0	80.2	87.4	89.6	86.2	97.8	88.1
1971	80.7	90.5	82.7	87.9	91.8	89.2	97.6	91.4
1972	86.1	93.2	85.5	90.7	94.9	92.4	100.7	91.8
1973	91.8	96.8	89.1	94.3	97.3	94.7	103.0	92.0
1974	89.9	97.3	92.2	95.6	94.1	92.5	97.6	94.8
1975	88.2	93.3	94.2	93.6	94.2	94.5	93.6	101.0
1976	93.8	96.0	96.8	96.3	97.4	97.6	96.9	100.8
1977	100.0	100.0	100.0	100.0	100.0	100.0	100.0	100.0
1978	105.5	104.9	103.4	104.4	101.1	100.6	102.0	98.6
1979	107.8	108.2	107.3	107.9	99.9	99.6	100.5	99.2
1980	106.2	107.4	110.5	108.4	98.0	98.9	96.2	102.8
1981	108.9	108.2	114.0	110.1	98.9	100.7	95.5	105.4
1982	106.4	105.4	116.6	109.0	97.6	101.0	91.3	110.6

Source: American Productivity Center.

tables showing annual estimates of output, inputs, and productivity ratios for the U.S. business economy and major sectors (see tables C.1–C.7). Quarterly sector estimates, and annual estimates for the thirty-one industry groups discussed in chapter 9, are available from the APC.

The concept of total factor productivity was explained in chapter 2 and need not be repeated. It was renamed multi-input productivity by the APC in recognition of the fact that the ratios relate real gross product (value

TABLE C.2
Indexes of Real Output, Inputs, and Productivity Ratios: Goods-Producing Sector
(1977 = 100.0)

Year	Output and Inputs				Productivity Ratios			
	Real Output	Labor Input	Capital Input	Total Factor Input	Total Factor Productivity	Output per Unit Labor	Output per Unit Capital	Capital-Labor Ratio
1948	41.1	104.4	49.2	90.3	45.4	39.4	83.5	47.2
1949	39.3	98.5	49.8	86.2	45.6	39.9	78.9	50.5
1950	44.0	100.5	51.5	88.1	50.0	43.8	85.4	51.3
1951	48.1	104.1	54.0	91.4	52.6	46.2	89.1	51.9
1952	49.5	103.6	55.6	91.5	54.1	47.8	89.0	53.7
1953	52.4	104.2	56.8	92.3	56.8	50.3	92.3	54.6
1954	50.1	97.5	57.8	87.7	57.2	51.4	86.8	59.3
1955	54.7	101.9	59.9	91.5	59.8	53.7	91.3	58.8
1956	55.7	102.4	61.8	92.4	60.3	54.4	90.1	60.3
1957	55.7	99.1	63.4	90.3	61.7	56.2	87.9	63.9
1958	52.7	91.6	64.1	85.0	62.0	57.6	82.3	70.0
1959	57.3	96.0	65.6	88.7	64.6	59.7	87.4	68.3
1960	58.0	94.7	66.7	88.0	65.9	61.2	86.9	70.4
1961	58.1	91.8	67.6	86.1	67.5	63.3	86.0	73.6
1962	61.9	93.7	69.0	87.8	70.4	66.0	89.8	73.6
1963	66.0	93.8	70.2	88.2	74.8	70.4	94.0	74.8
1964	69.8	94.5	72.0	89.2	78.2	73.8	97.0	76.1
1965	75.1	98.1	74.1	92.4	81.3	76.5	101.4	75.5
1966	79.1	101.2	76.9	95.4	82.9	78.2	102.8	76.0
1967	79.1	99.9	79.6	95.1	83.1	79.2	99.4	79.6
1968	83.0	100.7	81.6	96.2	86.2	82.4	101.7	81.0
1969	85.0	102.3	83.7	98.0	86.8	83.1	101.6	81.8
1970	81.4	97.3	85.1	94.4	86.2	83.7	95.6	87.5
1971	84.0	94.7	86.2	92.7	90.5	88.6	97.4	91.0
1972	90.0	98.4	87.7	95.9	93.9	91.5	102.7	89.1
1973	97.6	102.8	90.2	99.9	97.7	94.9	108.2	87.7
1974	93.0	101.5	93.0	99.6	93.4	91.6	100.0	91.6
1975	87.3	92.7	94.9	93.2	93.6	94.1	92.0	102.3
1976	94.3	95.9	97.1	96.2	98.0	98.3	97.1	101.2
1977	100.0	100.0	100.0	100.0	100.0	100.0	100.0	100.0
1978	104.9	105.2	102.6	104.6	100.4	99.7	102.3	97.5
1979	107.6	107.9	107.4	107.7	99.9	99.7	100.1	99.6
1980	103.1	104.0	110.8	105.5	97.7	99.1	93.0	106.6
1981	105.7	103.4	114.9	106.3	99.5	102.3	92.0	111.1
1982	97.7	96.0	117.2	101.3	96.5	102.8	83.4	122.0

Source: See table C.1.

added) to the *tangible* factor inputs of labor and capital, the latter including land and other natural resources as well as manmade structures, equipment, and inventories. But intangible capital, such as that resulting from human investments in education and training, is not included, nor are financial assets. The term is also broad enough to cover ratios of gross output to all tangible inputs — energy and other intermediate goods and services as well as the basic productive factors. The APC is currently engaged

TABLE C.3
Indexes of Real Output, Inputs, and Productivity Ratios: Service-Producing Sector
(1977 = 100.0)

Year	Output and Inputs				Productivity Ratios			
	Real Output	Labor Input	Capital Input	Total Factor Input	Total Factor Produc- tivity	Output per Unit Labor	Output per Unit Capital	Capital- Labor Ratio
1948	34.3	63.6	37.4	53.9	63.8	54.0	92.0	58.7
1949	34.5	63.2	38.1	53.9	64.0	54.5	90.4	60.3
1950	36.8	63.4	39.4	54.4	67.7	58.1	93.5	61.2
1951	37.9	64.8	40.3	55.6	68.1	58.5	94.0	62.2
1952	39.2	65.3	41.1	56.2	69.8	60.1	95.4	63.0
1953	40.4	66.3	42.1	57.2	70.6	60.9	95.9	63.5
1954	40.6	66.4	43.1	57.6	70.5	61.2	94.2	64.9
1955	43.4	68.4	44.6	59.4	73.0	63.4	97.3	65.2
1956	44.8	70.2	45.9	61.0	73.5	63.9	97.7	65.4
1957	45.7	70.5	47.3	61.7	74.0	64.8	96.5	67.1
1958	46.4	69.5	48.5	61.4	75.6	66.8	95.8	69.7
1959	49.3	71.7	50.0	63.3	77.8	68.8	98.5	69.8
1960	50.3	72.9	51.6	64.7	77.8	69.0	97.5	70.8
1961	51.8	72.8	53.2	65.2	79.3	71.1	97.3	73.1
1962	54.2	73.7	55.2	66.5	81.5	73.6	98.2	74.9
1963	55.6	74.5	57.3	67.8	81.9	74.6	97.0	76.9
1964	59.0	76.3	59.6	69.8	84.5	77.4	99.0	78.2
1965	62.6	78.2	62.4	72.1	86.9	80.0	100.4	79.7
1966	66.2	79.5	65.3	74.0	89.4	83.3	101.3	82.2
1967	68.9	80.4	68.0	75.6	91.2	85.7	101.4	84.5
1968	72.5	82.4	71.1	78.0	92.9	88.0	101.9	86.3
1969	74.8	85.3	74.6	81.1	92.2	87.7	100.3	87.4
1970	76.3	86.4	77.6	83.0	91.9	88.2	98.2	89.8
1971	78.5	87.4	80.9	84.9	92.5	89.8	97.0	92.5
1972	83.3	89.4	84.4	87.5	95.2	93.2	98.7	94.4
1973	87.7	92.5	88.6	91.0	96.3	94.7	99.0	95.7
1974	87.8	94.2	91.7	93.2	94.2	93.2	95.7	97.4
1975	88.8	93.7	93.8	93.7	94.7	94.8	94.6	100.2
1976	93.4	96.1	96.6	96.3	97.0	97.2	96.7	100.5
1977	100.0	100.0	100.0	100.0	100.0	100.0	100.0	100.0
1978	105.8	104.6	103.8	104.3	101.5	101.2	102.0	99.2
1979	108.0	108.5	107.3	108.0	100.0	99.6	100.7	98.9
1980	108.5	109.9	110.3	110.1	98.5	98.7	98.3	100.4
1981	111.1	111.6	113.5	112.4	98.8	99.5	97.8	101.7
1982	112.6	112.1	116.2	113.8	99.0	100.4	96.9	103.7

Source: See table C.1.

in the development of these broader multiple- and associated partial-productivity ratios.

The estimates are confined to the U.S. business economy, which comprises 85% of the GNP, since output in the nonbusiness sectors of general government, households, and private nonprofit institutions, and the rest-of-the-world sector cannot yet be measured independently of the input estimates. Further, the rental value of owner-occupied nonfarm housing

TABLE C.4
Indexes of Real Output, Inputs, and Productivity Ratios: Nonfinancial Corporate Business
(1977 = 100.0)

Year	Output and Inputs				Productivity Ratios			
	Real Output	Labor Input	Capital Input	Total Factor Input	Total Factor Productivity	Output per Unit Labor	Output per Unit Capital	Capital-Labor Ratio
1948	28.9	58.9	32.6	51.4	56.2	49.0	88.5	55.4
1949	27.6	55.4	33.3	49.1	56.3	49.9	83.1	60.0
1950	31.1	58.1	34.6	51.4	60.5	53.5	89.9	59.5
1951	34.0	61.8	36.3	54.5	62.3	55.0	93.6	58.7
1952	34.6	62.6	37.5	55.4	62.4	55.2	92.2	59.9
1953	36.7	64.4	38.7	57.1	64.3	57.0	94.8	60.1
1954	35.6	60.8	39.6	54.8	64.9	58.5	89.9	65.1
1955	39.6	63.8	41.2	57.4	69.1	62.2	96.2	64.6
1956	40.7	65.2	42.9	58.9	69.0	62.4	94.8	65.8
1957	41.2	64.5	44.2	58.8	70.1	63.9	93.2	68.6
1958	39.3	61.6	44.9	57.0	68.9	63.7	87.4	72.9
1959	43.7	65.4	46.1	60.0	72.7	66.7	94.6	70.5
1960	45.0	66.3	47.4	61.0	73.8	68.0	94.9	71.6
1961	46.1	65.6	48.6	60.9	75.8	70.3	95.0	74.0
1962	50.2	68.2	51.3	63.5	79.1	73.6	97.9	75.2
1963	53.6	69.8	53.7	65.4	81.9	76.7	99.7	77.0
1964	57.2	72.1	56.7	67.8	84.4	79.4	101.0	78.7
1965	62.2	75.9	60.6	71.7	86.8	81.9	102.7	79.7
1966	66.7	80.2	66.3	76.4	87.3	83.2	100.5	82.8
1967	68.2	81.2	70.7	78.4	87.1	84.1	96.5	87.1
1968	72.7	83.7	74.5	81.3	89.5	86.9	97.6	89.0
1969	75.9	87.2	78.4	84.9	89.4	87.1	96.8	90.0
1970	75.3	86.2	81.1	84.9	88.7	87.4	92.9	94.0
1971	78.8	86.1	83.4	85.4	92.2	91.5	94.5	96.8
1972	85.2	90.5	86.8	89.6	95.1	94.1	98.2	95.8
1973	92.0	95.4	90.3	94.1	97.8	96.4	101.8	94.6
1974	89.0	95.9	92.5	95.0	93.6	92.8	96.2	96.5
1975	87.2	91.4	92.7	91.7	95.1	95.5	94.1	101.5
1976	93.7	95.3	95.8	95.5	98.1	98.2	97.8	100.4
1977	100.0	100.0	100.0	100.0	100.0	100.0	100.0	100.0
1978	106.3	105.4	104.0	105.0	101.3	100.9	102.3	98.7
1979	110.1	109.3	105.4	108.3	101.7	100.7	104.4	96.4
1980	108.1	107.8	106.3	107.4	100.7	100.3	101.7	98.6
1981	110.7	108.5	110.1	108.9	101.6	102.0	100.5	101.5
1982	107.6	104.5	110.8	106.2	101.4	103.0	97.1	106.1

Source: See table C.1.

and of nonprofit real estate is removed from total gross business product (as in the Labor Department series) and from gross product originating in real estate, since the output and input estimates show the same movements. Even with this adjustment, the productivity estimates in the services sector are probably subject to some downward bias since there are still some types of outputs for which input estimates are used as proxies.

The output, or real gross product (value added) estimates for the

TABLE C.5
Indexes of Real Output, Inputs, and Productivity Ratios: Farming (1977 = 100.0)

Year	Output and Inputs				Productivity Ratios			
	Real Output	Labor Input	Capital Input	Total Factor Input	Total Factor Productivity	Output per Unit Labor	Output per Unit Capital	Capital-Labor Ratio
1948	75.4	309.2	72.0	205.0	36.8	24.4	104.6	23.3
1949	74.1	306.5	72.5	203.7	36.4	24.2	102.2	23.6
1950	78.2	283.6	74.5	191.7	40.8	27.6	104.9	26.3
1951	74.3	268.7	75.8	183.9	40.4	27.6	98.1	28.2
1952	76.2	255.5	77.1	177.1	43.0	29.8	98.8	30.2
1953	80.1	236.5	77.6	166.6	48.1	33.9	103.3	32.8
1954	82.0	229.7	78.3	163.1	50.3	35.7	104.8	34.1
1955	84.5	233.6	80.6	166.2	50.8	36.2	104.9	34.5
1956	83.3	222.4	81.1	160.2	52.0	37.5	102.8	36.4
1957	81.1	204.6	82.2	150.6	53.8	39.6	98.7	40.2
1958	84.7	189.7	82.8	142.6	59.4	44.6	102.2	43.7
1959	80.1	189.9	84.5	143.4	55.9	42.2	94.9	44.5
1960	84.7	183.2	85.4	139.9	60.5	46.2	99.2	46.6
1961	84.2	173.4	85.4	134.2	62.8	48.6	98.6	49.3
1962	83.8	168.1	86.0	131.3	63.8	49.9	97.4	51.2
1963	86.5	161.0	86.7	127.5	67.9	53.7	99.7	53.9
1964	84.4	152.3	87.6	122.7	68.8	55.5	96.4	57.5
1965	87.5	148.3	88.3	120.7	72.5	59.0	99.1	59.5
1966	82.6	134.4	88.7	112.8	73.3	61.5	93.1	66.0
1967	86.8	129.6	89.5	110.3	78.7	67.0	97.1	69.0
1968	85.1	126.8	90.1	108.9	78.2	67.2	94.5	71.1
1969	87.0	120.6	90.6	105.5	82.4	72.1	96.0	75.1
1970	91.7	113.7	91.5	102.5	89.4	80.6	100.2	80.4
1971	97.0	110.3	92.5	101.4	95.7	87.9	104.8	83.9
1972	94.8	111.4	92.9	102.1	92.8	85.1	102.0	83.4
1973	94.2	109.4	94.8	102.0	92.3	86.1	99.3	86.7
1974	94.9	109.3	95.8	102.5	92.6	86.8	99.0	87.7
1975	100.9	105.6	98.2	101.9	99.0	95.5	102.7	93.0
1976	96.3	100.9	98.9	99.9	96.4	95.4	97.4	98.0
1977	100.0	100.0	100.0	100.0	100.0	100.0	100.0	100.0
1978	98.6	101.8	98.8	100.0	98.6	96.9	99.8	97.1
1979	103.9	99.7	103.7	101.4	102.4	104.2	100.2	104.0
1980	104.5	97.2	104.1	100.4	104.1	107.5	100.3	107.2
1981	118.3	96.8	105.4	100.8	117.3	122.2	112.2	108.9
1982	123.4	93.9	105.6	101.0	122.2	131.4	116.8	112.4

Source: See table C.1.

business economy, as adjusted, and its major sectors and industries are
those prepared by the Bureau of Economic Analysis (BEA) in the Commerce Department, published annually for industries and quarterly for
sectors. These are used in the BLS sector productivity estimates. The APC
also ties into the BLS estimates of labor-hours in each sector. The
industry hours are estimated by the APC as the product of BLS estimates
of employment and average hours worked per week, plus unpublished

TABLE C.6
Indexes of Real Output, Inputs, and Productivity Ratios: Manufacturing Industry
(1977 = 100.0)

Year	Output and Inputs				Productivity Ratios			
	Real Output	Labor Input	Capital Input	Total Factor Input	Total Factor Produc- tivity	Output per Unit Labor	Output per Unit Capital	Capital- Labor Ratio
1948	35.8	79.4	39.2	68.5	52.2	45.1	91.4	49.3
1949	33.9	72.4	39.8	63.7	53.3	46.9	85.2	55.0
1950	38.6	78.2	41.3	68.3	56.6	49.4	93.5	52.9
1951	43.0	84.2	44.6	73.6	58.5	51.1	96.5	53.0
1952	44.5	85.4	46.4	75.0	59.3	52.0	95.7	54.4
1953	47.5	89.8	48.1	78.6	60.4	52.9	98.8	53.5
1954	44.1	82.1	48.9	73.3	60.2	53.7	90.3	59.5
1955	48.9	86.6	50.8	77.1	63.3	56.4	96.1	58.7
1956	49.2	87.9	53.3	78.8	62.5	56.0	92.4	60.6
1957	49.5	86.5	54.8	78.2	63.2	57.1	90.3	63.3
1958	45.2	79.4	55.1	73.3	61.7	56.9	82.0	69.4
1959	50.5	84.7	56.2	77.3	65.3	59.6	89.8	66.4
1960	50.7	84.4	57.1	77.4	65.5	60.0	88.7	67.7
1961	50.7	82.3	58.1	76.1	66.7	61.6	87.3	70.6
1962	55.1	85.6	59.5	78.9	69.7	64.3	92.5	69.5
1963	59.6	86.5	60.8	79.9	74.6	68.9	98.0	70.3
1964	63.9	88.4	62.7	81.8	78.1	72.3	101.9	70.9
1965	69.8	93.6	65.5	86.4	80.7	74.5	106.5	70.0
1966	75.1	99.8	69.8	92.1	81.6	75.3	107.6	70.0
1967	75.0	99.6	73.7	93.0	80.6	75.3	101.7	74.1
1968	79.1	101.4	76.6	95.1	83.1	78.0	103.3	75.5
1969	81.7	103.1	79.6	97.1	84.1	79.3	102.7	77.2
1970	77.0	97.3	81.4	93.3	82.5	79.1	94.6	83.7
1971	78.7	93.7	82.5	90.9	86.6	83.9	95.4	88.0
1972	86.2	97.8	84.6	94.5	91.3	88.2	102.0	86.5
1973	95.9	103.2	87.7	99.3	96.6	93.0	109.4	85.0
1974	91.9	101.2	92.1	98.9	92.9	90.8	99.8	90.9
1975	85.4	91.4	93.6	92.0	92.8	93.4	91.3	102.3
1976	93.6	96.0	96.5	96.1	97.4	97.5	96.9	100.6
1977	100.0	100.0	100.0	100.0	100.0	100.0	100.0	100.0
1978	105.3	104.4	104.2	104.4	100.9	100.9	101.1	99.8
1979	108.2	106.5	109.4	107.3	100.9	101.5	98.9	102.7
1980	103.6	101.8	114.5	105.0	98.6	101.7	90.4	112.5
1981	105.9	101.3	120.1	106.5	99.5	104.5	88.2	118.6
1982	96.5	93.3	123.1	101.5	95.1	103.5	78.4	132.0

Source: See table C.1.

estimates of hours worked by proprietors and unpaid family workers. These are adjusted to the sector totals. It should be noted that the employee hours are those paid for, which have risen faster than hours worked, whereas the hours of proprietors and unpaid family workers (about 10% of the total) are those actually worked.

The estimates of fixed capital for the farm and manufacturing sectors are those published by the BEA, based on the perpetual inventory method.

TABLE C.7
Indexes of Real Output, Inputs, and Productivity Ratios: Nonfarm,
Nonmanufacturing Industry (1977 = 100.0)

Year	Output and Inputs				Productivity Ratios			
	Real Output	Labor Input	Capital Input	Total Factor Input	Total Factor Productivity	Output per Unit Labor	Output per Unit Capital	Capital-Labor Ratio
1948	36.1	64.7	37.2	55.3	65.3	55.9	97.0	57.6
1949	36.0	64.0	38.0	55.1	65.4	56.3	94.8	59.4
1950	38.7	64.4	39.3	55.8	69.4	60.0	98.4	61.0
1951	40.2	66.3	40.3	57.4	70.1	60.7	99.8	60.8
1952	41.6	66.9	41.2	58.0	71.7	62.2	101.0	61.6
1953	42.8	67.6	42.2	58.8	72.8	63.4	101.5	62.4
1954	43.1	67.4	43.3	59.0	73.1	64.0	99.6	64.2
1955	46.1	69.6	44.8	61.0	75.6	66.2	102.9	64.4
1956	47.9	71.8	46.2	62.9	76.1	66.7	103.6	64.4
1957	48.6	71.8	47.7	63.4	76.7	67.7	101.9	66.5
1958	49.3	70.4	48.9	62.8	78.6	70.1	100.8	69.5
1959	52.4	72.8	50.6	64.9	80.8	72.1	103.7	69.5
1960	53.5	73.6	52.2	66.0	81.0	72.6	102.4	71.0
1961	54.9	73.4	53.9	66.5	82.5	74.8	101.8	73.5
1962	57.4	74.3	56.0	67.8	84.7	77.3	102.5	75.3
1963	58.9	75.1	58.0	69.1	85.2	78.4	101.4	77.2
1964	62.4	77.0	60.5	71.1	87.7	81.0	103.2	78.5
1965	66.0	78.9	63.2	73.3	90.0	83.6	104.4	80.0
1966	69.3	80.3	66.1	75.2	92.1	86.4	104.8	82.4
1967	71.6	80.7	68.7	76.4	93.7	88.8	104.2	85.2
1968	75.4	82.3	71.8	78.6	96.0	91.6	105.0	87.2
1969	77.4	85.7	75.2	81.9	94.5	90.4	103.0	87.8
1970	78.5	86.5	78.1	83.5	94.0	90.8	100.5	90.3
1971	81.1	87.6	81.2	85.3	95.0	92.6	99.8	92.8
1972	85.7	89.8	84.6	88.0	97.4	95.4	101.2	94.2
1973	89.7	93.1	88.6	91.5	98.0	96.3	101.2	95.2
1974	88.8	94.6	91.6	93.5	95.0	93.9	96.9	96.9
1975	89.0	93.2	93.7	93.4	95.3	95.5	94.9	100.6
1976	93.8	95.7	96.5	96.0	97.7	98.0	97.2	100.8
1977	100.1	100.0	100.0	100.0	100.1	100.1	100.1	100.0
1978	105.9	105.3	103.8	104.8	101.1	100.6	102.0	98.6
1979	107.9	109.6	107.4	108.8	99.1	98.4	100.5	97.9
1980	107.7	110.7	110.4	110.6	97.3	97.3	97.5	99.8
1981	110.0	112.1	113.8	112.7	97.6	98.1	96.6	101.5
1982	110.5	111.6	116.5	113.4	97.4	99.0	94.8	104.4

Source: See table C.1.

By this method, to real stocks at the end of the prior period is added real gross investment for a given period less estimated retirements (based on a retirement rate applied to the stock estimate) in order to arrive at real gross stock at the end of the current period. The estimates for the twenty two-digit manufacturing industries were those prepared by Daniel Creamer for the Conference Board for selected years, adjusted to the BEA totals, and interpolated and extrapolated by means of the perpetual inventory method using investment estimates from the Annual Survey of Manufactures and the BEA Plant and Equipment Survey. The investment numbers were deflated by the implicit GNP deflators for new nonresidential structures and producers' durable equipment. The real inventory stock estimates, by sector, are from the BEA, with industry allocations as required based on Internal Revenue Service data on the book value of business inventories, by industry. The farmland estimates are from the Agriculture Department. For land used in the other industries (primarily site-land) the 1972 ratios of the value of land to that of fixed capital from IRS reports were applied to the real fixed capital estimates for all years.[8]

The real capital and labor input index numbers were combined by weighting each by its base-year ratio to gross national income in the sector or industry as estimated by the BEA. The labor compensation estimates were adjusted to include the imputed value of the time spent by proprietors and unpaid family workers, assuming the same average compensation per hour as that earned by employees. The base years used were 1948, 1958, 1969, and 1978, and the resulting real dollar estimates for the periods 1948–59, 1959–69, 1969–78, and 1978 to the present were linked together by their ratios in the overlapping years. The output, input, and productivity estimates were then converted to index numbers with the year 1977 as the comparison base.

Appendix D

PRODUCTIVITY AND QUALITY OF WORKING LIFE CENTERS IN THE UNITED STATES AND ABROAD

Centers in the United States

American Center for Quality of Work Life
3301 New Mexico Ave., N.W., Suite 202
Washington, DC 20016
Ted Mills, Director
202/338-2933

Assessment, education, and training in QWL programs for unionized organizations.

American Productivity Center
123 N. Post Oak La.
Houston, TX 77024
Dr. C. Jackson Grayson, Chairman   713/681-4020

Public seminars, video-based training programs, information services, and broad range of consulting services.

Center for Government and Public Affairs
Auburn University
Montgomery, AL 36117

Dr. Raymond B. Wells, Director
205/279-9110

Technical assistance and consultation to state and local governments in Alabama.

Center for Manufacturing Productivity and Technology Transfer
Jonsson Engineering Center
Rensselaer Polytechnic Institute
Troy, NY 12181
Dr. Leo E. Hanifin, Director
518/270-6000

Solutions to specific manufacturing problems through applied engineering and the transfer of new technology.

Center for Productivity and Quality of Working Life
Utah State University, UMC 35
Logan, UT 84322
Dr. Gary B. Hansen, Director
801/752-4100

Research, education and training,

and consultation on human resource approaches.

Center for Productivity Studies
Kogod College of
Business Administration
The American University
Washington, DC 20016
David S. Bushnell, Director
202/686-2149

Research and consultation on labor-management and public-private sector relationships and the transfer of new technology.

**Center for Quality of
Working Life**
Pennsylvania State University
Capitol Campus
Middletown, PA 17057
Dr. Rupert F. Chisholm, Director
717/787-7746

Education, information, and assistance on QWL programs for Pennsylvania organizations.

**Center for Quality of
Working Life**
Institute of Industrial Relations,
UCLA
405 Hilgard Avenue
Los Angeles, CA 90024
Prof. Louis E. Davis, Chairman
213/825-1095

Information, training, and assistance in organization and job design approaches.

**Computer Integrated Design
Manufacturing and Automation
Center**
Grissom Hall
Purdue University
West Lafayette, IN 49707
Dean John C. Hancock, Director
317/494-5346

Research into advanced computer-aided design and manufacturing systems.

**Department of Commerce
Productivity Center**
U.S. Department of Commerce,
Room 7413
Washington, DC 20230
States L. Clawson, Manager
202/377-3653

Georgia Productivity Center
Georgia Tech Engineering
Experiment Station
Atlanta, GA 30332
Rudolph L. Yobs, Director
404/894-3404

Transfer of technology and safety, environmental, and human resource counseling to Georgia businesses.

**Harvard Project on Technology,
Work, and Character**
1710 Connecticut Avenue, N.W.
Washington, DC 20009
Dr. Michael Maccoby, Director
202/462-3003

Research into the relationship between work and human development.

Hospital Productivity Center
Texas Hospital Association
P.O. Box 15587
Austin, TX 78761
Dr. Karl L. Shaner
512/453-7204

Dissemination of techniques to improve hospital productivity.

Institute for Productivity
592 DeHostos Ave., Baldrich
Hato Ray, PR 00918

Mrs. Milagros Guzman, President
809/764-5145

Research, training, and consulting in human resource approaches to improvement.

Laboratory for Manufacturing and Productivity
Massachusetts Institute of Technology, Room 35-136
Cambridge, MA 02139
617/253-2225

Research into innovative manufacturing processes and systems and development of productivity analysis approaches.

Management and Behavioral Science Center
Wharton School
University of Pennsylvania
3733 Spruce St.
Philadelphia, PA 19174
Charles E. Dwyer, Director
215/243-5736

Research and consultation in organizational behavior, job design, and labor-management cooperation.

Manufacturing Productivity Center
IIT Center
10 West 35th Street
Chicago, IL 60616
Dr. Keith McKee, Director
312/567-4800

Application of advanced technologies to manufacturing.

Maryland Center for Productivity and Quality of Working Life
University of Maryland
College Park, MD 20742
Dr. Thomas C. Tuttle, Director
301/454-6688

Training and education, information services, and assistance in program development for Maryland organizations.

National Center for Public Productivity
John Jay College of Criminal Justice
445 W. 59th Street
New York, NY 10019
Dr. Marc Holzer, Director
212/489-5030

Information clearinghouse, education and training, and technical assistance for the public sector.

Northeast Labor-Management Center
30 Church Street
Boston, MA 02178
Dr. Michael J. Brower, Director
617/489-4002

Consultation and training in labor-management and employee involvement programs.

Oklahoma Productivity Center
Engineering North
Oklahoma State University
Stillwater, OK 74078
Dr. Earl J. Ferguson, Director
405/624-6055

Training and consultation in both technical and human resource approaches for organizations in Oklahoma and adjoining areas.

Oregon Productivity Center
100 Merryfield Hall
Oregon State University
Corvallis, OR 97331
James L. Riggs, Director
503/754-3249

Consulting and technical

assistance to small- and medium-sized firms in Oregon.

Pennsylvania Technical Assistance Program
J. Orvis Keller Building
University Park, PA 16802
Dr. H. LeRoy Marlow, Director
814/865-0427
Assistance to Pennsylvania organizations in solving specific technical problems.

Productivity Center
Chamber of Commerce of the United States
1615 H Street, N.W.
Washington, DC 20062
202/659-3163
Initiatives to influence public policy and organization of conferences.

The Productivity Center
University of Miami
P.O. Box 248294
Coral Gables, FL 33124
Dr. David J. Sumanth, Director
305/284-2344
Seminars and publications.

Productivity Council of the Southwest
5151 State University Drive, STF 124
Los Angeles, CA 90032
John R. Frost, Director
213/224-2975
Information, education, and consultation to organizations in southwestern region.

Productivity Evaluation Center
302 Whitmore Hall
Virginia Tech
Blacksburg, VA 24061

Dr. P. M. Ghare, Director
703/961-6656
Education and program development in industrial engineering and participative approaches.

Productivity Institute
College of Business Administration
Arizona State University
Tempe, AZ 85281
Dr. Eileen Burton, Director
602/965-7626
Research, information, training, and problem identification services.

Productivity Research and Extension Program
North Carolina State University
P.O. Box 5511
Raleigh, NC 27607
Dr. William A. Smith, Director
919/733-2370
Information and operations improvement projects with emphasis on manufacturing.

Puerto Rico Economic Development Administration
G.P.O. Box 2350
San Juan, PR 00936

Quality of Working Life Program
Ohio State University
1375 Perry Street
Columbus, OH 43201
Dr. Don Ronchi, Director
614/422-3390
Research and consultation in labor-management cooperation.

State Government Productivity Research Center
Council of State Governments

P.O. Box 11910
Lexington, KY 40578
James E. Jarrett, Director
606/252-2291
Information on state government
projects and productivity
approaches nationwide.

**Texas Center for Productivity and
Quality of Work Life**
Texas Tech University
P.O. Box 4320
Lubbock, TX 74909

Barry A. Macy, Director
806/742-1538
Information and consultation on
work innovation and
organizational change.

Work in America Institute
700 White Plains Road
Scarsdale, NY 10583
Jerome M. Rosow, President
914/472-9600
Education and training, technical
assistance, and information on
work practices.

International and Foreign Country Centers

International and Regional

Arab League Industrial
Development Organization
El-Phairr Square
Cairo, Egypt

Asian Productivity Organization
4–14 Akasaka 8-Chome
Minato-Ku, Tokyo, 107 Japan
Hiroshi Yokota, Secretary-
General
Contact: Mr. George C. Shen,
Director of Administration and
Public Relations

European Association of National
Productivity Centres
Rue de la Concorde, 60
1050 Brussels, Belgium

Contact: Mr. A. C. Hubert,
Secretary-General

Inter-American Productivity
Association
Casilla 13120
Santiago, Chile
Contact: Mr. Kovacevitz

International Labor Organization
Geneva, Switzerland

United Nations Industrial
Development Organization
Lerchenfelderstrasse #1, A-1070
Vienna, Austria
Contact: H. Abdul-Rahman,
Secretary-General

Country Programs by Region

Europe

Office Belge pour l'Accroissement
de la Productivité (OBAP)
Rue de la Concorde, 60
1050 Brussels, **Belgium**
Contact: M. Pierre F. Verlinden

Nationales Zentrum fur
Arbeitsproducktivitat
52 Boulevard 9 Dimitrov
Sofia, **Bulgaria**
Contact: V. Kunchev

Denmarks Erhversfond
Codamhus - Gl. Kongevej 60
DK-1850 Copenhagen V.,
Denmark
Contact: P. Assam, Director

British Council of Productivity
Associations
8 Southhampton Row
London WC1B 4AQ, **England**
Mr. D. F. Bailey, Chief Executive

British Institute of Management
Management House Parker Street
London WC 2B 5PT, **England**
Roy Close, Director General
Correspondence contact: William
Bree, Deputy Director General

Finland Foundation of
Productivity Research, Federation
of Finnish Industries
Etelaranta 10
00130 Helsinki 13, **Finland**

Centre National d'Information
pour le Progress Economique
(CNIPE)
Tour Europe, Cedex 07
92080 Paris, La Defense, **France**

Greek Productivity Center
28, Copodistriou Street
Athens, **Greece**
Contact: D. Talellis

Hungarian Institute for Industry
and Industrial Education Society
V, Szechenyi rakpart 3
Budapest, **Hungary**

Industrial Development Institute
of Iceland
Skipholt 37
Reykjavik, **Iceland**
Contact: S. Bjornsson

European Foundation for the
Improvement of Living and
Working Conditions
Loughlinstown House
Shankhill, co. Dublin, **Ireland**
Contact: Mrs. W. O. Conghaile

Irish Productivity Centre
IPC House, 35–39
Shelbourne Road
Dublin 4, **Ireland**
Contact: J. Ryan

Instituto Nazionale per
l'Incremento della Produttivita
(INIP)
Piazza Indipendenza 11/8
00185 Rome, **Italy**
Contact: S. Cimmino

Office Luxembourgeois pour
l'Accroissement de la Productivité
(OLAP)
18, rue Auguste Limiere
Luxembourg
Contact: J. Faltz

Commissie Opvoering
Produktiviteit Van de Sociaal-
Economische Radd
Bezuidenhoutseweg 60
Den Haag, **The Netherlands**
Contact: C.A.M. Mul

Norsk Produktivitetsinstitutt
(NPI)
Postboks 8401
Hammersborg
Oslo 1, **Norway**
Contact: S. Dalen, Director

Instytut Prezemyslu U
Drobnego i Rzemiosla
aleje Jerozolimskire 87
02–0001 Warsaw, **Poland**

Conselho Nacional de
Produtividade

Avenido Don Carlos I 126–3
Lisbon, **Portugal**

Subdireccion General de
Technologia y Productividad
Industrial
Ayala, 3
Madrid 1, **Spain**

National Productivity Center
(MPM) 46 Mithatpasa Caddesi
Yenisehir
Ankara, **Turkey**
Contact: A. Ulubay,
Secretary-General

Turkey Training and
Productivity Centre
P.O. Box 554 Nicosia
via Mersin 10, **Turkey**
Contact: H. M. Ateskin, Director

Rationalisierungskuratorium der
Deutschen Wirtschaft (RKW)
Dusseldorf Strasse
6236 Eschborn, **West Germany**
Dr. V. Ruhle, professor

Jugoslpvenski Zavoda Za
Produktivnost Rada
1, Uzun Mirkova
Belgrade, **Yugoslavia**
Contact: V. Odovic, Director

North America (not including U.S.)

Canada Department of Industry,
Trade and Commerce
Productivity Branch
235 Queen Street
Ottawa, Ontario
Canada K1A 0H5
Contact: Dr. Imre Bernolak

Department of Regional Economic
Expansion
43rd Floor, 800 Place Victoria
Montreal, Quebec
Canada H42 1E8
Contact: Roger Fournier

Institut National de Productivité
51 rue d'Auteuil
Quebec, **Canada** G1R 4C2

Correspondence contact:
Jacinthe Belisle

Centro Nacional de Productividad
de Mexico, A.C.
Anillo Periferico Sur 2143
Mexico 20, D.F.
Correspondence contact:
Dr. Gustavo Polit, Programa
Editorial e Informacion
Internacional

Monterrey Productivity Center
Edificio de las Instituciones
Campo 250, Pte 4⁰ Plso
Monterrey, Nuevo Leon, **Mexico**
Contact: Hugo Mier Arrieta

Central and South America

National Productivity Center
of Brazil
Ministry of Industry, Commerce
and Labor
Brazilia, **Brazil**

Servicio de Cooperacion Tecnica
Huerfanos 1117–1147, 9⁰ piso

Casilla 276, Correo Central
Santiago, **Chile**

Centro De Desaroolo Industrial
del Ecuador (CENDES)
Avenida Orellana 1297
P.O. Box 2321
Quito, **Ecuador**

Instituto Tecnico de Capicitacion
y Productividad (Intecap)
12 Calle 4–17
Zone 1
Guatemala City, **Guatemala**

Centro de Desarrollo y
Productividad Industrial de
Panama
Ministerio de Industrie
Apartado 7639
Panama City, **Panama** 5

Centro Nacional de Productividad
Presidencia de la Republica
Pablo Bermudez 214, Piso 10
Lima, **Peru**
Contact: George Succar, Director

Fundacion Instituto Venezalano de
Productividad
Avenida Libertador
Edificio Nuevo Centro-Chacao
Caracas, **Venezuela**

Asia

East Asia

Hong Kong Productivity Centre
20th & 21st Floors, Sincere Bldg.
173 Des Voeux Road
P.O. Box 16132
Central Hong Kong, **Hong Kong**
Dr. J. C. Wright,
Executive Director
Correspondence contact:
Ms. Cangidi Chan, Public
Relations Officer

Japan Productivity Center
No. 1–1. Shibuya 3-Chome
Shibuya-ku
Tokyo 150, **Japan**
K. Goshi, Chairman

Productivity and Development
Center
Development Academy of the
Philippines (IDP-DAP)
P.O. Box 5160
Makati Rizal, **The Philippines**
Mr. Arturo L. Tolentino,
Managing Director

National Productivity Board
6th Floor, Cuppage Centre
55 Cuppage Rd.
Singapore 0922

Dr. Goh Keng Leng,
Executive Director
Contact: Mrs. Lau Wai Ying,
Administrative Manager

Korea Productivity Center
10, 2-ka, Pil-Dong
Chung-Ku
Seoul, **South Korea**
Eun Bok Rhee, President
Contact: Mr. Kwan Won Rhim,
Managing Director

China Productivity Center
11th Floor, 201–26 Tun Hua
North Rd.
Taipei, **Taiwan** 100
Contact: Mr. Wang Sze-Cheh,
General Manager

Thailand Management
Development and Productivity
Centre
Department of Industrial
Promotion
Ministry of Industry
Government of Thailand
Rama 6 Road
Bangkok 4, **Thailand**
Mr. Thamnu Vasinonta, Director

South Asia

National Productivity Council
Productivity House
5–6 Institutional Area
Lodi Road
New Delhi, **India** 11003
Mr. K. T. Chandy, Chairman
Correspondence contact:
S. L. Mehta, International
Projects & Services Officer

National Productivity Centre
Ministry of Manpower,
Transmigration and Cooperatives
Jalan Letjen Haryono M.T.
(Kantor Ditjen Transmigrasi)
P.O. Box 358-kby
Jakarta Selatan, **Indonesia**
Mr. Rusli Syarif, Director

Industrial Management Institute
Bahlavie Road
Jame Jam Avenue
Tehran, **Iran**
Jamshid Gharajedaghi,
Managing Director

Malaysia National Productivity
Centre
P.O. Box 64
Yalan Sultan
Petaling Yaya, **Malaysia**

Industrial Services Centre
Post Box-1318
Kathmandu, **Nepal**
Mr. Ajit N. S. Thapa, Chairman
Correspondence contact:
Keshab P. Sharma, Chief
Industrial Extension Services
Division

Pakistan Industrial Technical
Assistance Centre
Maulana Jalal-Ud-Din Roomi
Road
Post Office, La hore 16, **Pakistan**
Brig. M. A. Faruqui,
General Manager

Economic Affairs Division
Ministry of Planning & Economic
Affairs
P.O. Bos 1689
Colombo, **Sri Lanka**
G.P.H. Leelananda de Silva,
Senior Assistant Secretary &
Director

Sri Lanka National Institute
of Management
7, Kollupitya Station Road
Calombo-3, **Sri Lanka**

Australasia

Australia Department of
Productivity
Ministry of Industry, Anzac Park
West Building
Constitution Avenue
Parkes A.C.T. 2600, **Australia**
Contact: Vernon White

Nepean Productivity Center
P.O. Box 10
Kingswood 2750, **Australia**
Contact: Dr. M. R. Ramsay,
director

Productivity Promotion Council
of Australia
Head Office 339 Swanston Street
GPO Box 475D
Melbourne, Victoria 3000, **Australia**
Contact: Mr. D. L. Casey,
Executive Director

Department of Trade and Industry
Productivity and Technology
Division
Private Bag
Wellington, **New Zealand**

Middle East

Israel Institute of Productivity
4 Szold Street
Tel-Aviv, **Israel**
Dr. Israel Meidan,
Executive Director
Correspondence contact:
Ms. G. Simon, Information
Officer

Syria Management Development
and Productivity Centre
Abdlghani Tollo Bldg.
Mohajrin
Damascus, **Syria**

Africa

Ghana Management Development
and Productivity Institute
P.O. Box 297
Accra, **Ghana**

Sudan Management Development
and Productivity Centre
P.O. Box 2308
Khartoum, **Sudan**

National Productivity Institute
P.O. Box 3971
Pretoria 0001
Republic of South Africa
Dr. Jan Visser, Executive Director

Tunisia Institut National
de Productivité
Rue bel Hassen Ben Chaabane
el Omrane
Tunis, **Tunisia**

Appendix E

GLOSSARY

Numbers in parentheses refer to definitions of other terms in this glossary.

1. Capital: In the context of the present study, the investment in natural resources, reproducible capital (structures, machinery, equipment, and inventories), and financial assets excluding investments in government debt and in securities of other enterprises. Compare **Input, capital (15)**

2. Capital, fixed: Sum of the value of land, structures, machinery, and equipment.

3. Capital, working: Sum of the value of cash, accounts and notes receivable, and inventories.

4. Capital compensation: The income accruing to owners of property in the form of interest, rent, royalties, and profits.

5. Capital consumption: Using up stored services and the resulting decline in value of reproducible durable capital as a result of aging, deterioration, and obsolescence; not to be confused with capital input **(15)**, which represents the use of extant capital goods.

6. Constant price (dollars): See **Deflation (7)**.

7. Deflation (price): Dividing an economic time series expressed in value terms by an index **(13)** of prices of the underlying physical units (combined by appropriate quantity weights) in order to convert the series to "real" terms or constant prices. Compare **Real gross product (42)**

8. Employee involvement (EI) plan: Program to secure increased productivity of labor, usually through group meetings to discuss problems and possible solutions. The plans vary, sometimes not involving financial incentives, as in quality control circles **(41)** and joint labor-management teams **(20)**; or they may involve group financial incentives, as in productivity gainsharing plans **(11, 43, 44)** and, less directly, in profit-sharing or employee stock-ownership plans.

9. Gross domestic business product: Gross product originating in the business sector, which comprises about 85% of U.S. GNP **(10)**; the remainder originates in general government, households, and nonprofit institutions and the rest-of-the-world sector. Gross domestic business product may be viewed as value added in the business sector, equal to the gross value of production less costs of intermediate products consumed.

10. Gross national product (GNP): Market value of all final goods and services produced in the nation's economy, gross of capital consumption allowances; the sum of value added (gross factor income plus indirect business taxes less subsidies) in all sectors and industries of the economy.

11. Improshare: Plan developed by industrial engineer Mitchell Fein for sharing value of productivity gains 50–50 between company and workers based on physical performance measures rather than on "economic productivity" ratios, as in the Scanlon Plan. The formula requires estimates of the value of the difference between actual hours worked by covered employees in a given period and those that would have been required at the productivity of a base period prior to installation of Improshare.

12. Index-number problem: Differences in movement of a quantity (price) index resulting from the use of different weight bases if there is a systematic relationship between relative changes in quantities sold and prices.

13. Index number: Device for measuring proportionate changes or differences in simple or complex quantities relative to their "base" magnitude. Index numbers of a time series, the most common type, represent magnitudes in given periods as percentages of their value in a base period.

14. Industry: Economically significant group of establishments engaged primarily in the same or similar lines of productive activity, generally characterised by the products made or the manufacturing processes employed. (The establishment is a single location where a distinctive, reportable activity takes place.) Government reports generally employ the groupings of the Standard Industrial Classification.

15. Input, capital: Volume of real capital stocks **(1)** used by an industry or company or available for production. Aggregates of capital in different industries or companies may be combined by the relative compensations **(4)** accruing to the capital stocks in each.

16. Input, labor: Hours paid for or worked by persons engaged in production in a given occupational or industry classification; different types of labor hours are usually combined by weights, such as the average compensation per hour in a base period, that indicate their relative importance **(23)**.

17.   Input: Physical unit of resource used in the production process **(28)**.

18.   Input, factor (services): Stock of the productive factors (labor and capital, including natural resources) employed in production over successive time periods, weighted by the compensation per time unit earned by each distinguishable type of factor in a particular base period.

19.   Input, intermediate product: Physical volume of purchased materials and services, direct and indirect, consumed in production (purchases of materials, less net additions to raw materials inventories during the period, plus purchased business services, including subcontracting); may be construed to include capital consumption.

20.   Joint labor-management productivity team: Type of employee involvement plan **(8)**. Productivity teams have been provided for in union-management agreements, notably in the 1971 and subsequent contracts with the United Steelworkers of America.

21.   Labor, direct: Includes all workers engaged in successive phases of the production process and any others customarily charged to measured output. Principal direct labor categories include fabricating, inspecting, receiving, packing, warehousing, and shipping functions.

22.   Labor, indirect: Includes personnel engaged in plant management and administration, product development, testing and in-plant R&D, machine setup and servicing, maintenance, yard labor, janitorial and clean-up work, as well as security guards, office workers, computer operators and programmers, etc., unless regularly charged to a cost center or department and to measured output.

23.   Labor compensation: Personal income from work consisting of employee wages and salaries, including premium pay and supplements to wages and salaries such as employer contributions to welfare funds and other "fringe benefits"; also the imputed compensation for the labor of proprietors and family workers (usually based on rates of employee compensation in the same industry).

24.   Labor efficiency: Changes in the efficiency of labor itself, within a given technological setting, as revealed by "work measurements." Changes in labor efficiency are only one aspect of changes in productive efficiency generally, as revealed by total factor productivity indexes **(38)**, or the so-called labor productivity indexes of output per labor-hour **(33)**.

25.   Labor force: Those persons in the population who are able and willing to work, and who are either employed or are unemployed but seeking work; not to be confused with labor input **(16)**, which takes account of hours worked and of the differing rates of compensation per hour in different industries and occupations.

26. Output, gross: Physical volume (or value in constant prices) of goods and services produced for sales, intraplant transfer, or for addition to inventories of finished or semifinished (in-process) goods during the accounting period; sometimes called "real gross output."

27. Output, net (real product): Gross output in constant prices, less the real value of intermediate goods and services consumed in production **(19)**; sometimes referred to as "real value added." For the economy as a whole, it equals the market value of all final goods and services produced – the national product in constant prices.

28. Production: Process of transforming resources (inputs) into products (outputs) that satisfy human wants; sometimes used as a synonym for output, which is the result of the production process.

29. Production worker: Defined by the Bureau of Labor Statistics to include workers (up through the working foreman level) engaged in fabricating, processing, assembling, inspecting, receiving, storing, handling, packing and warehousing, shipping (but not delivering), maintaining, and repairing, as well as janitorial work, security services, product development, auxiliary production for the plant's own use, record-keeping, and other services closely associated with these production operations.

30. Productivity: Ratio of physical volumes of output **(26, 27)** to one or more classes of input **(17)** used in the production process, usually expressed in terms of index numbers **(13)**.

31. Productivity, capital: Output per unit of capital input **(15)**.

32. Productivity, energy: Gross output per unit of energy, as distinct from other purchased intermediate products **(19)**.

33. Productivity, labor: Output per unit of labor input **(18)**; not to be confused with the narrower concept of labor efficiency **(24)**.

34. Productivity, materials: Gross output per unit of purchased intermediate products **(19)** excluding energy.

35. Productivity, multiple-input: Ratio of output to two or more input classes, as in total productivity **(37)** and total factor productivity **(38)** ratios, as distinguished from partial productivity **(36)**.

36. Productivity, partial: Ratio of gross or net output **(26, 27)** to one class of input.

37. Productivity, total: Ratio of real gross output **(26)** to a combination of all corresponding inputs: labor, capital, and intermediate products purchased outside the firm or industry.

38. Productivity, total factor: Ratio of the real product **(27)** originating in the economy, industry, or firm to the sum of associated labor and capital (factor) inputs **(18)**.

39.   Productivity improvement program: Systematic program designed to involve employees **(8)** at all levels of an organization in promoting its objectives such as increasing efficiency and reducing costs; the effort is usually headed by a "productivity coordinator" or other company official.

40.   Profitability analysis: Explanation of changes in profits in terms of changes in total productivity **(37)** and in "price-recovery" defined as the ratio of prices received for outputs **(26)** to prices paid for inputs **(17)**.

41.   Quality (control) circle: Small voluntary group of coworkers from a plant or office who meet periodically to formulate and solve problems and thus raise productivity. In Japan, where this approach has been highly developed, the circle members are given special training in various problem-solving techniques.

42.   Real gross product: Gross product in nominal values **(10)** after "deflation" to remove the effects of price changes and reveal the effect of changes in the physical volume of production. Real product is equivalent to a price-weighted quantity aggregate.

43.   Rucker Plan: Similar to Scanlon plan, except that productivity gains are measured by increases over a base period in the ratio of value added (rather than total value of production) to labor compensation.

44.   Scanlon Plan: Based on formula devised in latter 1930s by union official for sharing productivity gains between company and workers as measured by reductions in ratio of labor compensation to value of production relative to a base-period ratio. Committees set up to screen suggestions, and recommend management implementation of good ones.

45.   Weight base: Period from which relative weights **(46)** are drawn. It may or may not be the same as the "comparison base" from which values are set equal to 100.0 for index number construction **(13)**.

46.   Weight: Indicator of relative importance such as prices, by which physical units of outputs **(26)** or of inputs **(17)** are combined to provide aggregate measures.

Notes

Chapter 3

1. See "Measurement of Unit Man-hour Requirements," *Monthly Labor Review,* February 1950.

Chapter 4

1. See Everett E. Adam, Jr., James G. Hershauer, and William A. Ruch, *Productivity and Quality: Measurement as a Basis for Improvement* (Englewood Cliffs, N.J.: Prentice-Hall, 1981).
2. Zvi Grilliches, "Hedonic Price Indexes for Automobiles: An Econometric Analysis of Quality Change," published as a staff paper in "The Price Statistics of the Federal Government," prepared by the Price Statistics Review Committee of the National Bureau of Economic Research, 1961.

Chapter 6

1. See *Indexes of Output per Man-hour, Selected Industries* (U.S. Department of Labor, Bureau of Labor Statistics, annual).
2. *Improving Productivity through Industry and Company Measurement* (Washington, D.C.: National Center for Productivity and Quality of Working Life, October 1976), p. 40.

Chapter 8

1. The package of quartile and industry averages for eight industries is available from Information Services, American Productivity Center, 123 North Post Oak Lane, Houston, Texas 77024.
2. George E. Sadler et al., "How to Measure Your Manufacturing Productivity," *Plastics Technology* 28, no. 1 (January 1982): 74–81.
3. Again, the specific examples recorded in illustrations in ibid. may be helpful. There, table 6 is an example of output weighting for a multiple-product plastics plant. Table 7 illustrates one approach to shaping a weighted labor input reflecting relative skill levels in the work force. Table 8 outlines a useful summary of the approaches to weighting and index calculation for both "partial" and "multi-input" measures of productivity trends.

Chapter 9

1. Sources and methods underlying the estimates are described in John W. Kendrick and Elliot S. Grossman, *Productivity in the United States: Trends and Cycles* (Baltimore: Johns Hopkins University Press, 1980). The estimates have been revised and updated by Dr. Grossman for the APC in Houston.

2. John W. Kendrick, *Productivity Trends in the United States* (Princeton: Princeton University Press, for the National Bureau of Economic Research, 1961), and idem, *Postwar Productivity Trends* (Washington, D.C.: National Bureau of Economic Research, 1973).

3. John W. Kendrick, "International Productivity Comparisons," in *Contemporary Economic Problems, 1981,* ed. William Fellner (Washington, D.C.: American Enterprise Institute, 1981).

4. See John W. Kendrick, "Productivity Trends and the Recent Slowdown: Historical Perspective, Causal Factors, and Policy Options," in *Contemporary Economic Problems, 1979,* ed. William Fellner (Washington, D.C.: American Enterprise Institute, 1979).

5. Ibid.

6. See Kendrick and Grossman, *Productivity in the United States,* chap. 5.

7. Let X = changes in total factor productivity, and Y = changes in the implicit price deflators. The estimating equation is $Y = 4.61 - 8.99\ X$; $\bar{R}^2$ is 0.727.

8. Let X = price changes and Y = output changes. The estimating equation is $Y = 5.51 - 0.66\ X$; $\bar{R}^2$ is 0.137, significant at the 0.05 level. For the 1966–79 subperiod, $\bar{R}^2$ is 0.242, significant at the 0.01 level.

9. Let Y = output changes and X = productivity changes. The estimating equation is $X = 1.10 + 1.11\ Y$; $\bar{R}^2 = 0.358$, significant at the 0.01 level.

10. Kendrick and Grossman, *Productivity in the United States,* chap. 6.

11. Wesley C. Mitchell, *Business Cycles* (Berkeley and Los Angeles: University of California Press, 1913).

12. Frank M. Gollop and Dale W. Jorgenson, "U.S. Productivity Growth by Industry, 1947–1973," in *New Developments in Productivity Measurement and Analysis,* ed. John W. Kendrick and Beatrice N. Vaccara (Chicago: University of Chicago Press, 1980).

Chapter 11

1. C. Jackson Grayson, Jr., "A 'Hands-on' Approach to Management Productivity," *Chief Executive,* no. 15 (Spring 1981), pp. 36–38.

2. See John W. Kendrick, "Background and Overview of Productivity Improvement Programs," in *Productivity Improvement: Case Studies of Proven Practice,* ed. Vernon M. Buehler and V. Krishna Shetty (New York: AMACOM, 1981).

Appendix B

1. Since this case was prepared, Solar Turbines International has been sold to the Caterpillar Tractor Company.

Appendix C

1. See *Economic Indicators of the Farm Sector: Production and Efficiency Statistics, 1980* (U.S. Department of Agriculture, Economic Research Service, Statistical Bulletin No. 679, January 1982).

2. *Productivity and Costs,* U.S. Private Business Economy by Sector (U.S. Department of Labor, Bureau of Labor Statistics, quarterly).

3. *Indexes of Output per Man-Hour, Selected Industries* (U.S. Department of Labor, Bureau of Labor Statistics, annual).

4. See *Report of a Panel on the Concept of Measurement of Productivity* (National Academy of Sciences, National Research Council, 1979).

5. John W. Kendrick, *Productivity Trends in the United States* (New York: National Bureau of Economic Research, 1961), and *Postwar Productivity Trends in the United States, 1948-1969* (New York: National Bureau of Economic Research, 1973); John W. Kendrick and Elliot S. Grossman, *Productivity in the United States: Trends and Cycles* (Baltimore: Johns Hopkins University Press, 1980).

6. Elliot S. Grossman, *The American Productivity Center Measure of Multiple-Input Productivity Index: Methodology and Sources of Data* (Houston: American Productivity Center, 1981).

7. The summary was also used by Kendrick in his monograph "Interindustry Differences in Productivity Growth Rates," in *Essays in Contemporary Economic Problems, 1982,* ed. William Fellner (Washington, D.C.: American Enterprise Institute, 1982).

8. See U.S. Internal Revenue Service, *1972 Sourcebook of Statistics of Income.*

Bibliography

Adam, Everett E., Jr.; Hershauer, James G.; and Ruch, William A. *Productivity and Quality: Measurement as a Basis for Improvement.* Englewood Cliffs, N.J.: Prentice-Hall, 1981.

Buehler, Vernon M., and Shetty, V. Krishna, eds. *Productivity Improvement: Case Studies of Proven Practices.* New York: AMACOM, 1981.

Christopher, William F. *The Achieving Enterprise.* New York: AMACOM, 1974.

Davis, Hiram. *Productivity Accounting.* Reprint. Philadelphia: University of Pennsylvania Press, 1978.

Fabricant, Solomon. *Primer on Productivity.* New York: Random House, 1971.

Gollop, Frank M., and Jorgenson, Dale W. "U.S. Productivity Growth by Industry, 1947–1973." In *New Developments in Productivity Measurement and Analysis,* edited by John W. Kendrick and Beatrice N. Vaccara. Chicago: University of Chicago Press, 1980.

Greenberg, Leon. *A Practical Guide to Productivity Measurement.* Washington, D.C.: Bureau of National Affairs, 1973.

Griliches, Zvi. "Hedonic Price Indexes for Automobiles: An Econometric Analysis of Quality Change." In "The Price Statistics of the Federal Government," edited by the Price Statistics Review Committee of the National Bureau of Economic Research. New York: NBER, 1961.

Hogan, John D., and Craig, Anna, eds. *Dimensions of Productivity Research.* 2 vols. Conference proceedings. Houston: American Productivity Center, 1980.

Kendrick, John W. *Postwar Productivity Trends.* Washington, D.C.: National Bureau of Economic Research, 1973.

_____. *Productivity Trends in the United States.* Princeton: Princeton University Press, for the National Bureau of Economic Research, 1961.

_____. "Productivity Trends and the Recent Slowdown: Historical Perspective, Causal Factors, and Policy Options." In *Contemporary Economic Problems, 1979,* edited by William Fellner. Washington, D.C.: American Enterprise Institute, 1979.

_____. "International Productivity Comparisons." In *Contemporary Economic Problems, 1981,* edited by William Fellner. Washington, D.C.: American Enterprise Institute, 1981.

_____. "Background and Overview of Productivity Improvement Programs." In *Productivity Improvement: Case Studies of Proven Practice,* edited by Vernon M. Buehler and V. Krishna Shetty. New York: AMACOM, 1981.

Kendrick, John W., and Grossman, Elliot S. *Productivity in the United States: Trends and Cycles.* Baltimore: Johns Hopkins University Press, 1980. The estimates contained in this volume have been revised and updated by Dr. Grossman for the American Productivity Center in Houston.

Metzger, Bert L. *Increasing Productivity through Profit Sharing.* Evanston, Ill.: Profit Sharing Research Foundation, 1980.

Mitchell, Wesley C. *Business Cycles.* Berkeley and Los Angeles: University of California Press, 1913.

Moore, Brian E. *Sharing the Gains of Productivity.* Work in American Institute Studies in Productivity 24. New York: Pergamon Press, 1982.

Moore, Brian E., and Ross, Timothy L. *The Scanlon Way to Improved Productivity: A Practical Guide.* New York: John Wiley & Sons, 1978.

National Center for Productivity and Quality of Working Life. *Improving Productivity through Industry and Company Measurement.* Washington, D.C.: NCPQWL, October 1976.

New York Stock Exchange. *People and Productivity: A Challenge to Corporate America.* New York: NYSE, Office of Economic Research, 1982.

Ouchi, William. *Theory Z: How American Business Can Meet the Japanese Challenge.* Reading, Pa.: Addison-Wesley, 1981.

Pascale, Richard T., and Athos, Anthony G. *The Art of Japanese Management: Applications for American Executives.* New York: Simon & Schuster, 1981.

Salter, W. E. G. *Productivity and Technical Change.* Cambridge, Mass.: Harvard University Press, 1965; paperback edition, 1969.

Siegel, Irving. *Company Productivity: Measuring for Improvement.* Kalamazoo, Mich.: W. E. Upjohn Institute for Employment Research, 1980.

Sutermeister, R. A. *Productivity and People,* 3d ed. New York: John Wiley & Sons, 1978.

U.S. Department of Labor, Bureau of Labor Statistics. *Indexes of Output per Man-hour, Selected Industries.* Washington, D.C.: Government Printing Office, annual indexes.

Index

217

Quality control circles *(cont.)*
    also Solar Turbines International, pro-
    ductivity improvement program at
Quality of work life, 112, 116–17, 163

Real national product, 12
REALST. *See* Data Resources, Inc.,
    REALST model of
Regression, 10
Regulation, 100
Research and development: role of, in
    productivity growth, 14, 100; treatment
    of expenditure for, 30
Return, rate of, as capital input, 30
Rucker plan, 113, 172–77, 210

Savings rate, 14
Scanlon plan, 113, 172–73, 210
Solar Turbines International, productivity
    improvement program at: description of,
    165–67; development of, 164–65; and
    employee suggestions, 169; future plans
    for, 168; organizational background and,
    163; results of, 167–68
South Africa, Republic of, interfirm com-
    parison in, 58, 69, 74, 75, 80
Southern California Edison, productivity
    pamphlets prepared by, 120
Sperry Corporation, productivity publi-
    cations by, 120
Standard Industrial Classification Codes, 54
Stock, 12
Strategic planning, use of productivity
    measures in, 63, 119, 128–29
Structures. *See* Capital inputs
Suggestion systems, 172

Taxes, treatment of, 36
Taylor, Frederick W., 18
Tektronix, Inc., quality circle concept at,
    118

Tenneco, Inc., productivity improvement
    program at: data analysis for, 182–83;
    data gathering for, 181; evaluation of,
    184–85; feedback of findings at, 183;
    history of, 178; identification of oppor-
    tunities in, 183; initial visit for, 180–81;
    planning during, 183; focus of, 178
Total factor productivity, 47, 142, 188;
    definition of, 209–10; example of, 143–
    50; recent results of, in U.S., 209–10
Total productivity, 11, 46–47; and APC
    Performance Measurement System, 57–
    64; definition of, 209. *See also* "Mideast
    Manufacturing Company," total produc-
    tivity measurement at
Turkey, interfirm comparison in, 75, 77, 79
Turner Construction Company, index com-
    piled by, 43

Unionization, and productivity growth, 99
United Kingdom, interfirm comparison in,
    69, 70, 75, 77, 79, 80
United States Gypsum Company, pro-
    ductivity philosophy of, 117
Uses of productivity measures, 51–56, 119

Value added, 144, 191
Von Loggerenberg, Basil, 58

Wage negotiations, role of productivity
    measures in, 55
Weighting, 9, 20; definition of, 210; of
    labor-hour, 39
West Germany, interfirm comparison in,
    75, 76, 78, 80
Western Electric Company. *See* Bell Tele-
    phone, productivity measurement sys-
    tems for
Work ethic, 13
Work measurement, 17, 53
Working capital. *See* Capital inputs
Works Progress Administration (WPA), 25